WAR AND THE ARME BLANCHE

WAR AND THE ARME BLANCHE

BY

ERSKINE CHILDERS

Author of 'The Riddle of the Sands'; Editor of Vol. V. of the '"Times" History of the War in South Africa.' etc.

With an introduction by the Right Hon. Field-Marshall
EARL ROBERTS, K.G.

The Naval & Military Press Ltd

published in association with

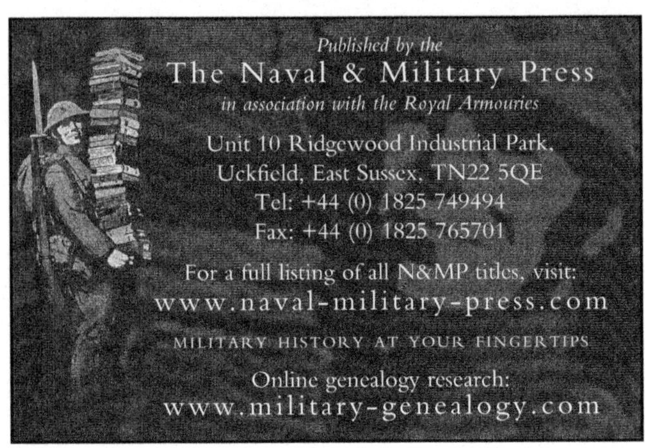

ROYAL ARMOURIES

The Library & Archives Department at the Royal Armouries Museum, Leeds, specialises in the history and development of armour and weapons from earliest times to the present day. Material relating to the development of artillery and modern fortifications is held at the Royal Armouries Museum, Fort Nelson.

For further information contact:
Royal Armouries Museum, Library, Armouries Drive,
Leeds, West Yorkshire LS10 1LT
Royal Armouries, Library, Fort Nelson, Down End Road, Fareham PO17 6AN

Or visit the Museum′s website at
www.armouries.org.uk

In reprinting in facsimile from the original, any imperfections are inevitably reproduced and the quality may fall short of modern type and cartographic standards.

Printed and bound by CPI Antony Rowe, Eastbourne

CONTENTS

INTRODUCTION

BY

FIELD-MARSHAL EARL ROBERTS, V.C., K.G.

I HAVE read with the greatest interest Mr. Childers's illuminating book " War and the Arme Blanche." My opinion of the subject with which it deals is already so well known throughout the army that I need not labour to say how entirely I agree with the author's main thesis ; indeed, anyone who will take the trouble to read " Cavalry Training " (1904), will see that I anticipated the arguments which he has so ably developed. This being so, it is not surprising that I should view the regulations laid down in " Cavalry Training " (1907), with some concern.

Let us consider briefly what the history of this question —the comparative value of steel weapons and firearms for Cavalry in war—is. Until within the last few years our Lancer regiments depended entirely on the lance and sword, while other Cavalry regiments depended almost entirely on the sword.* This was inevitable because of the inaccuracy and short range of the smooth-bore car· bine. Tentative changes were made when rifled arms

---

* No reference was made to the lance in the 1904 Regulations, because that weapon had been discarded as practically useless, owing to the introduction of breech-loading rifles. Now, unfortunately, the lance has been reintroduced—a retrograde movement. The lance is a positive impediment to dismounted action, as it adds greatly to the difficulty of led horses being moved forward when the men advance. In other words, it ties the men to the horses.

v

were adopted, but it is only within the last thirty years that Lancer regiments have had any firearm given to them save a pistol.* With such an equipment and such traditions it was perhaps but natural that the training of Cavalry should have been almost exclusively devoted to shock tactics and the use of the *arme blanche*.

But why now, with a different equipment, should Cavalry still be trained on the old tradition, and their rifles reside in buckets attached to the horse, only to be used on certain exceptional occasions to " supplement the sword or lance " ? (" Cavalry Training," sec. 142.)

The late Colonel Henderson, in his essay on the tactical employment of Cavalry, " Science of War," chapter iii., page 51, pointed out that, notwithstanding the introduction of gunpowder, the Cavalry was the arm that had undergone the least change. He went on to say that " shock-tactics, the charge, and the hand-to-hand encounter are still the one ideal of Cavalry action ; and the power of manœuvring in great masses, maintaining an absolute uniformity of pace and formation, and moving at the highest speed with accurately dressed ranks, is the criterion of excellence." He added : " to such an extent has this teaching been carried out, that the efficiency of the individual, especially in those duties which are performed by single men or small parties, cannot fairly be said to have received due attention."

After explaining how Cromwell's troopers " were taught the value of co-operation," and how " Cromwell built up his Cavalry on a foundation of high individual efficiency," he goes on to show that, " as time went on and armies became larger, and skill at arms, as a national characteristic, rarer, drill, discipline, manœuvre in mass, and a high degree of mobility came to outweigh all other

---

* When the 9th Lancers were ordered to join my column on Field Service in Kuram in 1879, carbines had to be served out to them, and the men had to be put through a hurried course of musketry.

considerations; and when the necessity of arming the nations brought about short service, the training of the individual, in any other branch of his business than that of riding boot-to-boot and of rendering instant obedience to the word or signal of his superior, fell more and more into abeyance. Shock-tactics filled the entire bill, and the Cavalry of Europe, admirably trained to manœuvre and attack, whether by the squadron of 150 sabres, or the division of 3,000 or 4,000, was practically unfitted for any other duty. The climax of incompetency may be said to have been reached during the cycle of European warfare, which began with the Crimea, and ended with the Russo-Turkish conflict of 1877-78. The old spirit of dash and daring under fire was still conspicuous, discipline and mobility were never higher. The regiments manœuvred with admirable precision at the highest speed, and never had great masses of horsemen been more easily controlled. And yet, in the whole history of war, it may be doubted whether the record of the Cavalry was ever more meagre."

Referring specially to the German Cavalry during the war of 1870-71, Henderson says: "The troopers knew nothing whatever of fighting on foot—their movements were impeded by their equipment—and a few *Francs-tireurs*, armed with the chassepot, were enough to paralyze a whole brigade. ... In fact, to the student who follows out the operations of the Cavalry of 1870-71 step by step, and who bears in mind its deficiencies in armament and training, it will appear very doubtful whether a strong body of mounted riflemen of the same type as the Boers, or better still, of Sheridan's or Stuart's Cavalry in the last years of the War of Secession, would not have held the German horsemen at bay from the first moment they crossed the frontier."

"Had the successes gained by shock-tactics been very numerous, it might possibly be argued that the sacrifice of efficiency in detached and dismounted duties, as well as the training of the individual, was fully justified. What are the facts ?" After enumerating the successes gained by shock-tactics from the days of the Crimea onwards, when anything larger than a regiment was engaged, Henderson adds : " Such is the record : one great tactical success gained at Custozza : a retreating army saved from annihilation at Königgrätz,* and five minor successes which may or may not have influenced the ultimate issue. Not one single instance of an effective and sustained pursuit ; not one single instance— except Custozza, and there the Infantry was armed with muzzle-loaders—of a charge decisive of the battle ; not one single instance of Infantry being scattered and cut down in panic flight ; not one single instance of a force larger than a brigade intervening at a critical moment. And how many failures ? How often were the Cavalry dashed vainly in reckless gallantry against the hail of a thin line of rifles ! How often were great masses held back inactive, without drawing a sabre or firing a shot, while the battle was decided by the Infantry and the guns ! How few the enterprises against the enemy's communications ! How few men killed or disabled, even when Cavalry met Cavalry in the mêlée ! Can it be said in face of these facts that the devotion to shock-tactics, the constant practice in massed movements, the discouragement of individualism, both in leaders and men, was repaid by results ? Does it not rather appear that there was some factor present on the modern battlefield which prevented the Cavalry, trained to a pitch hitherto unknown, from reaping the same harvest as the horsemen of previous eras ? Was not the attempt to apply the same principles to the battle of the breech-

---

* Of Königgrätz it would probably be more accurate to say that the Austrian Cavalry neutralized the Prussian Cavalry. It was the formidable row of Austrian guns that saved the Austrian army.

loader and the rifled cannon, as had been applied successfully to the battles of the smooth-bore, a mistake from
beginning to end ; and should not the Cavalry, confronted
by new and revolutionary conditions, have sought new
means of giving full effect to the mobility which makes it
formidable ?"*

Since Colonel Henderson, no one has dealt so exhaustively and so logically with this aspect of Cavalry in
war as Mr. Childers. He has gone thoroughly into the
achievements of our Cavalry in South Africa. It has
been said that this war was abnormal, but are not all
wars abnormal ? As, however, it was the first war in
which magazine rifles were made use of, and as the
weapon used in future wars is certain to be even more
effective, on account of the lower trajectory and auto-
matic mechanism about to be introduced, shall we not be
very unwise if we do not profit by the lessons we were
taught at such a heavy cost during that war ?

These, then, are Mr. Childers's conclusions in reviewing the period from the beginning of the campaign
up to March, 1900 :

" Widening our horizon to include the whole area of
the war at this period, we perceive that Cavalry theory,
so far as it was based on the *arme blanche*, had collapsed.
The only and not especially remarkable achievement of
that weapon is the pursuit at Elandslaagte on the second
day of hostilities. Everywhere else we have seen it
directly or indirectly crippling the Cavalry, and the
greater the numbers employed and the larger the measure
of independence permitted, the more unmistakable is
the weakness. When the Cavalry succeed strategically,

* Eight years have elapsed since Henderson wrote these words.
When they were penned the records of the South African War were not
at his disposal, and the Manchurian War had still to be fought. The
histories of these two campaigns only confirm his views, for during four
years of war it is impossible to find more than a few instances, and
these all trivial, of the successful use of the *arme blanche*.

as in the ride to Kimberley and back to Paardeberg, they succeed in spite of disabilities traceable to *arme blanche* doctrine. When they succeed tactically, as in the Colesberg operations, and in containing Cronje's force on the eve of Paardeberg, they succeed through the carbine, in spite of its inferiority as a weapon of precision. In tactical offence, the paramount *raison d'être* of the *arme blanche*, they fail, and in reconnaissance they fail."

With every word of this I agree, and it must be remembered that my judgment is based upon personal and first-hand knowledge. Why did our Cavalry fail ? Because they did not know, because they had never been required to know, how to use the principal and most useful weapon with which they were armed. Because they did not understand, because they had never been asked to understand, that their rôle should consist in attacking the enemy " exactly like the Infantry,* and to shoot their way up to him." †

In this matter of shooting their way up to their enemy, Cavalry possess great advantages owing to their mobility. General French's admirable movement at Klip Drift was essentially a rapid advance of fighting men carried out at extended intervals. It was a rapid advance of warriors who possessed the ability, by means of horses and rifles (not swords or lances), to place their enemy *hors de combat*. It was an ideal Cavalry operation, but it was not a " Cavalry charge," as this term is generally understood, and the *arme blanche* had nothing to say to it.

* I do not mean to reflect in any way on those in authority before the South African War for not having anticipated the power conferred by the magazine rifle and smokeless powder. But I submit that in " Cavalry Training " (1904) the lesson had been learnt, and the Manchurian War has surely confirmed the decision reached in 1904.

† Bernhardi, p. 60. Mr. Goldman's translation, second edition, of General von Bernhardi's " Cavalry in Future Wars."

In the preface to " Cavalry Training " (1904), I laid down that such an operation was sound in principle. I went farther—I encouraged it—and there is no doubt that on many occasions such an advance will have a far greater effect than a methodical advance on foot. But, such an advance must be essentially a rapid advance of fighting men armed with rifles, and the threat lies in the power of the rifle.

In the same Preface I pointed out that the rifle, which " will chiefly be required when dismounted, must be carried on the person of the soldier himself." The necessity for this was brought very prominently to my notice during the fight in the Chardeh Valley, near Kabul, on December 11, 1879. On that occasion more than forty carbines were lost by the 9th Lancers, two weak squadrons of which regiment, numbering only 213 men, took part in the engagement. Partly owing to the rough nature of the ground, and partly to the enemy's fire, several horses fell, and before the men could disengage the carbines from the buckets the Afghans were upon them. Without their firearms the dismounted Cavalry were quite helpless, and it was a sorry spectacle to behold these men, with their swords dangling between their legs and impeding their movements, while they vainly endeavoured to defend themselves with their lances. This incident confirmed the experience I had gained in the Mutiny as to the necessity for the firearm being attached to the man instead of to the horse, and I at once issued orders for this change to be made, and for the sword—which is only required to be used when the soldier is mounted—to be carried on the saddle.

The strongest opposition to these alterations was made by Cavalry officers in this country, and it was not until 1891 —twelve years after it had been adopted in Afghanistan— that sanction was accorded to the *men's* swords being carried on the saddles. Eleven years more had to pass before *officers* were authorized (Army Order, June 1, 1902) to have their swords similarly carried. But the rifle is still being carried on the horse, and, if this arrangement is not changed, the result will certainly be that, if a man gets upset and separated from his horse in a fight, he will have neither sword nor rifle with which to defend himself. This is not the case in India, where the rifle, supported by a small bucket, is attached to the man, so that when he dismounts the rifle goes with him.*

I trust that thirty years will not again be allowed to elapse before we take to heart and act upon the main lesson to be learned from the Boer and Russo-Japanese Wars, and in a lesser degree from every war that has taken place since the introduction of breech-loading arms. That lesson is, that knee to knee, close order charging is practically a thing of the past. There may be, there probably will be, mounted attacks, preferably in open order, against Cavalry caught unawares, or against broken Infantry. But, after reading Mr. Childers's book, backed by my own practical experience, I am driven to the conclusion that the only possible logical deduction from the history of late wars is, that all attacks can now be carried out far more effectually with the rifle than with the sword.

At the same time I do not go so far as the author in thinking that the sword should be done away with altogether. It is desirable that Cavalry soldiers, equally with their comrades in the Infantry, should have a steel weapon of some kind for use in the assault by night, in a mist, or on other occasions when a fire-fight might be impossible or inadvisable. Instead, however, of the present sword, the Cavalry soldier would be more suitably equipped with a sword-bayonet for fixing on the rifle when

* I may point out here that General von Bernhardi agrees with this. On page 176 (Mr. Goldman's translation) he says : " The sword should therefore be attached to the saddle, the carbine to the man, as is, in fact, the practice of all races of born horsemen."

fighting on foot—something like that with which our rifle regiments were formerly armed—but made with a substantial handle, large enough to be firmly gripped, so that in the event of its being required it could be used on horseback as well as on foot. This sword-bayonet must, of course, be attached to the man.

The two essentials of Cavalry in the present day are mobility and the power to use the rifle with effect. Unless Cavalry is mobile it is practically useless, as is proved over and over again in the pages of this book. It is by saving their horses in every possible way, and by skill in the use of the rifle, that Cavalry soldiers can hope to carry out properly the many important functions required of them in advance of, at a distance from, and in conjunction with, the main army. Further, as the rifle is the weapon which will enable Cavalry to be of the most real value in co-operating with the other arms on the actual field of battle, Cavalry soldiers must not only be good shots, but they must be taught how to fight as Infantry.

Owing to the enormous increase in recent years in the numbers which now constitute a modern army, the strategical area in which Cavalry will have to operate must inevitably be of considerable extent. Owing also to the increased size of armies on the actual battle-field, and to the extended formations necessitated by the long-reaching effect of modern weapons, the strain upon the Cavalry horses is infinitely greater than in former days, and unless men are taught to take every possible care of their horses, Cavalry will be unable to co-operate with the other arms when their services are most urgently needed —perhaps at a critical period of the fight—or to follow up and harass a retreating enemy.

It is impossible to over-estimate the value of Cavalry— trained as I should wish to see them trained—under the existing conditions of war. It is Cavalry that carries out the preliminary operations. It is frequently due to the information gained by Cavalry that a commander is enabled to make, or alter, his plan of action. It may often happen that Cavalry may help to decide the issue of a battle. It is by Cavalry that the fruits of a successful action are most completely reaped. And it is to the Cavalry that the army will look to save a retreat being turned into a rout or a disaster.

It is for these reasons, and because Cavalry is so frequently required to act alone, and often in quite small parties, at a considerable distance from the main force, that all ranks need the most careful training. The men should be intelligent and trustworthy; they require to have their wits about them even in a greater degree than other soldiers, for a single Cavalry soldier may at times have great responsibility thrown upon him. The officers should possess all the qualities of good sportsmen. They should be fine riders, careful horse-masters, have a keen eye for country, and be thoroughly well educated.*

In some recently written books on Cavalry great stress is laid on the necessity for inculcating the " true Cavalry spirit," and on the idea that " shock action alone gives decisive results." I cannot call to mind one single instance during the last half-century—ever since, indeed, arms of precision have been brought into use—when shock action alone has produced decisive results, and I doubt whether shock action, or, in other words, the *arme blanche* alone, will ever again be able to bring about such results against a highly trained enemy armed with magazine rifles. I confess I cannot follow the

* Unfortunately, the expenses connected with life in our Cavalry regiments are so heavy that only officers who have considerable means of their own can afford to belong to them, and but few of such go into the army as a profession. The only remedy is to make service in the Cavalry more attractive to those who are not well off by increasing the pay, and thus making it a prize for the Cadets at Sandhurst to struggle for as they now struggle for the Indian army.

train of thought which insists upon Cavalry requiring a "spirit" for "shock action," and a spirit different, it is presumed, to the soldierly spirit which it is essential for the other arms to possess if they are to behave with resolution and courage on the field of battle.

It is this soldierly spirit, which can only be produced by discipline and thorough training, that animates the Engineers to carry out the extremely dangerous duty of blowing open the gates of a walled city. It is this soldierly spirit that enables the Artillery to continue serving their guns until the last man of the party is shot down. It is the same soldierly spirit that enables the Infantry soldier to stand the strain of lying out in the open, possibly for hours, under a burning sun or in drenching rain, unable to move hand or foot without being shot at, a strain to which the order to charge the enemy's position comes as a distinct and welcome relief. And it is the same soldierly spirit which sustains the Cavalry soldier when employed on the important and hazardous duties of scouting and reconnoitring, in the carrying out of which he so often finds himself alone or with quite a small party. The "charge" doubtless requires "dash," but no special "Cavalry spirit"; the excitement of galloping at full speed, in company with a number of his comrades, is of itself sufficient to carry the Cavalry soldier forward.

I certainly would not venture to speak so decidedly on a matter, which has given rise to so much controversy of late years, did I not feel that I am justified in expressing an opinion from the fact that I have taken part in Cavalry combats, and have frequently had occasion to scout and reconnoitre with two, three, or perhaps half a dozen Cavalry soldiers, at a time when capture by the enemy meant certain death. And I have no hesitation in saying that scouting and reconnoitring try the nerves far more seriously than charging the enemy.

In conclusion, I would ask you, my brother officers, in whatever part of the Empire you may be serving, whether in the mounted or dismounted branches, whether in the Cavalry, Yeomanry, Mounted Infantry, or Colonial Mounted Corps, whether in the Artillery, Engineers, or Infantry, to read this book with an unbiassed mind, and not to be put off by the opening chapters, or to throw the book on one side with some such remark as, " This is written by a civilian, and what can he know of the subject ?"   Remember that most of our finest military histories have been written by civilians.   I would ask you to study the facts for yourselves, weigh the arguments, follow the deductions, note the conclusions, and then do one of two things.   Either traverse the facts, refute the deductions, and upset the conclusions, *or* admit the facts, agree to the arguments, acknowledge the deductions, and accept the conclusions.

WAR AND THE ARME BLANCHE

CHAPTER I

THE ISSUE AND ITS IMPORTANCE

My central purpose in this volume is to submit to searching criticism the armament of Cavalry. That armament now consists of a rifle and a sword in all regiments, with the addition of a lance in the case of Lancers. I shall argue that the steel weapons ought either to be discarded or denied all influence on tactics, and a pure type of mounted rifleman substituted for the existing hybrid type. I shall contrast the characteristics and achievements of this pure type with the characteristics and achievements of the hybrid type. I shall argue that a right decision in the case of Cavalry carries with it indirect consequences of the most far-reaching importance in regard to the efficient training of all our other mounted troops, regular or volunteer, home or colonial—troops which belong almost entirely to the pure type, but on whose training the mere existence of a hybrid type, with a theory of tactics derived from the steel, reacts unfavourably.

I cannot do better than begin by quoting two passages from page 187 of the latest edition of " Cavalry Training " (1907). They constitute an epitome of the case I wish to combat, and I challenge almost every proposition, express or implied, contained in them. The first runs as follows :

" From the foregoing it will be seen that thorough efficiency in the use of the rifle and in dismounted tactics

1

is an absolute necessity. At the same time the essence of the Cavalry spirit lies in holding the balance correctly between fire-power and shock action, and while training troops for the former, they must not be allowed to lose confidence in the latter."

Beginning with the first sentence, I challenge two assumptions implied in it : first, that " thorough efficiency in the use of the rifle and in dismounted tactics " (by hypothesis an absolute necessity) is compatible with thorough efficiency in shock action, also, by hypothesis, a necessity ; second, that thorough efficiency with the rifle is confined to what the compilers of the drill-book call " dismounted tactics." Passing to the second sentence of the same quotation, I challenge the definition of the " essence of the Cavalry spirit " there laid down. This definition is borrowed word for word from a German book, originally written before the Boer War and re-published in 1902, when the war was ending, by an officer —the distinguished General Bernhardi—who founded his conclusions not on experience but on report, and addressed those conclusions to the German Cavalry, whose tactics, training, and organization by his own admission were, and seemingly are still, so dangerously antiquated in the direction of excessive reliance on the steel as to present no parallel to our own Cavalry. I challenge the Cavalry spirit so defined because it is a hybrid spirit, impossible to instil and impossible to translate into " balanced " action, even if the steel deserved, as it does not deserve, to be " balanced " against the rifle. I challenge the definition still further, because it is not even an honest definition. Affecting to strike a just balance between the claims of the rifle and the steel, it does not represent the facts of existing Cavalry theory and practice in this country. Though borrowed from a German authority, it is even less to be relied on as representing the facts of German theory and practice, nor does it correspond to the general tenor of the very handbook—"Cavalry Training "—in which it appears. Those facts and that tenor find their really honest and truthful expression in the second quotation, which runs as follows :

"It must be accepted as a principle that the rifle, effective as it is, cannot replace the effect produced by the speed of the horse, the magnetism of the charge, and the terror of cold steel."

I challenge both the form and the essence of the statement : its form because the words imply that " the speed of the horse and the magnetism of the charge " are exclusively connected with the use of the cold steel ; its essence because the principle laid down is fundamentally unsound.

I want to induce all thinking men, whether professional soldiers or not, who take an interest in our military progress, to submit this theory of the *arme blanche* once and for all to drastic investigation, in the light of history —especially of South African history and Manchurian history—in the light of physical principles, and in the light of future Imperial needs. Above all, I want them to examine the case made for the theory by Cavalry men themselves, and to judge if that case rests upon an intelligent interpretation of new and valuable experience, or, rather, upon a stubborn adherence to an old tradition whose teaching they have indeed been forced to modify, but have not had the good sense to abandon. The principles laid down by professional men for the use of their own arm must of course exact the greatest respect, but they are not sacrosanct, and if they are found to rest on demonstrably false premisses they deserve to be discarded.

Of all military questions this question of the *arme blanche* and the rifle is one around which general or outside criticism may most appropriately centre. It is not merely a Cavalry question ; it cannot be disposed of by reference to the British regular Cavalry as it exists to-day.

The training of all mounted troops, regular or volunteer, home or colonial, however armed and trained, depends on clear notions as to the relative value of the two classes of weapon. As an example of what I mean, I suggest that it is shallow and unscientific to present the Yeomanry with the " Cavalry Training " handbook as a whole, and to inform them in a sort of postscript of three perfunctory pages that they should be " so trained as to be capable of performing all the duties allotted to Cavalry, except those connected with shock action." According to the inter-pretation of the words " duties connected with shock action," the injunction might mean anything or nothing. No clear interpretation of the words could be derived from the handbook itself. The Yeoman might turn for light to the Mounted Infantry Regulations, and ask if, in its opening words, he was " an Infantry soldier . . . " governed " in his tactical employment by the principles of Infantry training," and, if not, in exactly what sense and for what reasons he was supposed to differ from the Mounted Infantryman ; but he would ask in vain. In the end, he often concludes from the fact that he is " Cavalry," that he is in peril for lack of a sword, and appeals for the sword when he has barely mastered the rudiments of the rifle. The Mounted Infantryman, who has been first an Infantry soldier, nourished on " Infantry Train-ing," may well wonder why that manual encouraged him not to fear Cavalry, while directly he obtains a horse he is warned to fear the steel.

These are examples of confusion of thought at home. What of Greater Britain ? A critical time has arrived in our Imperial history. There is an universal sense of the necessity of closer union for Imperial defence. An Im-perial General Staff has been initiated which is to " stand-ardize " organization and training. One of its functions ought to be to formulate some clear, rational principles for the employment of mounted troops. We know we can get large numbers of these troops. From first to last in the Boer War we obtained upwards of 70,000 men outside Great Britain. We could obtain many in another great war, and make far more valuable use of them; if time and thought were to be given to their organization and training, with a special view to service in an Imperial Army. Inspiration in the first instance will naturally come from the home country. What are we going to ask of these troops, who, be it remembered, are designed to form an integral part of an Imperial Army, ready, without the confusion, waste, and inefficiency due to an improvised system, to take their place in the field for the performance of definite, specific duties? We shall hardly, it is to be presumed, recommend shock action with the steel weapon to men who have not even the sentimental tradition of shock action, much less any practical belief in its efficacy. In what light, then, is shock action to be presented to them? What is to be their rôle? Are they, like the Yeomanry, to be informed that they are unfit to perform an undefined range of duties for which shock action alone is a qualification, or are they to be held competent to act as "Cavalry," while the Yeomanry cannot claim that privilege? Again, are they, like the Mounted Infantry, to regard themselves on the one hand as "Infantry soldiers" mounted upon horses, and, on the other, as competent to perform regularly the duties of "Divisional Cavalry"? Or are they to be called Mounted Riflemen, a name officially unknown in England? And, if so, in what precise and positive way do Mounted Riflemen differ from Yeomanry, Mounted Infantry, and Cavalry? These questions must be answered, and they must be answered to the satisfaction of practical men whose ideas of war have been moulded by the South African War, where shock action, as they know very well, fell into complete disuse, where all classes of mounted troops,

home and colonial, performed according to their varying
degrees of ability, the same functions, and where the
rifle was the only weapon which counted.

This question of weapons for horsemen must be fairly
and squarely faced. It is a national and Imperial
question, upon which every shade of opinion, volunteer
or regular, should be consulted, and a verdict formed on
the evidence, historical and technical. Part only of the
rich and varied experience gained upon this question in
South Africa was gained by Cavalrymen. Gunners,
Sappers, and Infantrymen, to say nothing of volunteer
officers of every description, led mounted troops with
distinction. The most brilliant Boer leading came from
lawyers and farmers. The point is largely one for
common sense, applied to known and recent facts, and
everybody who takes any interest in military matters,
whether he bears arms or not, can and ought to form an
intelligent judgment on it.

But at present the situation is far from satisfactory,
and, unless the controversy can be brought to a head in
time, seems likely to grow more and more unsatisfactory.
General public interest in the details of the South African
War languished even before it was ended. After the
war was over the tendency was to banish a tedious
and unpleasant subject from memory. That, probably,
is only a phase, yet a phase which may be dangerously
overprolonged. The citizen army which fought in South
Africa side by side with the regular forces has disappeared.
A great number of its individual members still bear arms
as volunteers, but most of the organizations raised for
war purposes have perished as such, and with them many
of the sound, young traditions which were derived from
war experience. A new generation is slowly coming into
being, permeated, indeed, by growing enthusiasm for
military service, but not particularly interested in the
war, and taught on the highest authority to regard it as

abnormal. In the regular forces a somewhat similar tendency has been inevitable ; the causes which led to a general concentration of thought on mounted problems have disappeared. The war once over, the army naturally fell back into its normal organization. Men temporarily called to become leaders of horse from branches outside the Cavalry and regular Mounted Infantry returned to their former vocations and became reabsorbed in their old interests.

A great current of vital and original thought was irrevocably diverted. The ideas, no doubt, have lived on and thrived sporadically. At this moment there is probably much opinion in the army at large which is unfavourable to the official Cavalry view of the *arme blanche*, but the opposition is neither authoritative nor effectively articulate. In the natural course of things the regular Cavalry—a force centuries old and vested with immemorial traditions, the premier mounted force of the Empire—has reasserted its sway over theory and practice. Shock action, consigned to complete oblivion in South Africa and to equally complete oblivion in Manchuria, still holds the first place in the training of the Cavalry soldier. The reaction has been gradual but sure. In 1903, a year after our war, the lance, by official order, was relegated to the realm of " ceremony " and " recreation," and the sword was expressly subordinated to the firearm, which became the soldier's " principal weapon." Then the sword regained that place, and finally the lance returned to use as a combatant weapon in conjunction with the sword. It is true that the rifle has been substituted for the carbine, and that " thorough efficiency in the use of the rifle " is enjoined as an " absolute necessity " ; but, as I have pointed out, the spirit of the regulations suggests primary reliance on the steel as the main source of enterprise and dash. I lay stress on the spirit, for in the endeavour to make the best of both worlds, and to picture a perfect hybrid type, capable of doing all that first-class mounted riflemen can do, and all that first-class shock soldiers can do, the letter of the instructions for the employment of Cavalry in the field is often inexcusably evasive and ambiguous.

But if there were any doubt about the essential meaning, the published writings of Cavalry authorities like General Sir John French, when combating the advocates of the rifle, would dispel that doubt. At such times, the principle of balance is forgotten, and the ineradicable belief in the supreme efficacy of the steel is laid bare. Does this belief rest on a sound basis ? I want to show that it does not. It is a formidable task ; how formidable, the mere mention of the name of General French will show. Deservedly he commands widespread respect and confidence, not only as the most distinguished British Cavalry officer now living, but as a soldier of high general ability. To a vast number of minds his verdict on any military point would be decisive. In South Africa he was the incarnation of the soldierly virtues. His name is bound up with some of the best work done by the Cavalry during that war, so that any critic of the *arme blanche* who founds his criticism on that war, finds himself continually confronted by the seemingly unanswerable argument that our ablest Cavalry officer believes in the *arme blanche*, and our ablest Cavalry officer, himself endowed with long war experience, must be right. I ask the reader to reserve his judgment. No one who has not studied in a critical spirit this question of weapons for horsemen can realize the incalculable influence of purely sentimental conservatism upon even the ablest Cavalry soldiers. The whole history of the subject has been one of indifference to, or reaction from, war experience, with the result that every great war from the middle of the nineteenth century to the recent war in the Far East, with the solitary exception of the American Civil War, has produced a confession of comparative failure in the Cavalries employed, even from the Cavalry leaders themselves. General French himself would, I believe, be the first to admit that in South Africa he owed little or nothing to the *arme blanche*, and everything to the rifle. His case is that that war was abnormal. The *arme blanche*, indeed, is a religion in itself, comparable only to the religion of sails and wood which, in the affections of the old school of sailors—able sailors—long outlived the introduction of ironclads. This kind of conservatism must be analyzed, and, if need be, discounted, before we can arrive at the truth.

The published opinions of Sir John French may fairly be taken to represent the best, and in a sense the official, case for the steel weapon. In 1909 a new edition was issued in this country of Von Bernhardi's "Cavalry in Future Wars," the work from which the compilers of "Cavalry Training" have taken their definition of the hybrid "Cavalry spirit," and much more beside. It is admirably translated by Mr. Goldman, who wrote "With French in South Africa," after accompanying General French in the field during an important part of the South African campaign, who founded the *Cavalry Magazine*, and who may be regarded as the principal lay advocate of the *arme blanche*. Bernhardi's book is preceded by an introduction from the pen of General French himself. This introduction takes the form of an enthusiastic and absolutely unqualified eulogy of everything contained in the German publication, whose author is described as having, "with remarkable perspicacity and telling conviction, dealt in an exhaustive manner with every subject demanding a Cavalry soldier's study and thought."

Nor is the book only praised for its intrinsic merits. It is avowedly put forward as a conclusive answer to the English critics of shock manœuvre with the *arme blanche* —critics whom General French, in the earlier part of his introduction, takes special pains to answer with additional arguments of his own. Mr. Goldman, whose views may be presumed to have received the approval of General French, adds a preface, in which he pursues the same object. Here, then, we have a volume which correctly represents in a compact and convenient form the best professional opinion on this question. I propose to refer to it incidentally, and at a later stage to submit it to closer analysis ; but I urge my readers to read the book for themselves, only taking care to remember who Bernhardi was, when he wrote, why he wrote, and for whom he wrote. I venture to think that they will pronounce the representation of his volume as the last word of wisdom for British Cavalrymen, and as the supreme vindication of the *arme blanche*, an almost incredible phenomenon in a strange controversy. They will find it, indeed, profoundly suggestive and interesting, but unconsciously destructive of the very doctrines which its English sponsors believe it to uphold. A more genuine representation of Continental thought may be found in a book entitled " Cavalry in the Russo-Japanese War," by the Austrian authority, Count Wrangel, to which I shall also refer.

In submitting theory to the test of facts, I propose to concentrate attention on the modern evidence, and by " modern " I mean evidence since the introduction of the smokeless, long-range magazine rifle. Of the two great wars since that era, those in South Africa and Manchuria, I shall deal principally with the former. For Englishmen, bent on discovering from their own national experience the best weapons and tactics for mounted men of their *own race*, as distinguished from foreign races, the South African facts are the only modern facts strictly relevant to the inquiry. Aside from savage warfare, and disregarding the first Boer War as too brief and inconclusive to afford reliable evidence, we have to go back in our search for earlier experience as far as the Crimean War, when the firearm was a plaything as compared with the modern rifle. In the realm of foreign experience, there has been a great deal of controversy, much of it painfully sterile, on Cavalry work in the Austro-Prussian War of 1866, the Franco-German War of 1870, and the Russo-Turkish War of 1877-78. Here, too, the firearm, though considerably improved, was primitive compared with the Mauser or the Lee-Enfield rifles. Nor, in spite of the illuminating examples furnished by the American Civil War, had anything approaching the type we now know as mounted riflemen been initiated by the Continental soldiers. There was no means of testing the value of this type, because it simply did not exist. Cavalry training and manœuvres were still those of the Napoleonic era. The firearm carried by the Cavalry was inferior even to that carried by the Infantry, and scarcely an attempt was made to inculcate any effectual use of it. Hence the comparative impotence of the Cavalries.

The American Civil War of 1862-65, for Englishmen especially, stands in a class by itself.* The men engaged in it were men of Anglo-Saxon race, untrammelled by prejudices and traditions, working out mounted problems by the light of common sense. The firearm, poor weapon as it was, judged by our modern standard, became the most valuable part of Cavalry equipment, and the most fruitful source of dash and enterprise. Sheridan's Cavalry were said by Stuart, who was the best possible judge, to have fought better on foot than the Federal Infantry. The great Cavalry raids in which the war abounded, and of which the European wars which followed were conspicuously barren, depended absolutely for their success, as all such enterprises always must depend, on aggressive fire-efficiency. Fire from the saddle was constantly used by Morgan, Forrest, and other leaders.

* Colonel Denison's " History of Cavalry " gives an excellent account of Cavalry work in this war and others of the same period.

Infantry on both sides learnt to despise the sword, though for inter-Cavalry combats that weapon, owing to the imperfections of the firearm, remained a trusted auxiliary. Our modern rifle would have certainly produced the pure type of mounted rifleman which South Africa produced in both sets of belligerents. The example had no effect upon Continental tactics, a blind imitation of which has always been the besetting sin of our own Cavalry school. Thirty-four years later, when the rifle had enormously increased in power, we pitted ourselves against the born shots and hunters of the veld with as little regard for the Cavalry lessons of the American Civil War as though it had never been fought.

Lastly, we have the Russo-Japanese War of 1904-05. That, as I shall show, seals the doom of the *arme blanche,* and crowns the case for the mounted rifleman. But it is a foreign war, and not, therefore, so peculiarly applicable to ourselves as the Boer War, whose lessons, nevertheless, it drives home. I propose to discuss it at a later stage, and will only remark now that even the most ardent advocates of the sword and lance have to admit that those weapons played no part in the war, while, on the other hand, neither Cavalry, not even the Japanese, approached the standard of fire-action attained in the course of our own war.

One more general word about the history of the subject prior to 1899. A vast amount has been written upon it. There is much common ground. Nobody denies that the relative importance of shock manœuvre with the steel weapon has steadily declined for a century. It is generally admitted that the examples of successful shock action in the European wars of the sixties and seventies were relatively very few, and the performances of the Cavalries relatively poor to those of other arms. While persisting in the argument that, had certain conditions been fulfilled, Cavalry work, including shock work, might have been more distinguished, advocates of the steel now generally admit that even then the neglect of fire-action was the main cause of ill-success. Upon this point no one could speak more strongly than Bernhardi. But if there is much common agreement, we must make our minds absolutely clear as to the nature of this agreement. A great part of the controversy has raged round a comparatively narrow point : whether masses of Cavalry can any longer charge Infantry, and, if so, what are the limitations to the success of such a charge. It is agreed that since 1870 limitations are many and severe ; but the settlement of that point leaves the major issue untouched. The opportunities of the steel weapon may have diminished, but to the Cavalry school this weapon remains the weapon *par excellence* for the Cavalry, the indispensably decisive factor in inter-Cavalry combats, which are to take the form of shock duels, and the main inspiration for all the wide and important range of duties belonging to the arm. No historian has studied more profoundly, nor written more brilliantly upon, the development of mounted tactics than the late Colonel Henderson. He was deeply versed in the Civil War, and preached to deaf ears the great possibilities even of an imperfect firearm in the hands of Cavalry. In a masterly analysis of the mounted actions of the European wars from 1866 to 1878,* he pointed out the comparative failure of shock, and the magnificent opportunities which would have been open to any body of mounted troops as skilled in fire-tactics as Stuart's Confederates. He even goes so far as to say that " a few commandos of Boers could have reduced to utter impotence the whole French Cavalry." Yet, at the end of his inquiry, just when he seems to have proved to an impartial reader that the day of the steel weapon is over and the undivided reign of the rifle begun, he

* " Science of War," chap. iii., " Tactical Employment of Cavalry " (undated).

falters. There is a strange logical hiatus. Then the old dogma proves too strong. After all, he concludes, the source of the " Cavalry spirit " is, and must be, the steel. A precisely similar phenomenon, though springing from wholly different causes, and with more domestic justification, occurs in the case of Bernhardi and of Wrangel. Henderson's solution was that, if we are to have thoroughly expert mounted riflemen, they must be embodied in a separate force.

That compromise should have taken this particular form in Henderson is a circumstance I have never been able to understand.   It is utterly contrary to Civil War experience, as he himself interprets it. That he should recommend one pure type, armed with either weapon, or two pure types, each armed with a different weapon ; or one hybrid type, with *theoretical* perfection in both weapons, would be intelligible. That he should recommend a hybrid type, with the steel strongly dominant and the rifle admittedly inferior, plus a pure type of expert mounted riflemen, is strange indeed, after the conclusions he draws from history. But the *arme blanche* plays the strangest tricks with the acutest minds. Bernhardi and our own Cavalry school are shrewd enough to postulate theoretical perfection in the hybrid type, even if they make the sword the supreme source of dash. We do not know what Henderson's final opinions were. The essay in which he alludes to the Boers was written before the end of the war. In him we can easily trace the cause of the logical hiatus. He had to take into account the use of the steel by American horsemen in inter-Cavalry combats, but at a time when the imperfections of the firearm left a field to the steel which has since been shut off. Whether the South African War, with its mounted rifle-charges, modified his views, we are ignorant. His first volume of the " Official History " never saw the light, and he died in 1903. But we know this, that the last paper he ever wrote, the " British Army "—though he does not touch specifically on the mounted problem at all—insists primarily on the revolution wrought in all modern tactics by the deadly efficacy of the smokeless, long-range magazine rifle, a revolution whose essence was the substitution of individual skill and intelligence for those formal, machine-like movements of massed bodies which are best exemplified in the case of shock action.

Using the South African War as his primary source of illustration and guidance, I ask the reader to grapple seriously with the logic and history of this matter. I beg him not to be content, failing incontrovertible arguments, with the assurance of Cavalry men that, in spite of the lessened opportunities for the *arme blanche* and the greater importance of the rifle, the former weapon must still be regarded as the governing factor in Cavalry training. I ask him to take nothing for granted, but to examine every function of Cavalry, tactical or strategical, defensive or offensive, whether against Cavalry, Infantry, or guns, and with a pitllessly critical eye to investigate the evidence bearing upon this vital question : Which is the better weapon ?

: He will be discouraged and confused at the outset by the obscurities connected with nomenclature. Names sanctioned by time always have a strong influence in human affairs. Nowhere is this influence more disproportionately strong than in the case of mounted troops. The fine old word " Cavalry " simply means horse-soldiers without regard to weapon ; but by the tradition of centuries it has always been, and is still associated with the sword and lance, though, in fact, for a long time past all Cavalries have been accustomed to carry some sort of firearm as well. Then there are Mounted Infantry, a force, so to speak, improvised out of Infantry, with a short additional training as horsemen ; then the volunteer Yeomanry, and the Colonial Mounted Rifle-men.

Names apart, the reader must ask himself : What happens in action ? Does the rifle dictate tactics to the sword, or the sword to the rifle ? What precise part does the question of weapons play in the ascription to Cavalry and the denial to Mounted Infantry of all the difficult and important duties of the major reconnaissance, duties obviously requiring many faculties, mental and physical, which have no connection with the steel weapon ? Can a man ride quicker or better, be more observant, original, or intelligent because he carries a sword ? Finally, how is training to conform to weapons ? In the realm of tactics does the official language correspond with the truth ? Why should the expression " dismounted tactics," as opposed to " mounted tactics," be always used in reference to the use of the rifle by Cavalry ? Does not the common factor of mobility transcend the factor of weapons ? Cannot mounted riflemen " charge," not, of course, according to that narrow interpretation of the word which restricts it to shock, but in ways equally, if not more, efficacious ? And if, aside from the mobility derived from the horse, the dash shown in these and similar operations can demonstrably be shown to have been inspired by the rifle, is not the old Cavalry maxim that dash is derived from the sword seriously shaken ? It is all very well in printed instructions to inculcate perfection in both, but is it humanly possible to maintain unimpaired in the same body of soldiers, still defined as " Cavalry," the old standard of shock manœuvre, with all the rigorous training it demands, and all the specialized instincts and habits associated with it, while adding all the equally rigorous, and equally specialized education of body and mind, which is indispensable to the production of a good mounted rifleman ? If not, which weapon is likely to go to the wall ?

Seeking light on these and kindred matters, the student will find himself straying in a fog of loose definitions corresponding to loose thought. He will find the word " Cavalry " used in several different senses for several different purposes ; sometimes merely to mean armed horsemen, sometimes with special emphasis on the steel weapon, sometimes with particular reference to the rifle. He will find Bernhardi calling the Boers Cavalry, and his commentator, Mr. Goldman, gravely rebuking him for not seeing that they were Mounted Infantry. He will find General French hotly combating the heresy that " Cavalry duels " are a thing of the past, and confusing in his own mind duels decided by the *arme blanche* with those struggles for mastery between the rival mounted forces of two opposing armies which, everyone agrees, must be a preliminary factor of high importance in all campaigns ; and we find him becoming eloquent on the great and growing rôle of Cavalry in war, as though anybody had ever doubted that proposition, except in so far as it implied that Cavalry drew their power mainly from the *arme blanche*.

The South African War, no less than the Manchurian War, throws a flood of light on all these difficulties. It seems strange that it should be necessary to recommend a thorough sifting and weighing of the South African evidence. Yet it is necessary, for it is the fashion now to dismiss that war as abnormal, and throughout this volume I shall have to devote considerable space to arguing why, for the purposes of this controversy, it should not be regarded as abnormal. In the meantime, I appeal for the maintenance of some reasonable sense of proportion in this matter. The war lasted more than two and a half years. It cost upwards of 200,000,000 pounds sterling. It exacted supreme efforts, military and economic. The total number of male belligerents opposed to us from first to last, foreigners and rebels included, scarcely exceeded 87,000. The total number of soldiers put into the field to meet them from first to last exceeded 400,000. For us, as I have already reminded the reader, it was the first great war against a race of European descent since the Crimea. For us, and for everyone else, it was the first test on the grand scale of the smokeless magazine rifle, not only in the hands of Infantry, but in the hands of mounted troops, and in the hands of mounted troops operating against Cavalry of the old type. Artillery apart, our foes one and all were mounted riflemen of the pure type. By degrees all our own mounted troops, of whatever category, became merged in the same type. And the war gradually became a mounted war. Mounted efficiency became the touchstone of success. Unprepared in multitudes of ways for the great struggle, it was in this respect from first to last that our chief deficiency lay. On the other hand, it was by their skill in the use of the horse and rifle combined that the Boers were enabled to defy us for so long.

Merely to state these elementary and indisputable facts is to prove that the war cannot lightly be regarded as abnormal. Common self-respect, to say nothing of historical judgment, should forbid such a manner of thinking. We need to recognize both our faults and our merits as disclosed at that great turning-point in our Imperial history. Pushed, as it is pushed, to extremes, this idea of abnormality becomes a narcotic, lulling us into lethargy and reaction. This was *our war*, won only by a vast expenditure of *our* blood and treasure. It has its memories of bitter humiliation as of glorious achievement, and those memories are *ours*. The experience is mainly valuable to us in that it is *ours*. In moments of exaltation we congratulate ourselves, probably with sound justification, on having, in spite of many blunders, achieved what a Continental army could not have achieved. And yet, when it comes to reading the plainest technical lesson of the war, we find the leading exponents of Cavalry doctrine brushing aside our own priceless experience, appealing to Germany for light and guidance, and introducing German formulas—meaningless to Germans themselves—into British instructional handbooks.

One of the worst features of this insistence on abnormality is the tendency it breeds in Cavalry writers to read the mounted operations of the war from the Cavalry point of view only. Had things been otherwise, had there been the normal opportunities for shock manœuvre, how much more brilliant would have been the part played by the Cavalry ! That is the line of argument, prompted, as no one can fail to observe, not only by an abstract faith in the *arme blanche*, but by a very natural anxiety to place in the best light the achievements of the Cavalry in South Africa. Confined within proper limits, that motive is unexceptionable, but the moment it begins to have the effect of converting a technical question into a sentimental question it becomes vicious. That is what has happened. No one can doubt the fact who reads Mr. Goldman, General French's military biographer, and notes the laboured efforts to extract from the most unpromising material conclusions favourable to the *arme blanche*, and the deplorable loss of perspective which such an effort entails. May I say here, if Mr. Goldman will permit me, that, although controversy will compel me to criticize his work unsparingly, I gladly and sincerely recognize its value as a historical narrative. We differ, not about facts, but about the reading of facts. I think his very natural admiration and affection for the Cavalry have led him into the error of believing that their reputation, as a branch of the service, is bound up with the reputation of the steel weapon. Believing the contrary myself, I cannot help chafing sometimes under what seems a sort of coercion into assuming the rôle of a detractor of the Cavalry, while my sole desire is to attack their armament. I fancy that all critics of the *arme blanche* have to face the same disagreeable ordeal. I can only do my best throughout to make my attitude clear. The topic ought to present no difficulties. As a nation, we ought to be ashamed of ourselves if we cannot discuss a great theme like this dispassionately on its merits. The Cavalry, like every other body of mounted troops in the King's dominions, is an Imperial possession. We are all proud of them, and if we criticize their methods, it is with the single object of making sure that the energies of this splendid body of men are directed into the most fruitful channel. In all wars we know we can count on their setting a high example of the great soldierly qualities, but we also want to make sure of their taking their right place at the outset, and maintaining that place throughout, as the leading exponents of progressive thought applied to mounted problems, and in that capacity to serve as models to all their Imperial comrades, and to the world at large.

On its merits, then, and on broad lines, I propose to discuss this question, avoiding so far as possible everything tending to cloud the vision with prejudice or bias. When I illustrate from recent facts it is not with the barren and invidious purpose of apportioning blame or praise, but with the single aim of elucidating the truth.

CHAPTER II

THE THREEFOLD PROBLEM

I.—The Physical Problem.

In preparation for the historical evidence, I propose to state what I consider to be the constituent elements of a threefold problem.   There is the purely physical problem, which in the marshalling of rival sets of precedents, and in the formulation of rival definitions of the Cavalry spirit, has almost always been overlooked.   There is the psychological problem, and there is the problem of training.

The physical conditions are simple, so simple as scarcely to need comment, were not habit and usage apt to obscure the origin of long-accepted maxims.   I am almost afraid to submit my first proposition, so naked a truism must it appear.   The primary distinction between the horse-soldier and the foot-soldier lies in the horse, not in the weapon carried by the man.   No permanent, fundamental distinction, either before or after the invention of gunpowder, has ever existed between the weapons carried by foot-soldiers and horse-soldiers respectively. At this day both classes alike carry both a steel weapon and a firearm.   A vast amount may depend (and otherwise I should not be writing) on the way the weapon may be permitted to govern mounted tactics, but from time immemorial it has been the superior mobility derived from the horse that has given to Cavalry, using the word in its widest sense, all the special functions which distinguish it from Infantry.   Let us beware, then, if we find a writer coupling together the horse and the steel weapon as though, by some immutable law, they were inseparable factors of efficiency. Surely, they are not. The common denominator is the horse. To ignore the lance or sword is not, with all respect to Sir John French, to ignore the horse.* The sole issue is, by the agency of what weapon can the horse, in conjunction with the will and the manual skill and strength of the man, be used to the best advantage ?

If the horse has his merits, he has his drawbacks. Let us consider both, strictly in relation to the question of weapons. Let us remember at the outset what is too often forgotten, that the weapon is only used in actual combat. In all those phases of war which precede combat, for the rapid transportation from one point to another of any body of troops great or small, ease of movement and secrecy of movement are the paramount considerations. In a strategic raid or a tactical turning movement, in any operation, offensive or defensive, from the action of a patrol to the action of a division, the carriage of troops into the zone of combat is a problem of mobility and secrecy pure and simple. Any weapon which unduly burdens the horse or rider, or renders them unduly conspicuous, is an obstacle to those ends only to be justified by showing that it is indispensable for combat. Similarly, any system of training which is designed to facilitate combat with any particular weapon, but which reacts unfavourably upon mobility or secrecy prior to the phase of combat, is, to that extent, to be deprecated. The scout exemplifies the principle in its extreme form. Acting as a scout, he is not meant to fight, but to move quickly, and to see without being seen. It is quite possible that a few

* " Cavalry soldiers must of course learn to be expert rifle shots, but the attainment of this desirable object will be brought no nearer by ignoring the horse, the sword, or the lance " (Introduction to Bernhardi's " Cavalry in Future Wars," p. 22).

unarmed scouts might decide the fate of armies ; certainly scouts have, in fact, done so without recourse to weapons.

Hitherto, so far as the merits and drawbacks of the horse are involved, we are concerned only with his speed and endurance on the one hand, and his visibility on the other. But as soon as we regard the horse as entering the zone of combat, we are confronted with a new and serious qualification to his value—namely, his vulnerability. This, in one degree or another, is an invariable source of weakness. The danger to be incurred may be reduced to a minimum, as in the case of the pursuit of utterly demoralized troops. Surprise and stratagem may modify the risk to an indefinite extent, but the risk always exists, and can be overcome in the last resort only by a mobility so high as to transcend it. We arrive thus at the two opposing factors, mobility and vulnerability, the one tending to counteract the other ; and from the physical point of view it is upon the correct estimate of the relative strength of these two factors that the solution of every tactical mounted problem depends. It goes without saying that the invention and improvement of the firearm, by immensely extending the zone of vulnerability and immensely increasing the degree of vulnerability within that zone, has profoundly affected the conditions of this ever-present problem. The reader, no doubt, will add that the same general principle applies to Infantry. True ; but there is especially good reason to insist on its application to mounted troops.

Arrived at this point, we must, for the sake of clearness, disregard the hybrid type of horseman, and picture, for the time being, as separate personalities, the horseman armed with a steel weapon and the horseman armed with a firearm. Later on we will fuse the two personalities in one, when we come to consider training. But for the present I want to concentrate attention on the relative value in combat of fire and steel.

Let us take first the horseman armed with the steel weapon.

Two characteristics must be noted at once : (1) His steel weapon is used from horseback only ; (2) as against riflemen, whether mounted or dismounted, it is only used in *offence*.   In both these respects it differs from the bayonet.

In encounters on horseback with other steel horsemen (assumed, as before, to be pure steel horsemen) it may in a sense be said to be used both in defence and offence, but these encounters do not immediately concern us.   If two bodies of horse *agree* to settle accounts in that way, that is their own affair.   The best swordsmen and riders will win.   We are contrasting fire and steel, and the steel as against riflemen is only used in offence—why will soon appear.   We must picture, then, our steel horseman as acting offensively.

Now, in the physical sphere, while the improvements in the firearm have greatly increased both the zone and degree of the horseman's vulnerability, there is nothing to redress the balance in favour of the horse or the steel weapon.   Both the speed of the former and the efficacy of the latter remain practically constant quantities from age to age.   By comparison with firearms, steel weapons may be said to be incapable of improvement.   As missiles they have been obsolete for centuries.   As manual implements their range is the range of a man's arm, plus their own length.   They cannot be used at any point short of actual contact with the enemy, a point which must be reached with the rider in the saddle, while the growth in the destructive efficacy of the firearm, directed against so large a target as that presented by rider and animal combined, has steadily reduced the horseman's power of reaching that point without mishap.   Even after he reaches it, he still presents the same large area of vulnerable surface as compared with a man on foot.

On the other hand, if and when he obtains contact, he

gains in two ways. His weapon gains in efficacy relatively to the firearm, since for the moment the factor of range has been equalized, or almost equalized. Secondly, his horse has a new merit, its weight; but this is not an individual, but a collective merit, only developed by the combined weight of many horses.

That brings me to a consideration of the steel weapon's sole function in war—the shock charge. We are to regard the man now as a member of a mass. He and his comrades, by the impact due to the united momentum of their horses, aim at producing " shock," with its stunning physical effect on the defence. Aided by shock, they use their steel weapons.

Now, what are the necessary conditions for the production of genuine shock? First, the horsemen must attack in dense formation, precisely the formation which offers the best target for rifle-fire. Second, in order to make shock effective, the riflemen who are the object of attack must also be in tolerably dense formation, otherwise there is nothing substantial on which to exert shock. This, of course, is one of the greatest of the modern limitations to shock, for the whole tendency in war is towards loose and away from dense formations, the cause being the increased efficacy of firearms.

Thirdly, since the ground must be covered at high speed and with absolute cohesion in order to obtain momentum and to minimize vulnerability, the ground must in every case be such as to permit of high speed, fairly smooth, fairly level, fairly open, and, above all, continuously practicable up to the supreme moment of contact. Any concealed obstruction or entanglement met with in traversing the danger zone may irretrievably compromise the charge. For true shock a ragged, disjointed impact is useless. Clean, sharp, and shattering impact is the only end worth attainment. The ground may fulfil all these requirements up to the last few yards, but in the last few yards a sunk ditch, a wire fence, not to speak of more visible obstacles, such as hedges, walls, earthworks, or any of the common features of an ordinary defensive position, may render the whole enterprise nugatory. If the reader will bear in mind the average character of ground in European countries, he will recognize another serious limitation to the employment of shock.

Fourthly, supposing that all the conditions hitherto enumerated are satisfied, speed is still dependent on the freshness of the horses. Whatever their exertions in the performance of the innumerable and highly responsible duties of Cavalry not necessarily involving combat, the horses must be capable, whenever and wherever the opportunity occurs, of a vigorous gallop, ending with the super-gallop known as the "charge," at this supreme moment—the one and only moment in which the steel horseman fulfils his rôle. Modern war proves this standard of freshness to be chimerical. In peace-training you may compromise on speed as much as you please, and in point of fact the rigorous directions of "Cavalry Training" (p. 125) are often diluted to a canter ending in a short gallop. Futile compromise! The less speed, the greater and longer the vulnerability of the mass, and the *less shock*.

Here are four conditions for the effective exercise of shock, each stringent, and, since they must all be satisfied, of a fourfold cumulative stringency. Note again the absence of analogy with the bayonet, which is fixed to the rifle, and comes into use only at the climax of a fire-fight on foot. The four conditions may be mitigated genuinely by one circumstance, which I shall refer to later. At the moment I wish to refer to an alleged mitigation which embraces a profound fallacy, and I beg for the reader's particular attention to this point, for it is largely on that fallacy, at any rate in our own country, that the *arme blanche* continues to thrive.

Recall the first two conditions, which may be regarded as counterparts of one another—density of formation, both in the attacking and defending force. The reader will easily understand why the latter condition is so necessary. To propel a massed body of horsemen against an extended line of riflemen is a wasteful expenditure of effort. There will be no shock worth the name, while the mass in motion is almost as vulnerable a target to rifles as though the defence too were massed ; fire is convergent instead of direct, that is all. But supposing the horsemen follow suit, and charge in loose, extended order ? So they may, but in that case also *they will not produce shock*, which is the indispensable condition for the successful use of the steel weapon. Here is the heart of the whole matter. Though there is, of course, no fixed moment when shock may be said to disappear, it is plain that with every additional yard of extension, either in the attacking or defending line, or both, shock, which means the violent physical impact of a united body, must diminish. It is equally plain that in proportion to this diminution of shock the chances of the steel weapon rapidly dwindle and the retaliatory power of the rifleman rapidly increases. He is now an individual pitted against a rival individual who has lost the collective power due to mass, while he retains the vulnerability due to large surface presented by his horse. On these terms the rifleman has an immense advantage. He has room to move in, a longer range for his far more deadly weapon, and breathing-time. Let the student beware, then, when he finds it laid down in the textbook that Cavalry, when attacking Infantry, are to charge in " extended order " with the steel weapon.* No thoroughly logical upholder of shock—no German, for example—would be guilty of such a solecism. Bernhardi recommends, at the utmost, a " loosening of the files " from the jammed, knee-to-

* " Cavalry Training," p. 129.

knee rigidity of the charge, as it is to be employed against horsemen. "Only *closed* lines on a broad front can be relied upon for success."* Our idea of extension could only come from confusion of thought in a period of transition. The reader must watch this point most carefully when we come to illustrations from the South African War. Is there, then, no opportunity for horsemen to charge in extended order ? Of course there is ; but not for horsemen using the steel. I shall come to the other type in a moment.

I have dealt with the fallacious source of mitigation. Now for the true source—surprise. This factor of course favours the attack, not only of steel horsemen, but of all horsemen, and, indeed, of all troops in any phase of military effort. But it is the soul of mounted effort, because surprise is derived from mobility, and the horse is the instrument of mobility. Surprise, therefore, can mitigate any of the rigorous conditions imposed on shock. For example, the extended riflemen may be caught in flank so suddenly that they can neither develop fire before contact nor deploy frontally to meet it. Or massed infantry may be caught in column of route. But in all cases the degree of surprise requisite can only be measured by the rigour of the conditions, and experience proves, admittedly, that under modern conditions an enormous degree of surprise is necessary for the success of shock against riflemen. On the whole we shall not be far wrong if we lay it down, as Bernhardi plainly indicates, that the best, if not the only, opportunity for the steel against riflemen is in the pursuit of utterly demoralized troops. Here the least degree of shock is necessary, with a corresponding slackening in the rigour of the conditions of shock, but, be it noted, with a corresponding diminution in the efficacy of the steel, which, as I pointed out, is closely dependent on shock. If we reach a point

* " Cavalry in Future Wars," pp. 221-2 and 234 (4).

when no shock is possible, the steel becomes no more useful than the rifle.

So much for the steel, and the reader long before this will have seen why the steel is only used in offence. It requires shock, shock requires momentum, and momentum implies offence.

Now let us turn to the mounted rifleman, assumed to be of the pure type. But observe at the outset that we have already been dealing with his defensive rôle. Dismounted, he has the defensive power of Infantry, and the physical factors involved are precisely the same. Continue to regard him in defence, crediting him now with the additional mobility conferred by the horse. If it is only under the rarest circumstances that Infantry can be forced into combat on terms favourable to steel, still more rarely can mounted riflemen be so forced. They can extend more quickly, change front, or retire to better positions more easily—in a word, they have a tactical suppleness and elasticity unknown to Infantry. Of course, I am assuming that they are good mounted riflemen, skilled in the instantaneous transition from the mounted to the dismounted state, and able to manage their led horses adroitly and safely. It has always been the belief of the *arme blanche* school that steel horsemen if they cannot charge dismounted riflemen, can at any rate charge their led horses. All the facts, as I shall show, prove this idea to be illusory.

And now, on behalf of the rifle, let us carry the war into the enemy's camp, regarding the rifle, not as a defensive, but as an aggressive weapon in the hands of mounted men. Save for the elimination of weight, the physical merits and demerits of the horse remain precisely the same : speed on the one hand, vulnerability on the other. To exploit the first and minimize the second must be the effort here as always. But that is the only point of similarity in the two widely different problems presented by shock-tactics and fire-tactics. The sword can only be used in a hand-to-hand encounter ; the modern firearm has deadly effect at long distances. From this fundamental difference in the two weapons everything else follows. Shock, with its crushing limitations and disabilities, is totally eliminated. The very idea of shock is utterly foreign to the fire-tactics of mounted men, because there is no necessity for it.   There is no necessity, therefore, to comply with all the conditions which are required to produce shock, and which in their turn so dangerously enhance the vulnerability of horse and rider. Let us try to contrast the two systems of attack, with the steel and the firearm respectively, remembering that mounted riflemen, besides the defensive, have the offensive power of Infantry plus the mobility conferred by the horse.

As in defence so in offence, the firearm begins to be deadly when the steel weapon is only an encumbrance, and when the firer is still invisible. By the intelligent use of ground for the concealment of horses, and the development of fire at successive points, the attack may go through all the phases of Infantry attack with a vast increase of mobility, and with the vulnerability of the horse reduced by skill to a minimum.

But I need not dwell on the preliminary and intermediate phases of combat. It is only in the last phase—that of the final assault—that any parallel with shock-tactics begins. Up to this point the steel weapon has been idle, nor even now can it be brought into play unless all those four inexorable conditions are satisfied. The first two—close formation both in the attacking and defending force—do not apply at all to mounted riflemen, since there is no question of shock. The third and fourth have but a remote application.

Far from being a unique moment, this is merely a culmination. The enemy probably is already shaken, not by the fear of something which can only materialize after contact, but by positive casualties wrought by a long-range weapon. It remains to drive home the victory.

Contact may be desirable if feasible, but there is no imperative need for it. Under many conditions rifle-fire is more effective at 5, 50, even 100 yards' distance than in a mêlée. A victory may be crushingly conclusive without recourse to anything in the nature of a hand-to-hand encounter; but if nothing save a hand-to-hand encounter will secure a victory, the rifle provides scores of opportunities of obtaining that encounter where the *arme blanche* provides but one, if only the mounted riflemen are versed in that elementary part of their trade, which consists in knowing what and how to use, and when and how to discard, the horse. As compared with the steel horsemen, they are almost independent of ground. Instead of perpetually pining for level swards and open " Cavalry ground," they welcome inequalities and obstacles, for these are the true conditions of surprise. Indeed, they make use of these obstacles, instead of allowing them to baulk their efforts. Steep ascents often aid them, entrenchments and other defences, natural or artificial, at the point of contact, —hopeless barriers, however flimsy in their character, to shock—can be surmounted by them. But supposing the ground is open, level, and smooth, and a mêlée with the enemy obtainable by quadrupeds, suppose, in fact, the only topographical conditions which can render an *arme blanche* charge possible, is there no rôle open to them analogous to that of the steel horsemen ? Can they not charge home ? I shall prove by a quantity of facts drawn from experience that they can, and under conditions which would be fatal to an *arme blanche* charge. Not aiming at physical shock, not therefore presenting the vulnerable target produced by close formation, they do not need the same degree of speed, nor, consequently, that perpetual freshness in their mounts which is the chimera of theorists and the despair of practical men. Nor is the size of their horses—an important element in *genuine* shock—of any account to mounted riflemen. Within rational limits, the smaller they are the better. Finally, in the process of covering on horseback this last intervening space of open, level ground, when the *arme blanche*, remember, even at the eleventh hour is still idle, need the rifle, too, be idle ? Again, I shall bring ample modern testimony, which is fortified by much evidence from the American Civil War, to show that fire from the saddle, even if unaimed, may be used with signal effect, and in the case of the modern rifle, not merely moral effect, but physical effect. It may take the shape of aimed fire, as against horsemen at close quarters in pursuit, or against a Cavalry " mass," or groups of led horses ; while a few casualties, even from unaimed fire, in the defence, however constituted, produce great effect in daunting aim and nerves alike. Here, mark, is the crowning element of superiority in the rifle. Unlike the steel, which is used only from horseback, it can be used both from horseback and on foot. The first-class mounted rifleman—the ideal type we can construct from direct war experience—will be at home in both. He will use saddle-fire mainly in its unaimed or roughly-aimed form, and will dismount for effective killing.

The " charge," which is the sole function of the *arme blanche*, is no longer the monopoly of the *arme blanche*. It is one of the functions—the culminating function among many—of mounted riflemen. The word, of course, is an unsatisfactory one, because in its ordinary sense (derived originally from shock-tactics) it implies a mêlée or hand-to-hand encounter, while for mounted riflemen, as for Infantry, it has a far wider meaning. A charge ending within a few yards of the enemy—for example, just below the crest of an elevation on which the defending troops are stationed—is just as much a charge as if it were pushed beyond that intervening space into the sphere of physical contact, and it may be just as decisive. But examples, of which an infinity may be cited, will lead me too far afield at the present moment. I am regarding in isolation, so far as that is possible, the physical side of the problem, and I suggest that the physical factors give an immense superiority to the rifle over the steel as an offensive weapon for mounted men. Obviously it is possible to conceive cases when, from the physical point of view, the steel weapon may have an advantage. The point is, how often in modern conditions can such cases arise? I think that from the preceding analysis it will be clear that these cases can be narrowed down to the small class I have already mentioned—pursuits of thoroughly demoralized troops. Even then the advantage is exceedingly problematical, and is, in point of fact, not supported by any modern evidence. Under such extreme circumstances as Bernhardi describes on page 15 of " Cavalry in Future Wars " attack with any weapon whatsoever—battle-axe, revolver, club—will have approximately equal chances, if, indeed, any weapon at all is needed to secure surrender. What the rifle can effect in the way of sheer rapid killing I shall prove by facts.

Remember, too, another important point. Momentum is a continuing condition of the shock charge. Impetus must be sustained, the defence burst through, and a rally made on the farther side—a matter of time and difficulty—for another stroke which inevitably must be less effective than the first ; and the first, owing to dense formation, has struck a comparatively small area. The rifleman has nothing to do with continuing momentum, and the stereotyped "rally." His business is to use his rifle when, where, and how he can, mounted or dismounted, and with as large a radius as he can. He is always busy, and always formidable.

One more word on this contingency of the use of steel
in utterly demoralized retreat. It has always been the
favourite dream of Cavalrymen, but it is a dream which
in modern war never comes true. Panic is never universal. There are sections or groups always who have
nerve and spirit enough to fire, and show a decent front,
and directly any element of fire-defence enters in, the
power of the steel wanes to nothing, and the need for
mounted riflemen begins. It was so even in 1866 at
Königgrätz. It was so in South Africa and Manchuria.

I hope he is bearing in mind that it is only for the sake of
clearness that I have been taking pure types of steel horsemen and rifle horsemen respectively, and crediting both
with high excellence in their several *métiers*. The hybrid
horseman will, of course, have his share in the advantages,
defensive and offensive, of the pure mounted rifleman ;
what share is another matter. I am now contrasting fire
and steel in the physical sphere, and I ask, have I exhausted the cases of opposition between fire and steel ?
In reality I have, but I am too familiar with the *arme
blanche* sentiment not to be aware that I shall be held to
have ignored one important case. Again it is an imaginary case. Two solid masses of horsemen are pictured,
the one with swords, the other swordless, confronting one
another at close quarters on an open plain—" in the
open " runs the vague phrase—both blocks on *horseback*.
Palpably, so the argument runs, the steel must triumph.
Possibly, but the contingency never happens, never can
happen unless by one of those stunning surprises which
have no special relevance to mounted tactics, and which
argue scandalous neglect in the defence. For the steel
especially such stunning surprises are unattainable, because " open " ground, one of the conditions of shock,
is the worst ground for stunning surprise. But the
illusion does not stop here. It is elevated into that
complete conception of the inevitable shock duel which

is the very corner-stone of Cavalry theory. The idea
is this, that in the last resort shock alone can decide
the combats of mounted troops. It is true that this
unqualified generalization is so contrary to common
sense that it is rarely set forth in so many words, but
it comes to that, or there is no meaning in the theory.
The inter-Cavalry fight, says "Cavalry Training,"
whether in the phase of strategical reconnaissance, or
on the battle-field of all arms, must be decided by
shock. Fire-action at the best will have but a "negative
result."* I shall dispose of this fallacy, which has itself
paralyzed and sterilized Cavalries believing in it, by
illustration. Meanwhile the reader has probably detected
its inherent improbabilities. If there happens to be no
available ground for shock—and how much of England,
for example, is available ?—there must be *negative* effect
on both sides—a double stalemate, a deadlock—unless
both parties resort by agreement to a favourable place,
as in peace manœuvres they do in fact often resort.
But that is a secondary fallacy : the fundamental fallacy
is the supposition that the steel can impose tactics on the
rifle. It cannot. There is not a tittle of evidence to
prove that it can. All modern evidence proves that the
rifle imposes tactics on the steel, and the evidence only
confirms the plain physical principles.

II.—The Psychological Problem.

In war the moral advantage of a weapon, whether used
in offence or defence, depends absolutely on its physical
efficacy. It will inspire confidence in its possessor and
fear in his adversary in direct proportion to its average
working utility. Practical fighting men cannot be induced for long to retain either a sentimental affection or
a superstitious awe for a weapon of proved inferiority.

* "Cavalry Training," p. 194.

3—2

In the early days of a war, when the merits of new weapons, or of old weapons in new hands, are still in doubt, such irrational feelings have been known to operate ; but they do not last.   At the beginning of the South African War the Boers feared the horseman's sword, but the fear did not last.   The physical capabilities of the weapon, in harmony with the physical capabilities of the horse, determine the moral impulse of the horseman and the moral effect upon the enemy.

In endeavouring to apply this simple criterion to the case of the *arme blanche* and the rifle, we are confronted at once with two formidable obstacles, the " Cavalry spirit " and the " terror of cold steel "—the former a subjective idea, the latter its objective corollary.

No one but a Cavalryman, perhaps, can fully appreciate the depth and intensity of the old tactical tradition of the Cavalry, a tradition many centuries old, the treasured heritage of many glorious fields.   There is nothing which exactly corresponds to it in other arms.   Both the Infantry and Artillery have been accustomed to rely continuously on improvements in their weapons and to modify their field training accordingly.   But, as I have pointed out, the steel weapons of Cavalry are not susceptible of improvement.   With stereotyped weapons, however great the traditions behind them, the tactics have tended to be stereotyped, not absolutely, of course, but relatively to the progress made in other arms.   Hence there has grown up what is known as the " Cavalry spirit."   This consecrates the past, and entrenches the type behind an impregnable rampart of sentiment.   Let us note that in relation to other branches of the service the " Cavalry spirit " is something of an anomaly.   No one speaks, at any rate with the same peculiar emphasis, of an " Infantry spirit " or an " Artillery spirit," though the peculiar traditions of these arms are no less glorious, their *esprit de corps* no less admirable, their ardour in action no less great. No; the Cavalry spirit in latter days has come to be an unconscious tribute to change, and at the same time the symbol of resistance to change.

Let us be quite clear about the nature of this spirit, otherwise we may be misled by a mere point of nomenclature. I pass by that bilateral definition, referred to in the beginning of this volume, which, as I pointed out, represented mere lip-service to the rifle, and is not seriously accepted by Cavalrymen themselves. Historically, here and on the Continent the Cavalry spirit dates back to a time when there was but one category of mounted troops, that known as " Cavalry," to which all the war duties naturally belonging to men provided with horses were assigned, and whose primary weapons were the steel weapons. It has outlived the intrusion of the rifle into mounted tactics and the introduction of new pure types under the names of Mounted Infantry and Mounted Riflemen. Outliving these innovations, it has naturally retained, for Cavalrymen at any rate, a wider significance than present conditions warrant. It implies in the larger sense dash, speed, audacity, resource, nerve—qualities which should be the possession of all soldiers vested with the high mobility given by the horse. And it covers, in the larger sense again, all the duties still arbitrarily assigned to Cavalry and arbitrarily withheld from mounted riflemen—duties many of which have only the remotest connection with the steel weapon, and could be—have been, in fact—performed equally well, and better, by troops relying on the rifle. But, stripped of all these confusing elements, which are due to the secular association of the horse and the steel weapon as inseparable corollaries of one another, the Cavalry spirit, in its inmost essence, means the spirit of fighting *on horseback* with a steel weapon, in contradistinction to the spirit of fighting on foot with a firearm. As I have said before, with opposing bodies of horse who both deliberately elect to contend on horseback with the steel we have nothing to do. Our sole concern is to estimate the influence of the modern rifle upon that method of fighting. Now, in view of the physical principles set forth above, is the Cavalry spirit, as I have defined it, a sensible thing to inculcate ?

I shall prove that the " terror of cold steel," the objective counterpart of the " Cavalry spirit," is a myth. Cold steel, no doubt, may seem terrible enough to troops taught to rely on it, but no Infantryman worth his salt feels any terror of the horseman's steel. Infantry are taught in our own country to despise it, not to fear it. *A fortiori* mounted riflemen, with the combative power of Infantry plus high mobility, should be taught not to fear it. They are not so taught.

Strangely enough, the refutation of the theory of terror, and incidentally of the whole theory of the *arme blanche*, is contained within the covers of the Training Handbooks. Let the reader study carefully the whole of page 92 of " Infantry Training " (" Meeting an Attack by Cavalry "), noting specially the opening words about " open ground " and " broken ground " in the case of a foot-soldier versus an individual trooper. Forming square to meet shock has, of course, long been abolished. Then let him read pages 60 and 61 of " Mounted Infantry Training," where he will actually find gravely set forth directions for forming square to resist Cavalry, so vulnerable are Mounted Infantry taught to regard themselves when " surprised in the open " (the vague old phrase !) by Cavalry. Why give Mounted Infantry horses at all ? Meanwhile some zealot for the horse and the rifle has been allowed to insert on page 57 a direction for Mounted Infantry to use saddle-fire, though only in the case of " scouts and picked men." So near we are to common sense, and yet so far ! Fancy a scout, whose aim is secrecy, using saddle-fire !

In all this insistence on imaginary sources of awe the true moral factors underlying mounted action are forgotten. The greatest of these is surprise. Behind the weapon is the horse, and the horse is common to all mounted troops. Properly handled, mounted men will always be able to exert a strong moral effect upon non-mounted men, simply from their mobility, from their power to change or gain ground rapidly, to feint, raid, and swoop, envelop, outflank, mystify, outmanoeuvre—in a word, to surprise their slow-moving antagonists. It is the horse which invests them with this power, not the weapon, and if we are to speak of "terror," it is primarily the terror of surprise—in its widest sense—which hampers and daunts unmounted troops in dealing with mounted troops. Conversely, it is primarily the power of inflicting surprise which instils dash into horsemen, however armed. Nor is surprise merely an aggressive aim of horsemen; it is a defensive instinct, since the mobility which gives surprise is set off to some extent by the vulnerability of that engine of mobility, the horse. Here we come back to physical conditions. Surprise is useless unless materialized through the agency of a deadly weapon. For the materialization of surprise what comparison can there be between a smokeless, accurate magazine rifle and a weapon which is harmless unless and until physical contact is attained, especially if it be remembered that the sort of physical contact indispensable to success can only be brought about under such a rare combination of exceptional circumstances as I have described ?

To mounted riflemen surprise presents a whole world of activity unknown to shock horsemen. In extreme, but not at all abnormal cases, they can initiate, elaborate, and carry a surprise to complete and crushing victory without even so much as being clearly seen by the defence. In intermediate cases they can always be content with a far less *degree* of surprise than shock horsemen, for whom surprise only materializes at the supreme moment of a shock charge home. In remoter cases still they can exercise a strong moral effect even at great distances by a threat upon flanks or communications, when shock-trained horsemen would leave the nerves of the enemy absolutely undisturbed.

III.—THE PROBLEM OF TRAINING.

Here we gather up the threads of the two preceding sections. I have hitherto regarded fire-tactics and shock-tactics as distinct functions attributable to distinct categories of troops. Initially, that is the only way, I believe, of dissipating the mist of ambiguity cast over the subject by the loose employment of undefined terms like " Cavalry," and by that obsession of thought which cannot conceive of the employment of the horse to the best advantage without the accompaniment of a steel weapon. But the question has to be faced : Cannot shock-tactics, for what they are worth, and fire-tactics be har-moniously combined in a hybrid type ? We have at present only one category of troops which professes to combine both functions—namely, our regular Cavalry, who carry both a steel weapon and a good firearm. I can imagine a reader saying, " Granted that your analysis of the rival merits of the two weapons is correct ; you admit that the steel may conceivably have a remote sphere of utility : cannot the Cavalry do all that you picture mounted riflemen as doing, and, in addition, when the rare opportunities present themselves, use the steel effectively ?" Or I can imagine the convinced advocate of the *arme blanche* saying : " Your analysis is all wrong : the steel has a nobler and wider sphere than the rifle ; still, for what it is worth, we can use the rifle in the way you describe. We can do all your mounted riflemen can do, and a great deal more besides." As with the physical and moral problems, when theory has said her last word, war experience only can provide a final answer to these questions. Meanwhile I suggest for the reader's consideration that a profound fallacy underlies this notion that you can train the same set of men to become perfect in the use of weapons so different as the modern magazine rifle and the sword or lance, no matter from which weapon they are taught to derive their " spirit," or which weapon is supposed to give them the most numerous or valuable opportunities. If you favour one you prejudice the other ; and the more you endeavour to trim and compromise the less efficient the hybrid you produce. As Count Wrangel truly says, you cannot serve these two masters.* Both are equally exacting, and the types of education they exact are as far apart as the poles. Until quite recent times, outside a little perfunctory attention to the use of a short carbine, training based on the steel occupied almost the entire time of European Cavalries, including our own. Perfection in that training, whatever its war value, requires hard, continuous training extending over years. Manual practice in a steel weapon is an art in itself. To teach men to handle in concert steel weapons from horseback with safely to themselves, to say nothing of damage to their enemy, is a long and difficult matter. To teach them the shock charge under peace conditions and on selected ground and selected horses, with no bullets flying, and with no unforeseen obstacles to mar the symmetry, speed and cohesion which are the conditions of success, can be the outcome only of immense patience and application in sheer mechanical drill. If anyone doubts this let him go to " Cavalry Training " for confirmation. Whether the charge be used rarely or often makes no difference. What is worth doing at all is worth doing well, and to train men to do this thing well is a very

* "Cavalry in the Russo-Japanese War," p. 55.

big business. If they cannot do it well, they will be beaten at their own game by troops who can. It is futile to postulate an ideal balance between shock-tactics and the loose fire-tactics imposed by the modern rifle. For troops trained to rely mainly on the " terror of cold steel " the shock charge cannot be a side-issue. It is, and must be, the central aim of Cavalry education. It must govern drill, and through drill its influence reacts upon and permeates all functions of Cavalry to their remotest ramifications. The ideas behind it, the impulses directing it, are ideas and impulses totally different from, and, under modern conditions, fundamentally antagonistic to, those which inspire fire-tactics.

What is true of specializing in shock-tactics is still more true of specializing in fire-tactics. The art of the mounted rifleman, carried to the point of perfection to which by war experience we know that it can be carried, demands an exclusive education. Here, too, is a very big business, inexperience in which cost us scores of millions of pounds in South Africa. You cannot, by a stroke of the pen, as it were, graft this art on to the art of steel and shock by merely re-editing the pre-war Drill-Book. Marksmanship, though very important, is a comparatively small part of the education. Civilians can become good marksmen. Our Cavalry have proved latterly, to their high credit, that they can become good target marksmen without an excessive sacrifice of time. Nor could anyone who witnessed the general manœuvres of 1909 dream of saying that the Cavalry had not made remarkable strides in fire-tactics in the last few years. The advance, with its proof of the adaptability of our men to the art, only renders the squandering of energy on shock the more painful. We know that they can never learn enough of fire-tactics. What cannot be taught unless it be made a highly-specialized branch of study and training is the field-craft, the head, eye, and instinct for mounted work with the rifle, to say nothing of the more purely technical requirements—the special formations, the handling of led horses, fire from the saddle, and the like. The work involves a special way of looking at all field problems ; it is inspired, as I have said, by ideas and impulses of an altogether different category from those which inspire shock. It requires less machine-like drill, more individual intelligence, less crude exertion of muscle, more reliance on the wits, and withal just as good riding, just as careful horsemastership, and just as much self-sacrifice, audacity, and dash. I shall prove this up to the hilt by direct illustration from modern wars ; but is it not self-evident ? For here are men vested with the offensive and defensive power of Infantry, together with a mobility which is several times that of Infantry. Infantry have plenty to do to become good at their trade. How imperious and exacting must be the demands upon mounted infantry ! I have slipped into one of the conventional definitions. Let us give it capitals, and ask how the fire-duties of Cavalry differ essentially from those of Mounted Infantry, or any other category of mounted riflemen ?

Fog hangs heavy on that most pertinent inquiry. But the answer, of course, is that there is no difference whatever. And it follows necessarily that, however seldom or often fire-duties may be required of Cavalry, Cavalry will be excelled by mounted riflemen in the performance of those duties, just as they will be excelled in shock by troops who have more practice in shock. In either sphere the hybrid type must succumb to the pure type, and the moral is all the easier to see and enforce because the pure type of mounted rifleman, however arbitrary and fanciful the limits assigned to its utility, is actually and officially recognized at this moment, whereas no such thing as a pure type of shock horseman exists.

Nor is it only a case of competition with other mounted riflemen or other hybrid Cavalry. Let the reader extract from " Cavalry Training," tabulate, and analyze all the fire-duties now theoretically allotted to Cavalry. It will take some little trouble, because they are not marshalled compactly or given the emphasis they deserve. He will find that they cover almost the entire range of war, and it goes without saying that in every one of these duties the trooper must be prepared to fight approximately as well as the riflemen opposed to him, whether they be Infantry or mounted men. Otherwise he will fail. Troops cannot be manipulated in war so that each class meets only its corresponding type. Each class must be prepared to meet any other, both in defence and offence. I am not constructing an academical dilemma, but a dilemma forced upon us by the facts of modern war. Bernhardi sees it clearly, and goes much farther, accordingly, than " Cavalry Training " dares go, in postulating that utterly unattainable perfection in both weapons which is the only way out of the dilemma. More on that point later.

The truth is that, in this country, behind all the inconsequent reasoning which pervades conventional theories of mounted training, there lies the disastrous hallucination that skill with the rifle is a comparatively easy thing to learn, a thing which is essentially appropriate to imperfectly trained troops—volunteers, irregulars of all sorts— and which can be taken in their stride, so to speak, by regulars, whose crown and glory is shock. If this view were upheld only by the regular Cavalry it would be bad enough, but there is a tendency to uphold it among the volunteers too, so that we daily have the heart-breaking spectacle of men who have not yet come to the point of realizing the tremendous possibilities of the rifle crying aloud like children for a steel weapon. The responsibility for that fatal discontent rests absolutely on the Cavalry.

Lastly, let it be remembered that this is not merely a question of carrying weapons of debatable combat-value. It is a question of mobility, transcending weapons, but at the same time hinging on weapons. I began this chapter by insisting on the pre-combat or non-combat phases of war as distinguished from the combat phase, in which alone weapons are useful. Nobody suggests dispensing with the rifle. Can we dispense with the sword and lance ? Their weight alone is something, especially when both are carried. But besides that, they are the very weapons which add to visibility and injure general mobility. The more closely you adhere to the idea of shock—and, in strict logic, you should adhere to it if you admit the steel weapon at all—the more you are bound in strict logic to favour big horses and correspondingly heavy men. If you disregard logic, as we instinctively disregard it now, except in the case of the *élite* of our regiments, you risk overthrow in the theoretically inevitable shock duel with a more logical Cavalry. That is a small risk, because, as I shall prove, modern war does not favour that class of encounter. The great evil is the deadening effect of the shock theory on that direct aggressive power with the firearm which modern war insists on exacting. The result is either that humiliating inaction which extorted the puzzled censure of Von Moltke as long ago as 1866, or a dissipation of the physical energy of horses and men on circumventions and evasions which only postpone without facilitating combat. It is a matter of experience, too, that in time of peace the galloping standard for the shock charge, the instinctive aversion to dismounting, and other corollaries of the artificial shock system and the " spirit " founded on it, tend to produce under real campaigning conditions defective horse management and faults of a like character.

In the last resort the training of all our mounted troops turns on *Cavalry* training. If there is error there, error positive or negative will penetrate every class. Is there error ? The tests of peace are illusory. Let us examine the tests of war.

CHAPTER III

In reviewing the mounted operations of the South African War, I must impress upon the reader the necessity of regarding the war as a whole, and not as a series of episodes gradually decreasing in dramatic and technical interest, and ending in a long and dreary period, profitless for study, of sporadic hostilities known as the " guerilla war." A guerilla war really began within the first six months of hostilities. For serious students of the war, interest in its mounted tactics increases from first to last, because the war gradually became more and more a mounted war, and mounted tactics underwent a steady and progressive development. It would be unnecessary to begin with any such exhortation as this were it not for the sheer ignorance, even in authoritative writers, of actual historical events during the latter part of the war, events which have a direct instructional bearing on preceding phases, and without a knowledge of which it is impossible to grasp issues and draw conclusions.

In a sense the war was always a mounted war, because the Boers were all mounted. By tradition and choice they carried no steel weapon. Apart from a small but very efficient artillery they relied on the rifle, in the use of which they were highly proficient, and on the horse. They were, in short, mounted riflemen. In that character they did, to the best of their ability, all the work allotted in our own army to Infantry, Mounted Infantry, Mounted

Rifles, and Cavalry. This must constantly be borne in mind when we compare them with our own categories of troops, either in numbers or in efficiency. We cannot, for example, in comparing them to our regular Cavalry, lay stress on their numerical superiority over the latter arm, considered by itself. To make the comparison pertinent we must throw into our scale the whole of our Infantry, Mounted Infantry, and irregular horsemen, who supplemented the regular Cavalry in the performance of those functions which the Boers united in a single class of troops. The false basis of comparison constantly appears in criticism of the war, even professional criticism.

The Boers had very few regular troops, and what they had were mainly Artillery, the rest permanent police of a highly efficient quality. Their army was a national militia, organized on a territorial system admirably adapted for local warfare, but for united action on the grand scale possessing grave defects. In combat, individual skill and intelligence were remarkably high, the hunting and tracking instinct, taking military shape in the skirmishing and scouting instinct, being well developed. The habit of riding long distances over a thinly-peopled pastoral country, on short commons, and in all weathers, bore military fruit in endurance and in a skill in the care of horses which was of incalculable value to them. Without any stereotyped system of tactics or formations, there was a generally diffused common sense as to what to do and how to do it in any given military conditions of a tactical character, a *flair* for opportunities and dangers, an eye for ground, and above all an enormous belief, founded on knowledge and practice, in the efficacy of the rifle, especially in defence, and especially when the rifle was reinforced by the spade. Born shots and stalkers, they had also a natural genius for practical field entrenchment, a valuable gift in itself, but one which, in conjunction with moral causes, reacted unfavourably at first on their offensive impulse.

Nor, in the early part of the campaign, did the high potential mobility given to them by their horses act as compensation for this defect. Exactly how far they lacked offensive impulse is a point exceedingly difficult to determine, because it is complicated by their great numerical inferiority. At only two of the big actions of the regular war, the first and third, Talana and the battle of Ladysmith, had they as much as a numerical equality. They were greatly outnumbered in the rest of the Natal campaign, while in our central advance to Bloemfontein and Pretoria, and on to Komati Poort, their strength in action was rarely as much as a third of ours, often a quarter, and sometimes as low as a fifth. In guns we always had an enormous preponderance. Still, in consideration of their high skill as riflemen, we may certainly say that at first they were deficient in offensive impetus, and missed opportunities of victory. Siege-work particularly had a very bad effect on them. In other field-work they seem to have regarded the horse —or rather the pony—as a necessary and prosaic vehicle, without which life on the veld under any circumstances whatever, peaceful or warlike, would have been inconceivable. He was a commonplace means of transport rather than a direct source of tactical, or even of strategical, enterprise. In the tactical sphere, this failure to derive from the horse an aggressive ardour analogous in kind to the " Cavalry spirit " was not due to any embarrassment felt in disposing of led horses during the dismounted phases of a fight, for they were wonderfully expert in this important matter ; nor, certainly, as later experience proved, was it due to the lack of a steel weapon, which would have been alien to and destructive of their peculiar tactics. The failure was due partly to an innate affection for stalking and entrenchments, to a wholesome fear of the rifle, corresponding to an equally wholesome reliance upon it, and in some degree to a mere misapprehension of the physical risks involved. It was connected, too, with a rooted aversion to straying far from their slow and cumbrous transport waggons, concern for whose safety was an obsession in the mind of each individual burgher, since they were private, not public, property. But there was a graver obstacle than all these, indiscipline, unfitness for that swift and sure' collective action without which no troops can attain a high degree of aggressive mobility.

A tactical inertia, out of all proportion to their real mobile power, was only one symptom of a malady which infected the whole Boer organization, military and national. Indiscipline in one form or another paralyzed strategy, poisoned the springs of enterprise, set the man above the corps and the province above the State. It promoted selfishness, vacillation, and, in every commando in the field, a habit of desertion, for the most part temporary, but none the less paralyzing. If in all this there was a good deal of mere child-like levity, a tendency to regard war rather as a series of big picnics than as a sustained national effort, the moral evil was none the less far-reaching, and, so far as the integrity of the two Republics was concerned, mortal.

At this great crisis no deep common patriotism united the Boers. Their national spirit had not, in the truest sense, come into being. It was born later under new leaders and in the hour of disaster.

These phenomena are familiar in the struggle of primitive pastoral races against powerful nations. I only draw attention to them in order to link my own special topic with the wider moral study of which it forms an inseparable part. The Boers, as mounted riflemen, cannot be considered apart from the Boers as citizens of two States fighting for political independence, and it will be found that the vivification of their civic patriotism corresponded exactly with the vivification of their mounted tactics. Unhappily, the study of these tactics has generally broken off precisely at the point at which they begin to become most interesting—that is, at the turning-point between Boer despair and Boer hope ; and broken off merely because that hope, however stimulating to action in the field, was, in respect of its major objects, illusory.

It is a commonplace that both the merits and defects of the British regular army, at the time when war was declared, were diametrically opposite to those of the Boer militias. Imperial purpose was vigorous and sustained ; but the power of carrying out that purpose, even with vastly superior resources in men, money, and material, was disproportionately weak. Discipline was high, individual skill and intelligence, especially in the use of the rifle, relatively low. Excessive precision and formalism, the product of long years of peace, characterized the drill and manœuvre of all arms alike. Of the Artillery, which was by no means unaffected, I need say nothing here. The Infantry, by comparison with the Boers, may be said to have been wholly ignorant of the immense power of the modern rifle in modifying formal tactics and in exacting fieldcraft and loose, flexible extensions. Marksmanship was poor, the stalking instinct scarcely existed, and the art of field-entrenchment was in a rudimentary stage. On the other hand, disciplined valour and self-sacrifice, in a degree unknown as yet to the Boers, offered substantial compensation for these serious defects.

I pass to the Cavalry, the arm with which we are more immediately concerned. The " Cavalry spirit," when the war began, was essentially the spirit described in the last chapter—the spirit, that is, of fighting on horseback with a steel weapon. It was from this source that they were taught to draw their inspiration for the great Cavalry virtues which may all be summed up in the one word " dash." The shock charge, founded on high speed and knee-to-knee cohesion, was the supreme manifestation of this spirit, the end to which all training led, and on which all manœuvre was based. Reconnaissance and scouting nominally held a high place in the scheme of education, but were in fact seriously prejudiced by the excessive regard paid to the exactitude and precision of movements in mass, which were to prove impracticable in the face of the modern rifle. Individual training inevitably suffered. If fire-power in the enemy, as a hindrance to mass and shock, was under-estimated, fire-power as an auxiliary to the sword or lance was almost ignored. In the current " Drill-Book " (1898), out of 450 pages, five were devoted to " Dismounted Service," as compared with twelve for " Ceremonial Escorts." Fire-action was treated as abnormal, and expressly contrasted with " normal mounted action." An inferior firearm, the short carbine, was carried, but on the saddle, not, as it should be, on the back, and was held in low esteem as essentially a weapon of defence, in contradistinction to the steel, which is purely a weapon of offence. The men, naturally enough, were poor shots and unaccustomed to skirmishing. Their grand rôle was on horseback, not on foot. Fire-tactics signified to them " dismounted tactics " in the most sterile sense of the term—tactics, that is, devoid of aggressive mobility. Note the interesting difference between this view and the original Boer view. The Boers, too, may also be said to have regarded fire-tactics as " dismounted tactics," but only in this limited sense, that as yet they had scarcely begun to reinforce the aggressive power of the rifle with the aggressive mobility of the horse. In the minds of the Cavalry the horse and the steel weapon were joint and inseparable ingredients of aggressive tactical mobility. If we regard the horse

4—2

in isolation as a physical factor in combat, the Boers (following the formula suggested in Chapter II.) over-estimated his vulnerability and neglected his mobility. The Cavalry did the opposite.

The standard of military education among officers, as throughout the greater part of the army, was not high enough. If Bernhardi had written "Cavalry in Future Wars" one year earlier, and had excited the interest he has since excited, the difference might have been enormous, even if his fallacies as well as his truths had been embraced. As it was, the historical outlook was imitative of the Continental methods of the sixties and seventies, which in their turn were imitative of still more antiquated methods. The really great and stimulating Anglo-Saxon precedent, the American Civil War, had had scarcely any effect on Cavalry practice in this country, partly from inattention, partly perhaps from the same mistaken impression which pervaded the German and French schools, and was so soon to be shattered to pieces by our own experience, that the methods of self-made volunteer troops afford little or no instruction to regulars.

It is necessary to add that these observations are general. In every arm there always have been and always will be differences between different units, the consequence almost entirely of different degrees of ability and energy in the officers, and, above all, in the commanding officer. In the case of the Cavalry, methods being standardized throughout, the important question was, when and in what volume would come the fresh stream of initiative imperatively required? Very naturally, but most unfortunately (for in regular corps influence from the top downwards is of vital consequence), the senior men were the most conservative of all. The hope lay mainly in junior men. How it materialized we shall see. In the meantime ardour was universal, and the prime soldierly qualities of physical courage, discipline, and endurance were, throughout all ranks of the Cavalry, as in all branches of the service, at a high level.

The Mounted Infantry was a comparatively young, inadequately recognized force, with few war traditions. Trained by able and intelligent officers, themselves enthusiasts for the rifle, the force was eager to gain distinction in the field, and to show that the rifle and the horse could be vigorously and effectively combined. But the Cavalry theory, modified in practice, undisputed in principle, hung heavy over its prospects. The force was formed by abstractions from Infantry regiments—a radically false system ; it was taught deliberately that its functions must, in the nature of things, be wholly different from and subordinate to those of Cavalry ; that reconnaissance, except for its own protection, was outside its sphere ; and that there was one function, the " charge "—the noblest ideal of horsemen— to which it could never aspire. In so far as the charge implied " shock " in its true sense of the physical impact of one serried mass upon another serried mass, no fault could be found with this restriction. But, as I have suggested, to mounted riflemen who realize their full potentialities, the charge implies other things than shock. It denotes the culmination of aggressive mobility. Aggressive mobility, therefore, overclouded by this exterior motive of unattainable shock, was not before the war the supreme ideal which it should have been, and could have been, to the Mounted Infantry. Could have been, that is, if the magnitude of the task involved in the education of riflemen for mounted work, even with the limited aims in view, had been realized. Infantry soldiers, with all the defects as well as all the virtues of Infantry training, thoroughly imbued with the instinct for rigid formations, and at first unable to ride, were the raw material, and a few months' exercise with the horse was considered sufficient to convert them into mounted riflemen. The force, in short, as it entered the field, represented, both in organization and training, one of those indefensible compromises between foot-soldiers and horse-soldiers which will continue to be evolved as long as ideas are confused by the belief that the steel weapon is, and must be, the dominant weapon for horsemen. Happily for the Mounted Infantry, war proved to be a great clarifier of ideas.

From the regular mounted troops of the home country we pass to that great throng of volunteers—an army in itself—which, as the war progressed, poured in ever-increasing volume into South Africa from every part of the Queen's dominions, or were raised within the borders of South Africa itself. Known by a bewildering variety of names—Yeomanry, Sharp-shooters, Horse, Light Horse, Mounted Infantry, Mounted Rifles, Scouts, Borderers, Carbineers, Guides, and even Dragoons and Lancers—they all in fact belonged to one distinct type, that of the mounted rifleman. A small fraction carried steel weapons at the outset, but none were seriously trained to shock ; all relied on the rifle in conjunction with the horse.

Whether, when they first took the field, the minds of these men (regarded in the mass) were affected by a recognition, conscious or subconscious, of a higher power known as shock transcending the humbler functions of the rifle, and vested only in professional troops armed with steel weapons, it is exceedingly difficult to say. At first probably such a feeling had a strong, if unrecognized, effect on the outlook of the mounted volunteers from the home country, as it certainly affected that of the professional Mounted Infantry. The old territorial Yeomanry force, at the time of the outbreak of war, did in fact carry a steel weapon, and the new Yeomanry, improvised for the war, though they came mainly from totally different classes from the old, and had little in common with them but the name, could not be free from the associations linked with the sword.   To the Colonials, especially the South Africans, who were deeply imbued with the Boer belief in the rifle, the *arme blanche* was probably little more than a race tradition, exercising, perhaps, a sort of dim influence which they could not have explained in words, but not consciously brought into line with any practical scheme of mounted duties.   The established volunteer corps, from which the first Colonial mounted troops were derived, whether inside or outside South Africa, had been designed for local defence, not for Imperial co-operation.   By a wise choice, for which we cannot be too thankful, they had been trained, largely through the aid of Imperial officers, almost entirely as mounted riflemen, without any explicit understanding that they were to do functions subordinate or ancillary to those of steel-armed professional Cavalry.   As to aggressive mobility, that was for them simply a question of fighting efficiency and discipline, points in which they could not have been expected to reach the standard attainable in permanent professional organizations.

In respect of these two points, fighting efficiency and discipline, all writers have felt the difficulty of forming any general appreciation of the irregular mounted troops, so heterogeneous was their composition, so wide the variations of quality between contingents sent at different times from the same source, so distractingly complicated the vicissitudes both of name and composition through which many of the corps went.   It is enough for my purpose at this moment to note, first, that all were enlisted originally for limited terms, and, second, that the average excellence of the personnel was highest at the beginning, and underwent a distinct decline as the war progressed. The decline set in just when an opposite tendency was beginning to become visible among the Boers, not in their case connected with reinforcements, for they had none, but through a regeneration of existing elements.   These facts have a most important bearing on the development of mounted tactics.

These general observations on the volunteer mounted troops of the Empire necessarily carry us beyond the actual military situation at the outbreak of war. The Yeomanry and the vast majority of oversea organizations had not been heard of then. So complete was the confidence of the military authorities in the regular home troops that it was only under strong governmental pressure that small detachments from the self-governing colonies of Australasia and Canada were permitted to join the flag, and of these, in compliance with an intimation that Infantry would be preferred, only 775 officers and men, coming from Queensland, New South Wales, New Zealand, and Victoria, were mounted. Of the British Colonies in South Africa, Cape Colony had a normal volunteer force of about 7,000, but mainly composed of Infantry, together with two permanent mounted corps, the Cape Mounted Rifles and the Cape Mounted Police, of whom about 1,000 men in all were available for the war. Far away to the north two new volunteer regiments of mounted riflemen, the Protectorate Regiment and the Rhodesia Regiment, were rapidly recruited and trained in the two months preceding hostilities. Natal, by the expansion *ad hoc* of its normal volunteer force, was able to put a total of rather more than 1,000 mounted men into the field, together with 300 more drawn from the permanent Natal Mounted Police.

The Imperial Light Horse, with an original strength of 500, were ready to take the field at once. Formed and equipped in Natal, but recruited from among the best elements of the Uitlander population of the Rand, this famous corps reached at once a high pitch of military efficiency. Their Colonel was a brave and able Cavalry officer, who understood his men and the work they would have to do, and had made no attempt to impose upon them stereotyped Cavalry methods. Their strength lay in the rifle and in the horse.

Such were the mounted troops of the two belligerent races. All were new to civilized warfare on the scale now in prospect. All, with the single exception of the British Cavalry, may be truly described as irregulars, dependent mainly on their own native wit for the evolution of a good system of fighting. Behind a great deal of over-confidence on both sides, due to reciprocal misunderstandings of the lessons of the Majuba campaign, there were not a few reservations and much curiosity as to the relative value of weapons, as of many other things.

Before coming to actual hostilities I must deal briefly, even at this early stage, with a question which must occupy our minds continually in studying the mounted operations of the war, for upon the final answer to it hangs the verdict upon the weapons. Were the conditions " abnormal " ? Were they abnormal—that is, in the sense that they did not give a fair opportunity for testing the relative merits of the steel weapon and the rifle ? That is the narrow question before us, and I beg the reader to concentrate upon it, without allowing his mind to be influenced by the mass of irrelevant considerations which necessarily surround it. There need be no mistake as to what is meant by " normal " in the minds of the *arme blanche* school. Their normal war is a war against one of the great Continental armies, whose cavalries are penetrated with an even stronger belief in the *arme blanche* than our own. This is the special eventuality for which we are supposed to prepare. Without pausing to discuss the soundness of this view of " normality," or the logical consequences to which it would necessarily lead us, let us accept the chosen ground of argument. Let us constantly be asking ourselves why this or that set of conditions should not be reproduced in such a war, and if they were so reproduced, which type of Cavalry—that relying primarily on the " terror of cold steel," or that relying primarily on the rifle—would do the best. In these analogies let us picture Cavalry in all their various functions, strategical or tactical, offensive or protective, independent or in conjunction with other arms, and in collision either with Cavalry, Infantry, or Artillery, fixing our thought resolutely at every step on the weapon and the tactics associated with it, and refusing to be led astray by circumstances which have no direct or indirect bearing on these points. It is by no means an easy task. Every war is abnormal in the sense that it differs from every other war. The special peculiarities of the Boer War are on the surface, patent to the most careless observer. But do they affect the point at issue ?

At present I only wish to dwell on two broad considerations—*personnel* and *terrain*.

Humanly speaking, the Boers were very like ourselves. They were a white race, with white ideals, of European descent, allied to us by blood, and allied, if we are thinking of the German parallel, with the Germans. Their religion was our religion. Their democratic instincts were as strong as our own, and stronger than those of the Germans. In spite of a multitude of points of contrast, economic and social, there was in them no fundamental abnormality of race or custom which would justify, *prima facie,* the conclusion that their methods of warfare could never be, and should never be, our methods of warfare. They were neither savages on the one hand, nor Martians on the other.

The ground on which the war was fought was only abnormal in the sense that it was abnormally favourable to the *arme blanche.* As I pointed out in the last chapter, one of the four great conditions precedent to shock is open country. From a military point of view, no country in the world is more favourable to the *arme blanche* than South Africa. Whether in regard to natural topography, or topography as modified by man, it is incomparably more " open " than any possible European theatre of war, including Great Britain, the least open of all.   There are mountain ranges, one of which became the scene of Buller's long Natal campaign, and rugged hilly districts, as there are in Europe ; but the predominant characteristic is that of vast, undulating plains, varied by sharper inequalities, by ridges, isolated heights, and minor ranges of hills.   These features frequently became centres of conflict, simply because they supplied strong positions. Of features due to the presence of man or under the control of man, of woodlands, gardens, orchards, fences, walls, ditches, parks, enclosures, of towns and the intricate semi-urban environment of towns, of all the thousand-and-one obstructions to free mounted movement which characterize populous, highly-developed countries, South Africa may be said to have been almost destitute.   The barbed-wire boundary fences of the very extensive farms into which the country was divided were the commonest artificial obstacles.

So much for the tactical opportunities of the *arme blanche*.   By an unavoidable paradox, ground tactically fit for that weapon is the least favourable for scouting and reconnaissance.   It is a pity that the words which now head chapter vi. of " Cavalry Training " were not there in 1899.   " The increased power of modern firearms and the introduction of smokeless powder have made it both more difficult and more necessary to obtain information." In that open country and with their long rifles, the Boers outmatched our Cavalry scouts from the first.   As regards local intelligence, Natal and Cape Colony, the scenes of the most critical fighting, were British territory, where there was an abundance of skilled aid.   It is true that in parts of Cape Colony there was a large, and in Natal a small, unfriendly Dutch element.   But that is a more favourable state of things than a population entirely hostile. And when, later, the task of repulse ended, and that of invasion began, and we were faced with that very problem of a hostile population, even then it was never wholly hostile. Besides a sprinkling of farmers British by birth or sympathy, beside the lower class of Dutch *bywoner*, which from the first showed signs of pliancy, and as time went on supplied us with an increasing number of spies, besides the native races from whom we ultimately obtained far more aid than the Boers, we derived enormous advantage from the large urban British element in the Transvaal, which gave us intelligence officers like Woolls-Sampson, and fine corps like the Imperial Light Horse, composed of men who knew the language and customs of the country. But supposing every soul in the country, white and native, man, woman, and child, had been bitterly hostile from the first, that surely is not to be regarded as an abnormal circumstance in war. On the contrary, it is one of the very difficulties which Cavalry exist to overcome. Bernhardi, it is interesting to note, lays special emphasis on this difficulty as one likely to prove increasingly serious in future wars.* After all, the object of war is to conquer, and people resent being conquered.

For my facts I shall rely mainly on our own " Official History," so far as it has progressed, and on the *Times* History, which is already complete. Though they often differ in criticism, these two histories tally with remarkable closeness in matters of fact. The official volume dealing with the greater part of the guerilla war is not yet published.

* " Cavalry in Future Wars," p. 10, and elsewhere.

CHAPTER IV

ELANDSLAAGTE

Note on Nomenclature.—Throughout the chapters dealing with the Boer War I use the expression " Cavalry " to mean British regular Cavalry. I use the expression " Mounted Infantry " to mean regular British Mounted Infantry (*i.e.*, drawn from Infantry battalions). I use the general expression "mounted riflemen " to cover all mounted troops, Boer or British, armed only with the rifle.

THE campaign opened in Natal with the attempt of General Sir W. Penn Symons, with 4,000 men and 18 guns, to hold the untenable Northern position at Dundee against a greatly superior converging force of Joubert's Transvaalers. Sir George White, who only with reluctance had consented to this attempt, was concentrating at Ladysmith, and facing the Free Staters ; while midway between White and Symons a detached Boer force, 900 strong, under Koch, was about to plant itself upon the railway connecting Dundee and Ladysmith. Symons's mounted troops were one regiment of Cavalry, three companies of Mounted Infantry drawn from the three battalions which formed his Infantry brigade, a squadron of Natal Carbineers, and a few picked Guides. Joubert's southward advance from the frontier was excessively slow—seventy miles in a week. Watched and reported by Cavalry and other patrols, it nevertheless culminated in a complete surprise of the British camp at dawn on October 20, 1899, by Meyer's force of some 4,000 men and 8 guns. The General's overconfidence was the principal cause of this surprise, and it is interesting to note that his reason for not establishing more Cavalry pickets to supplement the inadequate system of defence in the heights above the Dundee valley was that he wished to keep the Cavalry fresh—fresh, that is, for shock action. The battle of Talana was, from our point of view, an Infantry fight, fought with splendid spirit and tenacity, and, for the moment, a victory. From the Boer point of view, in this case, as in all others, it was a mounted rifleman's fight. Our own mounted troops were employed with an aggressive purpose, that of turning the Boer right and intercepting the Boer retreat. They consisted of Cavalry and Mounted Infantry acting in concert, the latter, according to the regulations of that period, being regarded as a " valuable auxiliary to the former." The movement began well. An admirable, but also a somewhat dangerous position, was gained well behind the main Boer force, within range of its led horses and commanding its line of retreat, at a moment when retreat was just setting in. Stratagem and fire-action combined might have produced great results. Shock was preferred. A few Boers were sabred, some thirty prisoners were taken, and then the movement collapsed. The Boers took the offence. The commanding officer on our side lost his head, and, after much difficulty, half the Cavalry got back without their prisoners to the British lines ; the rest of the force, after a running fight, in which the rifles of the Mounted Infantry were the only effective means of defence, was surrounded and forced to surrender. It would be unjust and undiscerning to make too much of this opening episode. Nevertheless, in so far as the value of the *arme blanche* was concerned, not merely as a weapon, but as an inspiration of resourceful and effective manœuvre, the incident was of bad augury.

The next day, October 21, came Elandslaagte, fought on the line of communication connecting Dundee and Ladysmith between Koch's force of 900 men and 2 guns, planted astride the railway, and a mixed force of 3,500 men and 18 guns sent out by White from Ladysmith under command of General French. Our mounted troops were three squadrons of Cavalry, five of the Imperial Light Horse, and a few Natal volunteers. The fighting, which ended brilliantly for ourselves, was highly honourable to both sides. From the Boer point of view, it consisted in a magnificently stubborn defence of a strong position by an inferior force of mounted riflemen, fighting on foot up to the moment of actual contact, and under crushingly superior Artillery fire. From our point of view, with one interesting novelty, to which I shall refer later, it was a plain, hard, straightforward fight with the three arms co-operating on thoroughly conventional lines : the Infantry carrying through a well-planned frontal attack with remarkable dash ; the Artillery shelling the main position ; the Cavalry watching both flanks during the progress of the action, and, just at dusk, after the final repulse of the enemy from the main position, pursuing with the lance and sword. The pursuit, carried on for about a mile and a half with vigour and enthusiasm, touched only a portion of the retreating burghers, but, so far as it went, it was effective : it struck the " terror of cold steel " into the pursued with scarcely any loss to the two squadrons engaged ; it caused casualties and surrenders, though precisely to what extent is difficult to say. No figures exist. In short, the Cavalry had performed with considerable success the peculiar function traditionally assigned to their arm.

Now let us turn to the unconventional feature of this fight. The Imperial Light Horse, early on the same morning, had made the reconnaissance on which the battle scheme was founded, and had seized and held necessary tactical points. They had rushed the railway-station by a gallop in open order. Together with the Cavalry (who came out later with the main force from Ladysmith) they had prepared the way for the Infantry advance, and had helped to clear a flank during the early part of the action.   But in addition to these duties they dismounted and joined with the Infantry in the assault of the main position, took a prominent and, at one critical moment, a decisive share in the desperate fighting which wrested it from the Boers, and suffered losses (including that of their brave Colonel) heavier than most of the units engaged.

Mr. Goldman, in remarking on Elandslaagte, makes the strange comment that the Imperial Light Horse were " trained as Cavalry," and adduces their exploits on this occasion as an example of the value of that arm in South Africa.*   This is the first of many misinterpretations upon which I shall have to comment.   For all practical purposes the Imperial Light Horse were mounted riflemen, who used rifles, not carbines, and, as far as I know, never in all their history made or attempted to make an *arme blanche* charge, yet were very effective in action, and were very fair scouts.   Used for the bloody assault at Elandslaagte, they could not also be used for the pursuit.   If they had not joined in the assault, could they, or troops of their type, have been used in an equally effective way for the pursuit ?   The inquiry compels us to look back a little more closely at the conditions of the charge.

The following points should be noted :

1. For the troops engaged on both sides this was the first day of hostilities.   Steel-armed Cavalry was a new fact to the Boers.   The steel had the best chance it ever was to have of inspiring " terror."

2. There were no Boer reserves left to cover the retreat.

3. The light was failing, a circumstance favourable to the steel, unfavourable to fire.   (Contrast the broad daylight at Talana, when the Boers rallied and out-

* " With French in South Africa," p. 426.

manœuvred the cavalry.) *Some* light is necessary, of course, but, within obvious limits, the poorer the better.

4. The ground was as open and smooth as Cavalry on the average can expect. Dongas and rocks during the initial advance only ; from within 300 yards of the enemy and onwards (according to the " Official History ") not a lawn, but fair galloping ground.

5. Horses and men fresh, not hitherto seriously engaged. Why ? Because there had been no opportunity for the use of steel.

6. The enemy, already shaken and spent by a hard fire-fight on foot, were retreating at their usual ambling trot, in loose, formless groups ; " raggedly streaming," as the Official Historian correctly puts it. He adds that this objective, " a crowd in the loose disorder of defeat, seemed to offer an indefinite object for a charge," but " that there was no likelihood of a better whilst sufficient light remained." I must digress for a moment on that illuminating *obiter dictum*, because it gives a clue to the Cavalry view of Cavalry work. The historian is regretting the absence of a chance for " shock," in its literal and in its only accurate meaning, of the collision of *two* massed bodies ; two, and both massed. The Boers were not massed ; clearly, therefore, it was of no use for the Cavalry to adopt mass, and in point of fact they charged with " extended files." There could be no " shock," therefore—that is, violent physical impact—and there was in fact none. The Boers were ridden down individually. What the official commentator does not apprehend is that this absence of mass, in his view an unfortunate drawback, was in fact one of the very conditions which made the charge possible. It was a corollary to the beaten, spent state of the pursued. Ragged streaming away is a characteristic of defeated troops in retreat. Cohesion means morale, and morale means the will and power to retaliate. Nor is it only a question of morale. The physi-

cal conditions of the preceding fire-fight determine the nature of the retreat. In this case some 900 Boers, in widely extended order, had been defending a line nearly two miles long against an enemy proportionately extended, both extensions being truly normal—that is to say, dictated by the range and deadliness of the modern rifle. Retreat from such a line, immediately after a failure to withstand a punishing assault, pressed in some quarters to the bayonet's point, excludes cohesion in any troops, European or extra-European. Boers, as I pointed out in the previous chapter, never troubled much about set formations at any time, whether or no there was time for them, not through incapacity, but simply because they did not need them, and not needing them were better without them. For them, therefore, this kind of ragged retreat was not solely the result of the beating they had suffered. Normal in any troops, it was normal in a peculiar sense with them.

I dwell on this point at some length, not because of the intrinsic importance of this fight, or of the Official Historian's comment upon the pursuit (for he may have written thoughtlessly), but because it directly raises the big issue dealt with in my analysis of the physical problem in Chapter II. I enumerated there the many crushing limitations which surround the use of real shock against riflemen, mounted or on foot, and I instanced the pursuit of beaten troops as one of those rare cases where the steel weapon has its best opening. But I also pointed out that this was a case where any well-mounted troops, however armed, have a good opening ; and that brings us back to the point from which we started in comparing, for the sake of illustration, the work of the Imperial Light Horse and the Cavalry at Elandslaagte. First, however, let us recapitulate the six favourable conditions of this Cavalry pursuit :

(1) Novelty of the steel. (2) No Boer reserves.

(3) Bad light.   (4) Open and smooth ground.   (5) Fresh horses and men.   (6) Ragged retreat of beaten enemy.

This may be regarded as a rare combination of ideal conditions ; how rare will be seen as the war proceeds.

Now for the Imperial Light Horse, whom, let me say, I am regarding, not as an individual regimental unit, but as a type of what good riflemen can do, just as the Cavalry squadrons engaged were types of what Cavalry, decidedly good according to the standard of their time, could do.

I asked, would the Imperial Light Horse, if they had not been used for the fire-fight, have been capable of an equally effective pursuit without the use of steel weapons ?   The speculation, of course, though instructive, is largely academical, the crucial point being that they *had* been used for the preceding fire-fight.   However, for the sake of argument, we must vest them with favourable condition No. 5, " Fresh horses and men."   Nos. 2, 4, and 6 would have been equally applicable to them ; No. 1 is irrelevant.   There remains No. 3, " Failing light."   This would have been distinctly adverse to the accurate use of the rifle, but at the same time let us remember the fundamental distinction between the rifle and the steel—that is, range.   Posted, for the sake of argument, in the spot where the Cavalry were posted (threatening the enemy's right rear), the Imperial Light Horse would at once have had the first bodies of retreating Boers well within the range of vulnerability : 500 yards is the official estimate.   Yes, but fire at this moment would no doubt have meant delay, and caused less damage to the Boers than the undelayed steel-armed Cavalry.   Granted ; a point to the Cavalry.   Let us go on. After routing a first batch in a long gallop, the Cavalry turned on their tracks, met a second batch, and scattered and harassed these men also.   Would not the Imperial Light Horse meanwhile have had a good chance of intercepting these men ?   Finally, picture the irregular corps as capable of fire from the saddle, and keep that point in your mind for future illustration.

All this is the veriest sketch, suggestive of the factors inherent in mounted combats, but utterly unreal, because it is utterly impossible to postulate identical circumstances for steel-action and fire-action. The essence of the matter is that the Imperial Light Horse, by aptitude, training, and equipment, were capable of joining effectively in the Infantry assault of the main position, and that the Cavalry, by aptitude, training, and equipment (they carried the short carbine), were neither capable of, nor designed for, similar intervention. If the Colonials had not been used for the main assault, the course of the battle might have been changed. The assault might have failed (in the penultimate phase there was an exceedingly critical revival on the Boer left flank, checked by the Gordons and Imperial Light Horse combined), or the assault might have been consummated too late to give to the Cavalry the margin of light necessary for their pursuit. Or—and this is really the most pertinent and suggestive eventuality—the Imperial Light Horse used as their capacity deserved, might have operated actively on the enemy's rear at an earlier period, when the Cavalry was still passive. Result, a change of battle conditions, which defies speculation. On the other hand, we can, to a certain extent, isolate our view of the Cavalry exploit. They did, under ideal conditions, exactly what they were trained to do, and I do not think they, or any other Cavalry similarly trained, could have done it better.

In dwelling so long upon the topic of pursuit we must remember that there was no question at any moment of a charge by Cavalry either upon *unbroken* riflemen or upon led horses. Nor (save in the case of the rush upon the station by the Imperial Light Horse) was there any attempt on the part of the mounted riflemen on either side, Boer or British, to carry aggressive mobility to the point of charging on horseback into point-blank range of riflemen on foot.* Developments of that sort were still a long way off.

I have enlarged so much on this small fight in order to focus the reader's attention upon the principles it illustrates. Let him study it in conjunction with the action of Talana, which preceded it, and with all the multitude of fights which followed it, in the next two and a half years. Let him begin at once to picture parallels in European warfare, on a bigger scale or smaller scale, and ask whether they tell for or against the *arme blanche*, and why ? Imagine the 900 Boers as a German force, either of Cavalry or of the three arms in normal proportion, and without anything in the least degree resembling either our Imperial Light Horse or the militant burgher. Should we have won more or less easily ? Or imagine 3,500 Germans, constituted as before, tackling the 900 Boers. Instead of moderately open ground, suppose ground diversified with copses, walls, hedges, a sunk lane or two. Make any permutations or suppositions that you please, and test each by South African facts.

Finally, ask yourself at every step, on which method, that of the *arme blanche* or the rifle, will it pay best in the long-run to train mounted troops ?

* Unless the last Boer rush was of this character. The " Official History " (vol. i., p. 169) says that fifty Boers " charged boldly up-hill " to within twenty yards of the crest held by the Gordons and the Imperial Light Horse, and then used their rifles. Whether they charged mounted is not stated.

CHAPTER V

FROM ELANDSLAAGTE TO THE BLACK WEEK

October to December, 1899.

In these two opening combats of the war the steel weapon had had its first rebuff and its first success. What was to happen now ?

Immediately after Elandslaagte, French's force, having disposed of Koch, was recalled by White to Ladysmith (October 22). On the same night the Dundee force, now in a situation of great and growing peril from Joubert's united commandos, was forced to retreat hurriedly and secretly to Ladysmith. White sent out 5,300 men to cover the last stage of the retreat against any possible interruption from the 6,000 Free Staters who were threatening Ladysmith from the west. Hence the action of Rietfontein (October 24), a desultory fire-fight, for the most part at very long ranges, against an invisible and intangible enemy ; in its proof of the mysterious, far-reaching potency of the rifle, a pregnant contrast to the close encounters at Talana and Elandslaagte.

But it was six days later, at the battle of Ladysmith (or Lombard's Kop), that the most definite and sub-stantial proof was given of the superiority of the rifle over the steel. Joubert had closed on Ladysmith with 12,000 men. White, also with 12,000 men, of whom 3,000 were mounted, conceived a bold and elaborate plan of attack designed not merely to drive the Boers back, but to inflict a crushing defeat. To his two mounted brigades

70

(each composed of two Cavalry regiments and a corps of Colonial mounted riflemen) White assigned functions which were typical of the military theory of that day. One was to co-operate with the Infantry attack on the right, wheeling wide round the flank, and getting behind the enemy's left. The other, held in reserve behind our left Infantry attack, was designed, when both attacks had succeeded, to cut in upon the Boer line of retreat (which lay towards the left or north), and pursue the beaten burghers. In order to facilitate the scheme of pursuit, an Infantry force had been detached by night to seize a pass—Nicholson's Nek, of evil memory—which the Cavalry would have to surmount before debouching upon the plain. Since the force so detached suffered disaster, and the whole of White's attack, here and elsewhere, failed, the left mounted brigade had very little to do. The right mounted brigade, whose work began with daylight, failed to effect the purpose assigned to it. Fire-tactics were immediately imposed upon it by the enemy's mounted riflemen operating on rocky, bushy ground, and in fire-tactics the Mauser, in the words of the " Official History," at once " dominated the carbine." Advance was impossible; proper flank support to the Infantry was scarcely less difficult ; even the retreat at the end of the day's fighting was far from an able performance. French, who led the brigade, was not the French of a fortnight later, when the horse and the steel weapon were beginning to be dissociated after their long traditional partnership. For the present the fact was painfully obvious that the only professional troops endowed with the mobility of the Boers were the least capable of grappling with the Boers in action.

But did mobility, backed by the rifle, inspire dash in the Boers ? At this period, except in isolated cases, no. The inertia, so disproportionate to their tactical flexibility and brilliant skirmishing skill, was never more apparent than at the close of this battle outside Ladysmith, when White began his retreat.   No such opportunity was ever to present itself again for a really decisive victory. Joubert regarded the action as a defensive action, and had issued general orders against a pursuit.   On the other hand, a simple burgher, Christian de Wet, had inspired the one genuinely aggressive enterprise which distinguished the Boer movements on this day—namely, the attack and capture of the detached force at Nicholson's Nek.   This —like the capture of Majuba nearly twenty years earlier— was a feat of stalking pure and simple, with which the horse had little to do, save that it bore the riflemen rapidly from a distant part of the field into the outermost fringe of the zone of combat.   The outermost fringe—that is the point to watch.   Could horses penetrate the inner fringe under rifle-fire and so precipitate the decisive phase of a conflict ?   While waiting for the answer let us be sensible and remember that after all the main thing is to win fights.   Galloping under fire is only a means to an end.   Stalking under fire requires nearly as much dash to be effective.

The long siege of Ladysmith now virtually began. By an error of judgment all the mounted troops, including the Cavalry regiments, were retained within the lines, and were thus practically demobilized for five months.   Happily for our arms, however, French and his staff just succeeded in leaving the town for the south before investment was complete.   Happily, too, the strenuous efforts to raise more volunteer mounted troops within South Africa were now bearing fruit.   Two fine but wholly raw regiments, Thorneycroft's Mounted Infantry and Bethune's Mounted Infantry, were able to strengthen the miserably scanty forces which, pending the arrival of Buller and heavy reinforcements from England and the Cape, stood between Southern Natal and invasion.   Even so, there was nothing during the first half of November to stop Joubert with the forces at his disposal from a vigorous raid on Maritzburg, and even on Durban. But his tactical inertia was exceeded by his strategical inertia. Egged on by Louis Botha, he did indeed initiate a raid with a force of over 3,000 picked men on picked horses, but it degenerated into a leisurely foray for loot and cattle. The time for action slipped by. British troops were pouring into Natal to redress the strategical balance, and in the last week of November the Boer force withdrew behind the Tugela, there, aided by abstraction from the investing force, to begin their long and desperate struggle to prevent the relief of Ladysmith.

Colenso, fought on December 15, was the first great event in this historic conflict. From our point of view, like all the subsequent fights in Natal, it needs very little comment. Buller, commanding a force of 18,000 men, of whom 2,500 were mounted, made a frontal attack with his Infantry and guns upon an immensely strong entrenched position held by 6,000 Boers. He failed, inflicted only nominal loss on the enemy, suffered 1,100 casualties himself, and lost ten guns. Two Cavalry regiments formed the professional nucleus of the mounted brigade ; the rest were raw irregulars. There were Bethune's and Thorneycroft's Mounted Infantry, who, in the fighting around Estcourt three weeks earlier, had been just blooded and no more, a squadron of Imperial Light Horse and some Natal volunteers who had had much the same experience, and the newly enlisted South African Light Horse, who had not yet fired a shot. Reconnaissance prior to the battle had been little more than nominal. Pitted against the Boer outposts—expert shots all of them —our scouts had rarely been able to get near the enemy's lines. The Tugela fords were not properly known ; the enemy's principal positions were but dimly conjectured. Artillery fire was the substitute for reconnaissance, and that produced no response from the crafty burghers.

In the battle itself the rifle from first to last governed tactics. The aggressive task given to the mounted brigade was the attack upon Hlwangwane Mountain, the great natural outwork upon which the Boer left flank rested. The irregulars were chosen for this attack, and rightly chosen, because rifles were absolutely essential. They made a plucky but vain effort to carry a strong position strongly held, and extricated themselves with some difficulty at the end of the day. The work of the Cavalry was confined to covering their retreat. As at Ladysmith, there was no opportunity for the steel, not from any chance causes, but because the rifle saw to it that no such opportunity should be allowed to occur.

Colenso was one of the three defeats in that sad week of mid-December, when the nation first realized the magnitude of the enterprise it had undertaken in South Africa. Let us carry events in other quarters of the field of war up to the same point, with special emphasis on the use of mounted troops.

Far up in the north the investment of Mafeking had begun immediately after the declaration of war (October 12). In a week the whole of the railway from Mafeking to Orange River was in Boer hands, and on the 23rd Kimberley was definitely invested. On no portion of this line were there any regular mounted troops, and of the local levies the only mobile force outside a besieged town was the Rhodesian Regiment of mounted riflemen, 450 strong, based on Tuli and commanded by Plumer, who, with this little handful of men and his own nerve and resource, did extraordinarily good work in threatening the Northern Transvaal, and at a later period in aiding in the relief of Mafeking.

Meanwhile the Boer invasion of Southern Cape Colony hung fire for three full weeks, and when it at last began, on November 1, the day Buller landed in South Africa, it was dilatory and methodless. Still, the strategical situation for ourselves was serious. White's investment in Ladysmith, and the consequent danger to Southern Natal, had dislocated the entire scheme of British strategy, which was founded upon a resolve to land a whole Army Corps in Cape Colony and advance straight upon Bloemfontein and Pretoria. Buller's decision, as we know, was to divert the greater part of his Army Corps to Natal, take command there himself, and make the relief of Ladysmith the primary British object. Probably the decision was the best that could have been come to, but it involved the dissolution of the Army Corps as an organized instrument of conquest, and the reduction of the grand scheme of irruption upon the enemy's capital to a minor scheme of advance up the western railway line for the relief of Kimberley. In the meantime, and until a fresh army could be sent out from England, the vital portions of Cape Colony, comprising the great ports and the system of communications radiating therefrom, could only be protected against invasion by a mere demonstration of force exercised in the midst of districts teeming with disaffection.

Happily the Boers leaders had no eye for aggressive strategy, nor indeed any military organization on which to base aggressive strategy. Absorbed by the prospect of capturing Mafeking and Kimberley, just as in Natal they were absorbed by the prospect of capturing Ladysmith, they fell naturally in both cases into an attitude of strategical defence—defence against the relief of the towns they were investing. The same feebleness which characterized the raid upon Southern Natal early in November characterized the straggling invasion of Southern Cape Colony at the same period. Nevertheless, it was no light task for us to conceal our weakness in this quarter, and, with a thin containing line of troops gathered from the fragments of the old Army Corps, to hold in play greatly superior Boer forces. It was French who was called to undertake this delicate and difficult duty. How he performed it I shall relate in the next chapter. For the present, let us briefly review Methuen's advance from Orange River towards Kimberley.

Methuen started on November 20 with a total force of 10,000 men, including 7,000 Infantry, 16 guns, and only 1,000 mounted men. The professional mounted element was represented by one Cavalry regiment, and three companies of regular Mounted Infantry ; the irregular element by Rimington's Guides and a handful of New South Wales Lancers. Methuen, therefore, was relatively weaker in mounted troops than any leader in Natal, and his operations provide proportionately less material for criticizing mounted tactics and the weapons suitable thereto. I say " proportionately " less, because, as I pointed out in my preliminary chapter upon the numbers and quality of the British and Boer mounted troops, we cannot reckon the Boers twice over, once in their capacity as dismounted riflemen holding positions against our Infantry, and a second time as mobile riflemen available for mounted evolutions against our Cavalry. Yet that strange error has been constantly made, and among other cases in the case of Methuen's first three battles—Belmont (November 23), Graspan (November 25), and Modder River (November 28), in the first two of which the total British force engaged outnumbered the total Boer force engaged by nearly four to one, and in the third by more than two to one, while the British mounted troops, reckoned independently, amounted to half the Boer force and a quarter the Boer force respectively. The enemy, with something over 2,000 men at Graspan and Belmont, and with about 3,500 at Modder River, supported by Artillery which never exceeded three guns and two pompoms, had to make head against 7,000 British Infantry on the first two occasions, 6,800 on the second, and 7,500 on the third, backed by Artillery which rose from sixteen to twenty guns. The Infantry included the Brigade of Guards, and, taken as a whole, were as fine a body of troops of their class as could be found in any European country. These troops bore the brunt of all three battles. They stormed the rocky heights at Belmont and Enslin, and faced the yet more deadly fire which swept across the level plain from the sunken beds of the Modder and the Riet. Whatever tactical flexibility the Boers may have derived from their ponies in meeting these attacks, nearly the whole of their small force was pinned to its position until the crisis of each action, by the necessity of meeting Infantry and Artillery attacks in superior force.

The British mounted troops, on a reasonable calculation of relative strength, must be regarded as having been left approximately free for supplementary independent action on the enemy's flanks and rear. This is how Methuen regarded them and endeavoured to use them. In the event, though all worked their hardest, they had no appreciable effect on any of the actions. The steel weapon was useless, although the terrain for shock was ideal. The Cavalry were not adapted or properly trained for fire-action, and the Mounted Infantry and irregulars, though trained and adapted for it, were very backward in the art. Reconnaissance, too, was inadequate. Methuen never knew with accuracy the strength and position of the enemy, and at Modder River was totally at sea until his Infantry was actually under heavy fire. The conditions no doubt were exacting. It was not numbers, but a small quantity of picked scouts that was needed. But Cavalry training had not encouraged that kind of individual merit.

The conventional comment upon all these actions has been that, owing to the paucity and exhaustion of the mounted troops, we could not reap the fruits of victory by sustained and destructive pursuit. There is truth, of course, in the proposition, but only that sort of half-truth which for instructional purposes is often more misleading than error.

As an example of this sort of mistaken criticism I will take the Official Historian's remarks upon Graspan, on which occasion Methuen sent his mounted men in two bodies (one including two squadrons of Lancers, the other one squadron) six miles to the rear of the enemy's main position with a view of surprising their laager and cutting off their retreat. There were no Boer reserves here, save a small guard to the laager, which, though sighted by the stronger British detachment, was not attacked. The Boers ultimately dealt with were the same men who had held the main position almost to the bayonet's point against our Infantry, and who retreated after their defeat at that point. So far from intercepting or hampering the retreat, both bodies of mounted troops, unable to effect a junction, were attacked in detail by the fugitives, and put into dangerous positions, from which the fire-power of their Mounted Infantry and mounted riflemen were the principal means of extrication.

The Official Historian says: " At Graspan, as at Belmont, the open plains across which the enemy was compelled to retire were singularly favourable to Cavalry action, and had a satisfactory mounted brigade with a Horse Artillery battery been available, the Boers could not have effected their escape without suffering very heavy losses. Not only were the mounted troops at Lord Methuen's disposal insufficient numerically, but their horses were already worn out by the heavy reconnaissance duty which had of necessity been carried out day after day without relief under the adverse conditions of a sandy soil, great heat, and a scarcity of water."

There could be no better instance than this of the way

in which the *arme blanche* faith is perpetuated from generation to generation, in defiance of experience. Every schoolboy has been puzzled by that reiterated comment upon most of the battles of history, that the exhaustion, or insufficiency, or feeble handling of the Cavalry by the victorious side prevented the full fruits of victory being garnered in. Why does this phenomenon happen so very often ? he wonders. The historians rarely tell him two simple reasons—namely :

1. That troops armed even with a poor firearm are rarely so utterly and universally demoralized, even after a severe defeat, as to be unable to check the onset even of fresh Cavalry.

2. That Cavalry, who in all normally constituted armies form but a small proportion of the combatant troops, if they have worked hard in reconnaissance on previous days, not to speak of their action in prior phases of the battle, rarely find their horses fresh enough for long sustained gallops against a retreating army. (The reader will remember that this freshness is one of the four great conditions for the successful use of the steel.)

Both these limitations, which are cumulative, must be constantly borne in mind when criticizing mounted action in the South African War or any other war, and it must be noted that the second limitation applies to mounted riflemen, as well as to Cavalry, with this important reservation, that fire-action very often enables the former to dispense with long gallops, while for the steel weapon nothing short of a hand-to-hand *mêlée*, attained through the medium of the " charge," is of any use at all.

Now what moral does the Official Historian draw from Graspan ? His conclusion amounts to this, that if, in addition to our Infantry and sixteen field and naval guns, and in addition to about 900 mounted troops whose horses were worn out with reconnaissance, we had had a " satisfactory " mounted brigade (and the context shows that he means a brigade of Cavalry) and a battery of Horse Artillery, both fresh for pursuit and with an ideal terrain over which to pursue, the Boers, 2,000 to 3,000 in number, many of them just as tired as our men by long rides to the field and by reconnaissance, would not have effected their escape without heavy losses. If we could only have everything always as we wish it ! Unfortunately, in most wars the kind of conditions imagined by the critic are Utopian. If we count on obtaining anything like such a superiority over any European foe, we are living in a fool's paradise. Instead of complaining of our bad luck in fighting against the Boers, we ought to congratulate ourselves upon our advantages, and search coldly and unflinchingly for the causes which enabled so small a people to withstand a powerful Empire for so long.

In the light of common sense, what is the most striking feature of Graspan and of all these other fights ? Surely the power of a small number of mounted riflemen, skilled in the management of the horse and skilled in the use of the modern firearm, to withstand greatly superior forces framed upon the European model, even allowing for cases where the proportion of mounted troops did not reach the normal European standard. The one thing emphatically that these fights in South Africa do *not* prove is that we wanted more steel-armed horsemen. The only way of proving that we did involves that *reductio ad absurdum* of the steel weapon which the Official Historian unconsciously finds himself drawn to embrace. For that is what it comes to. Given a force of mounted troops approximately equal to the whole Boer force, plus a threefold superiority in Infantry and guns, and we should have turned defeat into destruction. During an important part of the campaign, as I shall afterwards show, we did actually obtain something like these very conditions, but in only one instance were able to make destructive use of them, and in that instance solely through the agency of the firearm.

Before leaving Graspan, let us note for future use that on two occasions parties of Boers tried to ride down British mounted troops (both Cavalry and Mounted Infantry) in the open. The attempts failed, but there was no retort in kind. De la Rey was in command of the Boer force on this day. It will be interesting to observe his use of the mounted charge at a later period of the war.

At Magersfontein, on December 10, Methuen's enterprise for the relief of Kimberley came to an abrupt end. Since the battle of Modder River, twelve days earlier, both sides had been reinforced. The Boers, holding a strong entrenched position under Cronje, were now some 7,000 in number with 5 guns and some pompoms. Methuen had received a brigade of Infantry, another Cavalry regiment, a fourth company of Mounted Infantry, and a battery of Horse Artillery. Altogether he had 11,000 Infantry, 1,600 mounted troops, and 33 guns (not counting a large number of machine guns)—that is to say, a total superiority of about two to one, and in guns of about six to one. Between a third and a quarter of the Boer force—representing their right—was not engaged in the battle. About seven-eighths of our force was engaged.

It is scarcely necessary to recall the tragic catastrophe which befell the Highland Brigade in their night attack upon the key of the Boer position, Magersfontein Hill, where the enemy's centre rested. The rest of the battle, from the British point of view, resolved itself into a successful effort to save this isolated brigade from total annihilation, and an unsuccessful effort to break through the Boer left, which was flung forward crescent-wise over undulating, bushy ground. The whole battle was a fire-battle ; the rifle supreme, the British guns of very little aggressive killing value, though potentially of high defensive value in preventing Boer counter-strokes. Horses on both sides were in the background. With the exception of some irregulars on our extreme left, all our mounted troops, including the Cavalry, fought on foot like the Infantry. The two Lancer regiments, their equipment and habits considered, did particularly well, but not, let it be remembered, in the capacity for which they had undergone nineteen-twentieths of their severe and elaborate training. I hope that here, as at Colenso, the reader will mentally figure his European parallels, substituting whatever categories of troops he pleases, in whatever relative strength, and on whatever terrain. We may remark that the topography of Magersfontein was in no sense peculiar. The position was not nearly as strong as at Colenso, where a river divided the combatants. Nor was it stronger than the averagely strong defensive position in Europe. The height of Magersfontein Kopje had no significance ; for, like shrewd soldiers, the Boers had discovered that it is the forward and lowest slopes of a hill which give the most deadly field of fire, and it was these which they defended. The position was entrenched with peculiar skill, and held by peculiarly steady and accurate marksmen—that was all. These marksmen were mounted riflemen, many of whom had ridden to join Cronje from distant points. If they had been shock-trained European horsemen, they could neither have entrenched nor held the position. Though they scarcely used their horses at all during the action, the horses (like their cumbrous and bulky transport) were there, out of range, in almost defenceless knots and groups, vulnerable to just the sort of attack which Cavalry are supposed to be able to deliver. Separation from their horses, it may be observed, did not perturb these riflemen in the manner in which mounted riflemen are always, in Cavalry theory, supposed to be perturbed. They sat in narrow ditches on nearly level ground, from which retreat meant exposure to a withering storm of gun and rifle fire. Nor on this occasion is it easy to impute lack of aggressive dash to the Boers. Very few troops so situated and so outmatched in numbers and Artillery could have launched counter-strokes, whether mounted or on foot. That is a point which must be kept in mind whenever we compare the action of a small force of high mobility against a large force of low mobility. The defensive power of the former is far greater in proportion than its offensive power.

While the Highland Brigade was moving " ghost-like to its doom " in the dark morning hours of December 10, Gatacre's force—200 miles away in Cape Colony—was approaching an even worse fate at Stormberg. This unhappy affair need not detain us long. It was a case of a mismanaged night attack by 1,850 Infantry, 450 regular Mounted Infantry, and 12 guns, upon 1,700 Boers. Although the surprise was complete, ignorance of the topography and the exhaustion of the troops involved our force in disastrous failure. Our Mounted Infantry escorted the guns and covered the final retreat, but took no part in the critical fighting. So far as mounted lessons are concerned, the moral was against the Boers. Here, certainly, they showed a marked lack of aggressive mobility. When total destruction of the British force was well within their grasp, they were content with a partial, if substantial, success. There was no real pursuit, even by two fresh commandos which appeared on the flank of the retreat. If the action stood alone, it might be plausibly conjectured that the absence of a steel weapon was accountable for this slackness. A review of the whole war disposes of the supposition.

6—2

Colenso, Magersfontein, Stormberg, three decided checks in three widely distant areas of the theatre of war, constituted the " Black Week " of mid-December, 1899. With the single exception of the charge at Elandslaagte, on the second day of hostilities, the sword and lance had effected nothing.

CHAPTER VI

COLESBERG AND KIMBERLEY

December, 1899, to February, 1900.

The immediate effects of these events may be put under four heads :

1. A national and Imperial awakening to the greatness of the emergency.

2. The appointment of Lord Roberts to the supreme command in South Africa.

3. Large additional reinforcements of regular troops of all three arms, and of militia.

4. The improvisation of large numbers of additional mounted troops. These belonged to three categories :

(*a*) Three thousand additional regular Mounted Infantry, improvised by abstraction from every Infantry battalion in South Africa, with additions from Great Britain.

(*b*) The enlistment and gradual despatch of large bodies of volunteer mounted riflemen ; from Great Britain (in the shape of 10,000 Yeomanry), and from Canada, Australia, New Zealand, and India.

(c) The enlistment in South Africa of a quantity of new irregular corps of mounted riflemen, including a local militia for the defence of Cape Colony, the latter force being backed by Town Guards partly composed of Infantry.

No question ever arose of training the mounted irregulars to the use of the steel weapon. The long postponed decision to raise Yeomanry, for example, was directly inspired by a telegram from Buller after Colenso, asking for " 8,000 irregular Mounted Infantry." This view of present requirements did not represent any radical change of military theory. There was a general impression abroad, first, that this was a " peculiar " war demanding peculiar expedients ; second, that it was a comparatively simple and easy matter to improvise mounted riflemen. The first proposition was a misleading half-truth, the second a profound fallacy, but the net result, however arrived at, was good. Outside the Cavalry itself, it was already generally recognized that the rifle must, in this war at any rate, be the dominant arm for mounted troops. Even among the Cavalry, reliance upon the carbine and upon the support of mounted riflemen had intensified with every day of hostilities.

As I explained in the previous chapter, the Natal entanglement, with the wholesale diversion of troops which it entailed, had left Cape Colony in mid-November almost defenceless against invasion, slowly and timidly as that invasion was proceeding. It came at two principal points : in the north-east by way of Aliwal North and Burgersdorp to Stormberg ; and in the centre by way of Norval's Pont to Colesberg, and on towards Naauwpoort. The former advance threatened only the East London railway-line. The latter advance was the more serious in that it endangered, not only Methuen's communications with the south, but the whole of the railway system from our two major ports, Cape Town and Port Elizabeth, with its three cardinal junctions— De Aar, Naauwpoort, and Rosmead. The three serious defeats of mid-December, and especially that of Gatacre at Stormberg, increased the danger. At least six weeks must elapse before sufficient reinforcements could be gathered for the great projected advance under Roberts. Torpid as the Boer strategy was, pusillanimity on our part might encourage them at any moment to greater efforts. Our one resource for the time being was " bluff." Buller had realized this from the first, and given instructions accordingly to French, who had taken up the command at Naauwpoort on November 20, with orders to " worry " the enemy, and make, if he could, a bold show of operating towards Colesberg.

French performed the difficult rôle allotted to him with complete success. His operations lasted ten weeks, and included a multitude of small schemes and enterprises, which it is impossible for me to recount in detail. I can only sketch his doings and methods in broad outline, with a special view to their bearing on the question of weapons for mounted men.

Aggression, perpetual but never rash, was the keynote of his action. As the handful of troops with which he started work slowly grew, by accretion from the base, to a substantial force, he steadily pushed forward, first to Arundel, then to Rensburg, then to a line immediately threatening Colesberg, all the time widening his protective net to right and left over the adjacent country. His system was to harass, surprise, impose upon the enemy constantly, with forays, reconnaissances, and stratagems. Except for the unhappy failure of an infantry night attack, no sensational fights occurred, but a great number of small engagements, which would repay close study.

The troops employed were of all arms—Infantry, Horse Artillery, regular Mounted Infantry, Australasian and South African mounted riflemen, and regular Cavalry. Numbers and composition varied from time to time. The total force at French's disposal for active operations rose from about 1,200, mainly Infantry, on November 20, to 2,000, half of them mounted, in the second week of December, and to 4,500 in the second week of January, 1900, when all immediate danger to the Colony was at an end, and he was firmly established in the positions round Colesberg, with his rear quite secure.

This force included four batteries of Artillery, and no less than 2,000 mounted men (an unusually high proportion), of whom some 1,200 were regular Cavalry.

The Boers, who were under the very poor leadership of D. Schoemann, were also progressively reinforced. Their available fighting strength at any given time is impossible to measure, since it varied from day to day, and week to week, with the energy or indifference of the burghers. But it is fairly safe to say that at the outset they outnumbered the British force by nearly two to one, held a distinct though lessening superiority for about three weeks—the really critical period of the operations—and in the second week of January were approximately equal to French's forces. At a somewhat later stage they were considerably reinforced.

Because French was a cavalryman, and because more than half the mounted troops engaged were regular Cavalry, it has often been too lightly assumed that the Colesberg operations proved the value of the training peculiar to Cavalry—that is, in the *arme blanche*. Mr. Goldman, for example, in the course of a contrast between the types of Cavalry and mounted riflemen, cites these operations as an example of the " successful use of Cavalry when properly employed."*

Observe the confusion caused by nomenclature. The *arme blanche* was not and could not have been used, though the terrain was perfect for it.† I think I am right in saying that only on one occasion, the fight of January 3 near Maeder's farm, was there any question of sabres, even in pursuit. The 10th Hussars and a squadron of Inniskilling Dragoons, with two horse batteries, were engaging a force under Piet de Wet, which had just failed

---

* " With French in South Africa," p. 421.

† Mr. Goldman complains that, although open, the country contained ridges, which provided successive lines of resistance to a retreating enemy. He does not see what ridicule he throws on Cavalry by such a line of argument.

in a surprise attack on an Infantry position. Suddenly the Boers lost heart, and bolted across the plain; the Cavalry followed in pursuit, but were checked by the fire of a small party who stopped to take cover in some rocky ground. By the time these men had been turned out their comrades were safe. This is a typical illustration of the weakness of Cavalry in pursuit.

The Cavalry, like the irregulars, acted throughout as mounted riflemen, and though, like all the troops engaged, they did well, they would have done much better if they had carried rifles instead of carbines, and had spent their professional life in practising rifle-tactics. In the same way the regular Mounted Infantry would have done better if in peace they had been regarded, not as a cross between Infantry and Cavalry, but as fully-fledged mounted troops, capable, with time and the proper education, of being of as much general practical utility as Cavalry. The 400 New Zealand Mounted Rifles, who formed the majority of the unprofessional mounted troops engaged, stood from the first on a footing of equality with the regulars, because they had nothing to unlearn, though, like everyone else, much to learn.

I must add three remarks upon the Colesberg operations :

1. Unlike the formal actions or battles we have hitherto been considering, these operations presented a multitude of minor tactical problems arising from the daily contact of small bodies of troops on a wide front. In all these small encounters down to those of patrols, the rifle, not the steel, governed tactics. If only those of our present Yeomanry officers who are asking for the sword, not so much for shock action on a big scale as for this very class of small encounters, would take the trouble to study the work of their own countrymen in such operations as those around Colesberg, they would, I believe, be converted to implicit faith in their rifles.

2. The operations, so far from being abnormal, bear a strong resemblance to the kind of work which, under our present system, Cavalry, unhelped by Infantry or mounted riflemen, will have to do in any European war, particularly during the initial stage of mobilization and concentration for a united advance. During this stage it is the duty of the Cavalry to form a screen, both protective and aggressive in character. This was exactly what French, with his composite force, did. Besides assisting to cover the rear of an existing force—Methuen's—he was in the position of covering the front of a hitherto partially mobilized and unconcentrated army. At first most of the army he was screening was still in England, his and its primary base. Gradually it collected in force behind him, at the Cape Peninsula or secondary base, until it swelled into the force which marched under Roberts to Bloemfontein. That an ocean intervened between the primary and secondary bases does not affect the analogy. In the light of the Colesberg operations, how grotesque seems the theory of the great preliminary shock duel which, according to " Cavalry Training " and the German theorists, is to be sought by the rival Cavalry screens !

3. The " spirit " which actuated our operations around Colesberg was not the " Cavalry spirit," which means essentially the spirit of fighting on horseback with a steel weapon. It was the spirit which should actuate all troops, but particularly mounted troops, simply because they possess horses—the spirit of aggressive mobility, backed by resource, stratagem, and dash. In French this *spirit*, not only now but throughout the war, was admirably exemplified, and we can only regret profoundly that it did not rest on a radical belief in the firearm as distinguished from the steel weapon, and that the Cavalry he led was not trained upon that principle.

4. That French's personality as an able and vigorous officer was a decisive factor in the success of the Colesberg

operations is proved by the narrative of other mounted work at the same period. The best mounted enterprise done by Methuen's troops during the long halt at the Modder was Pilcher's Sunnyside raid of January 1, 1900, by Queenslanders and Mounted Infantry. The Cavalry work, both in the reconnaissance of January 8, and at the Koedoesberg on February 7, was the reverse of vigorous.

THE RELIEF OF KIMBERLEY.

We now approach the principal Cavalry achievements in the South African War. To explain their origin I must refer to the general military situation at the beginning of February, 1900. The only substantial change which had occurred in the Boer dispositions since their successes of mid-December, 1899, was the gradual reinforcement of the Colesberg force, which French had been containing, from a strength of 2,000 to 7,000 ; elsewhere they had stood in an attitude of passive defence. Cronje had sat in his trenches at Magersfontein facing Methuen at Modder River. The Stormberg force, facing Gatacre, had been almost inactive, and behind Cronje the sieges of Kimberley and Mafeking had been carried on with no great vigour. In Natal the siege of Ladysmith had been maintained with diminished energy and steadily diminishing numbers, while Louis Botha held the line of the Tugela against the repeated attacks in ever-increasing strength of Buller's relieving force. At the beginning of February the third of these attacks, that by way of Vaal Krantz, had just failed.

Behind the screen so skilfully maintained by French the new army had been steadily collected. At the beginning of February it was sufficient for an advance.

By this time the last opportunity for aggressive Boer strategy on the grand scale had completely passed away. For general, not merely local aggression, brain and mobility combined could not have availed to counteract the numerical superiority which we had now gained, and were increasing daily. Our strength on paper in South Africa at that moment (about 130,000 men on a conservative estimate) approximately trebled the paper strength of the Boers, including their foreign and rebel auxiliaries.

Our effective fighting strength—100,000 men and 270 guns—was between double and treble the effective fighting strength of the Boers at the same period. Our " effective fighting men " in Cape Colony alone, given by Roberts in his despatch of February 4 as 51,900 (exclusive, as he said, of the garrisons of Mafeking and Kimberley and of seven militia battalions, and evidently exclusive also of all auxiliary non-combatant units), considerably exceeded the enemy's entire field-force, reckoned on a gross, not on a net, basis.*

* I have tried, as usual, to follow the figures of the "Official History," although for this period they are inadequate. Sometimes the considered estimate of the historian is given, sometimes the Intelligence estimate on the spot, with or without a warning that it was exaggerated, while in the case of particular operations the estimate is occasionally altogether omitted. It is not stated how much allowance is made for men detached on non-combatant duties, and for that leakage from particular commandos of burghers "on leave" which was such a grave source of weakness for the enemy.

On January 10, when Roberts landed, the historian's estimate of "total effective strength of Boers in the field " (vol. i., p. 409) is 46,500, thus disposed :

Joubert in Natal	21,000
Schoemann at Colesberg	5,000
Grobelaar around Stormberg	4,000
Cronje at Scholtz Nek	8,000
Ferreira besieging Kimberley	3,000
Snyman besieging Mafeking	2,500
H. Botha on Rhodesian border	1,000
" Reinforcements "	2,000
	46,500

But, although it was distinctly our turn for aggressive strategy, the problem which faced Roberts was one of extreme difficulty. The fall of any one of the three besieged towns, especially that of Ladysmith, would have involved a grave loss of prestige, and Ladysmith was hard pressed. Kimberley, in a far from heroic spirit, was actually threatening surrender, if not relieved immediately. Roberts had to operate on exterior lines with a hastily improvised army, deficient in staff arrangements, transport, commissariat, and, above all, trained and experienced mounted troops. He rose to the height of a great occasion.

His scheme, briefly, was to leave a skeleton force under Clements in front of Colesberg ; to turn the left flank of the Stormberg commandos with Brabant's Corps of 3,000 Cape Colony mounted volunteers ; and, with the bulk of his own army, to march by the western flank on Bloemfontein, smashing Cronje and relieving Kimberley

---

On February 16 (four days after Roberts began his move) an Intelligence estimate (" somewhat exaggerated ") is given to this effect :

Cronje (including Kimberley force)	12,000	20 guns
A. Cronje (detached by Cronje)*	1,300	2 guns
Near Goemansberg	300	1 gun
Reinforcements (*i.e.*, to Cronje) (" uncertain ") ..	5,000	
Colesberg	8,000	10 guns
Stormberg, etc...	2,000	
	28,600	

The Natal estimate is omitted, but by reference to the chapters on Natal at the same period the total Boer strength there cannot have been more than 12,000. Add, therefore, 12,000 + the forces of Snyman and H. Botha on January 10, *i.e.*, 3,500, and we get 15,500

Total .. 44,100

---

* These figures are certainly wrong. Andries Cronje's force should be included in the 12,000 credited to Cronje.

in one stroke. This stroke, he was well aware, would automatically lessen the pressure upon Natal.

All the Cavalry in Cape Colony, and, under the original scheme, nearly all the regular Mounted Infantry, together with Colonial mounted contingents, were to be formed into a semi-independent unit under French for the relief of Kimberley.

The preliminary movements were consummated with extraordinary secrecy and skill. By February 10 an army of 45,000 men and 118 guns* had been collected behind the Modder, of whom 37,000, representing approximately 30,000 combatant troops, afterwards took part in the invasion of the Free State.

The Infantry divisions, including that of Methuen, were four, with a gross strength of nearly 30,000, and 76 guns. The Cavalry division, which is our particular concern, with a gross strength of 8,000 men and 42 Horse Artillery guns, was divided into four brigades—three consisting of regular Cavalry, one consisting of regular Mounted Infantry and Colonial mounted riflemen. The regular Cavalry brigades contained altogether seven regiments and portions of two others, a total of about 3,000 sabres. The brigade of mounted riflemen was 2,250 strong.

A word about the force of regular Mounted Infantry, totalling 3,500, now under Roberts. Most of this force had been raised during the last two months, and was very raw and crude, a large proportion of the men being scarcely able to ride, while a few still wore trousers or kilts. The horses, too, were ill-trained and in bad condition. But the force had at last been given the outline of a regular organization, and was now distributed in eight battalions of 450 each, grouped in three divisions, under Colonels Alderson, Hannay, and Ridley. Roberts

---

* These and the subsequent figures are taken from Roberts's despatch of February 16. No figures of strength (only of units) are given either in the text or appendices of the " Official History."

had intended all of these to form part of the independent mounted force, but this plan, through lack of time, proved not to be feasible. Alderson's division alone, 870 strong, went with French, brigaded, as I have shown, with 1,400 Colonials. The rest of the regular Mounted Infantry stayed with the main army, in company with other volunteer mounted units (City Imperial Volunteers and Colonials), making up a total mounted reserve with Roberts of some 3,600 men.

Cronje's forces, including the men investing Kimberley and a detachment in the west under Liebenberg, numbered at the utmost 11,000, with 20 guns. Of these 7,500 were under his immediate control. Numerically, therefore, he was barely a quarter as strong as Roberts, without counting in the latter's force (as it should properly be counted) part at least of the Kimberley garrison. In respect of mounted men, if all Cronje's troops, including the Kimberley investing force, had been mounted, and all available for purely combatant duties, they would have been barely more than equal, numerically, to the mounted troops under Roberts—that is to say, to the Cavalry division and the mounted reserve reckoned together. Or, to put the case in another way, if we set off the Kimberley garrison against the Boer investing force, the Cavalry division, with its horse-gunners included, was equal to Cronje's main force. Behind the Cavalry division lay the mounted reserve, four divisions of Infantry, and 76 guns.

In point of fact, Cronje's main force was not all mounted, much less well mounted. Sandy soil and burning heat had played havoc among his horses during the last two months. Not more than a quarter of his burghers were well enough mounted to perform long and rapid marches ; about half were poorly mounted, and the rest were actually on foot. Regarded as a whole, moreover, his army was no more mobile than our own. It was supplied, like ours, through the agency of heavy ox-transport, in motion slow and cumbrous to the last degree.

I have to insist on these figures and facts because, obviously, they have a close bearing on our inquiry into the relative merits of the steel weapon and the firearm. On the whole the Cavalry division, when the operations began, was approximately as well off in the matter of horses as Cronje's force. They were in as good condition, probably, as the horses of an invading army coming 6,000 miles by sea to a different hemisphere can expect to be. The division was given a laborious task, though a strictly normal task, in the shape of a raid. The weather was very hot, water scarce, and the conditions exceedingly trying. The horses succumbed in hundreds, mainly from unpreventable causes. But we have to recognize a preventable cause. We may pass over the vexed question of overloading. Most contemporary critics seem to have agreed that the horses of all our mounted troops were overloaded ; but the light load is a counsel of perfection exceedingly difficult to work out in practice. I refer to faults under the heading of horse management, which was admittedly not up to the war standard. The defect was common to all our mounted troops, but in the case of the professionally trained Cavalry we can trace the indirect influence of the shock theory, which in time of peace had encouraged artificial manœuvre as opposed to work under real field conditions. And yet, by perverse reasoning, the destruction of horse-flesh has been twisted by some writers into a negative argument for the *arme blanche*. As we shall see, steel weapons at no period of the war had any combat-value, whatever the condition of the horses.

It is depressing to reflect that the short raid now proposed under the trying conditions described was not strategically necessary. Kimberley stood in no material danger. Roberts, in overwhelming force, only twenty miles away, and ready to strike at Cronje, would have been justified in disregarding the demands made by the civil population for immediate relief. Practically he could scarcely take this course. Facing the situation boldly and generously, he included the immediate, physical relief of the town in his scheme of attack on Cronje, asked the Cavalry Division to perform the task, and was enthusiastically and energetically obeyed. We must remember, however, that under normal conditions the situation could scarcely have arisen. Faced by 45,000 men, of whom, guns apart, a fifth were mounted, Cronje must have raised the siege, and, if he risked a battle, have concentrated every man for it. Even as it was, had our large mounted force been not only as mobile but as highly trained in the rifle as the enemy, it would surely have been used to secure the envelopment and defeat of Cronje where he stood, in the Magersfontein position. But it was not so highly trained. That was the governing factor and the true " abnormality." Kimberley could be given immediate relief only by a long, circuitous march which in the end wrecked the mobility of the division.

The position was this : The Modder separated Cronje from Roberts. Twenty miles north of the Modder, and behind Cronje, lay Kimberley ; but Cronje's communications did not lie in this direction. Though the force investing Kimberley was still supplied by rail from the Transvaal—that is, from the north—Cronje himself was now based by road on Bloemfontein, nearly 100 miles to the east—towards his left flank, that is—a thoroughly false and dangerous strategical position for the Boer leader. It lay with Roberts to cut this line of communication and envelop Cronje. North he must have operated, for Cronje might decide at any moment to cut adrift from Bloemfontein and retire north ; but there was nothing to be gained by operating as far north as Kimberley.

Cronje, stubborn in spirit, but slow in thought and

action, and, on this occasion, badly served by his scouts, was thoroughly mystified by the secrecy and suddenness of his enemy's stroke. Until the last moment he clung to the belief that he was to be attacked in the Magersfontein trenches, which he had defended so successfully two months earlier. When threatening symptoms appeared to his left front, he did his best to watch this quarter by despatching successively three small bodies of his best-mounted burghers, under A. Cronje, Lubbe, and Christian de Wet, some 1,200 in all; but he made no effort to set in motion his partly dismounted main force of about 6,000 men, with its unwieldy laager.

Ramdam, twenty miles south of the Modder, and forty miles by air-line from Kimberley, was the British point of concentration. French and the Cavalry division left this point for the north early on February 12, with the main army slowly following, less Methuen's division, which remained to confront Cronje. Two days' march brought French to the Modder, with his troops and gun-horses already much spent. According to the " Official History," forty horses were dead and 326 unfit to march. There had been barely more than a show of opposition at the crossing of the Riet and the Modder. De Wet, if he had chosen, might have done more to delay the advance with the 800 men whom at one moment he had under his hand, but he was daunted by the imposing array of horsemen and guns, and left Lubbe with only 250 men to dispute the passage of the Modder. He himself hung on the rear of the grand army, where he soon found his opportunity for a formidable stroke.

From the Modder at Klip Drift to Kimberley is twenty miles. Cronje, though he did not yet suspect French's objective, was beginning to be alarmed, and now detached another 800 men and 2 guns, under Froneman and

De Beer, who were joined by 100 men under Lubbe, to oppose him. French, on the morning of the 15th, after a day's rest, swept this little force aside by one abrupt and vigorous stroke, which has become famous as the " Klip Drift Charge." A mountain of error has been heaped upon this event. Let us examine the circumstances.

French, on the night of the 14th, had been joined, thanks to some splendid forced marching, by the sixth Infantry division and by most of Hannay's brigade of Mounted Infantry — that is to say, by about 6,000 Infantry, 20 guns, and 1,500 mounted men—a force in itself numerically superior to the whole of the main body now remaining with Cronje. With the Cavalry division added there were now at Klip Drift some 13,000 men and sixty-two guns. Cronje's communications with the east were definitely severed, the point of severance was held in force, and French was free for his independent spring on Kimberley. As it happened, Cronje on the same afternoon, dimly alarmed, had moved his headquarters and main laager a little east, so that it actually lay only six and a half miles west of Klip Drift, though the Cavalry, in spite of a day's rest, were too tired for the reconnaissance necessary to discover this fact. If the fact had been discovered, it would have shed a curious light on the proposal to relieve Kimberley.

However, the immediate problem was to open the road for French to that town. Nine hundred Boers (with 100 of Lubbe's men reckoned in) and two guns faced the large force at Klip Drift. They were disposed in an arc, concave from the British point of view, occupying two converging ridges, between which ran an expanse of open ground about a mile in width at the narrowest point, and gently rising to a " Nek." Both valley and Nek were good galloping ground, without wire or obstacles of any kind. Very few Boers were on the Nek—perhaps

a hundred; the majority were on the two ridges. Instead
of clearing them out in the manner usual at this period,
by a slow preliminary assault, French resolved to rush
his whole division through the valley and over the
Nek, under cover of Artillery fire.

It was a sensible resolve, promptly made and admirably
executed. At the moment when French formed it he
was about a mile distant from the Modder and about two
miles from the Nek. His division, in column of brigade
masses, had been checked by the fire of the two Boer guns
posted on the western or left-hand ridge, about 3,000
yards away, and by rifle-fire from the nearest part of the
eastern ridge, about 1,500 yards away. All seven
batteries of Horse Artillery, supported by two batteries
of the Infantry division and two naval guns—fifty-six guns
in all—had opened on the two ridges and the devoted
pair of Boer guns, and had temporarily silenced the latter.
It was now that French ordered the charge, and while it
lasted, all but two horse batteries, which were kept in
reserve, continued to bombard the Boer positions.
Gordon's brigade, less two squadrons, which were engaged
on the flanks, led the way, deployed in extended order—
eight yards between files, twenty yards between front
and rear rank—pace, fourteen miles an hour. Broadwood's brigade came next, 800 yards behind, and the
other two brigades (one of Cavalry, the other of mounted
riflemen) followed, though exactly at what interval and
in what formation we are not told precisely. But I think
we may assume that the fully deployed charge was made
only by Gordon's brigade, and that, at any rate, this was
enough to secure the object in view.*

* The *Times* History describes Broadwood's brigade as galloping
after Gordon's, half a mile behind. The German critic, who appears
to have been an eyewitness, speaks of 6,000 horsemen charging as
though in one body. I base my account on our own "Official
History."

It must be clearly understood that the objective of the charge was the lightly-held Nek, to reach which the division had to run the gauntlet of the flank fire from the two converging ridges. All went well. As the official account says : " The squadrons of the leading brigade came at once under a shower of bullets, both from front and flanks, yet few fell. The extended formation, the pace of the charge, and thick clouds of dust, puzzled the burghers, while the supporting fire of the batteries shook their aim." The Nek was reached and won, the burghers who held it fled, only a few remaining to " be struck down or made prisoners." (The *Times* History says about a score were " speared or made prisoners.") Their comrades on the flank ridges appear to have ridden off before the charge was well over. With only fifteen casualties, the whole division and its seven horse batteries passed the danger-point, and went on that same day to Kimberley. Ferreira and the investing force beat an immediate retreat, and the town was relieved.

Such was the charge at Klip Drift. What can we learn from it ? In the first place, let us try to grasp the realities that lie behind conventional phraseology. The movement was not a " charge " in the commonest sense of the word, as applied either to Cavalry, Infantry, or any other troops. Though offensive in character, it was not even in absolute strictness an attack; for upon the Nek, which was the objective of the movement, there was nothing worth the attack of a division. Least of all, as the *Times* History truly points out, was it a " Cavalry charge " in the sense of a shock charge with the steel weapon, for there was nothing substantial upon which to exert shock. This was perfectly realized by French, who was intentionally taking the line of least resistance, in accordance with his primary object, which was to get to Kimberley, not to defeat these Boers. With that end in view, he ran the gauntlet of fire, pierced the Boer line, and proceeded. There was no possibility or intention of producing shock, for the leading brigade charged with files eight yards apart, a formation which excludes anything approaching shock. Nor had the result anything to do with the steel weapon : necessarily not, for shock is the only real *raison d'être* of the steel weapon. The threat of any weapon would have served to drive the handful of Boers from the Nek in the face of such a deluge of horsemen. Their actual losses were as insignificant as our own. There was no pursuit of any part of the Boer force, for, as the Official Historian dryly remarks, " The British troopers, riding *seventeen stone*, and mounted on weak and blown horses, had no chance of catching an enemy riding *fourteen stone* on fresh animals." That should surely give cause for reflection. This was only the fourth day out from Ramdam : it had been preceded by a day's rest, and this was the first operation of the morning. Difficulties apart, in order to have converted the movement into such an attack as would have constituted a test of weapons, it would have been necessary for French either to pursue as best he could, or to use the position gained in order to turn upon Cronje's main laager, which now lay defenceless only six miles to his rear, or even upon the rear of Cronje's combatant force at Magersfontein. But, even if he had known that Cronje's transport was so near, his orders were explicit—to relieve Kimberley instantly. By an ironical coincidence, at this very moment De Wet was raiding the main army's transport at Waterval.

The direct result of neglecting the Boers who were driven away from Klip Drift was that a number of them returned shortly after the repulse, and took up an entrenched position north of the sixth division, where they curtailed the reconnaissances of our Mounted Infantry, and enabled Cronje's main force to march across our front during a bright moonlight night.

As far as weapons are concerned, the whole interest of the day centres in the rifle—the Boer rifle. For the first time in the war a large body of our mounted troops had deliberately entered and penetrated a fire-zone on horseback. That was the new fact. How had they done it ? What were the conditions ? What light is thrown on the age-old physical problem of vulnerability and mobility as modified by the modern magazine rifle ? These are the questions of really serious interest to students of mounted action. It must be admitted that Klip Drift by itself does not afford much foundation for argument. With every Boer rifle on the field reckoned as an effective factor, the disparity in the size of the forces engaged was so abnormal as to preclude far-reaching conclusions. Of course, every Boer rifle on the field was not effective. All the 900 burghers present cannot have been in the immediate firing-line, and the firing-line by no means wholly commanded the masses of moving horsemen. Unfortunately, none of the accounts are precise on these important points—volume of fire and range. One can make only rough inferences from a comparison of narratives and maps.

The official map represents the enemy's arc-shaped firing-line as covering five miles of ground. The *Times* History makes it nearer seven ; while the German Official Historian calls it two and a half. At any rate, it was a very thin, widely extended skirmishing-line, a part of which must have been out of range of the charge. I should imagine that half of the men on the western or left-hand ridge, which ran at right angles to the line of our advance, could not have fired an effective shot at the Cavalry. With the eastern or right-hand ridge it was different. This was the more strongly held, and ran parallel to the line of our advance ; but here, too, the average range must have been great, for the Boers (as on the western ridge) lined the summit, not the slopes, and (according to the official map) only the northerly half of the ridge directly overlooked the narrow part of the valley, or, rather, the exit from the amphitheatre. What was the width of this valley or amphitheatre ? Again we are left in doubt. The contours of the official map represent it roughly as diminishing from three miles to one and a half ; the narrative says that the Nek—that is, the narrowest point—was from 1,200 to 1,500 yards broad. No estimate is anywhere given of the average range and volume of the flank fire from the two converging ridges. One thing only is certain, that the direct frontal fire—that is, from the Nek—was insignificant. So few were the Boers at this point that the official map does not mark them at all.

Out of these scanty and conflicting data we may perhaps conclude that, allowing for the frontal extension of the Cavalry and for the position of the Boers on the summits of the ridges, the range was at no point less than 1,100 yards, and averaged about 1,300 from first to last, while the number of rifles brought into more or less effective play for a few minutes may be conjectured at 500 or 600. The ranges were long, therefore, and the rifles few, in consideration of the short time allowed for their use.

The next point to discover is : What were the physical and moral conditions under which the Boer fire was delivered ? Let us note three main circumstances, all normal in character, but—in two cases, at any rate—abnormal in degree.

1. *Artillery Fire.*—Bombardment by fifty-six guns, although it appears to have caused little or no loss to the Boer riflemen, must have rendered accurate and steady shooting almost impossible. The German historian quotes a Boer present as saying that " the fire from the English guns was such that we were scarcely able to shoot at all at the advancing Cavalry."

2. *Dust.*—This may be regarded as a normal circumstance, rightly to be counted on by any leader of horse who plans a mounted movement under fire. In later stages of the war the Boers used to fire the grass for a similar purpose.

3. *Surprise.*—This, everywhere and always, is the soul of offensive mounted action. It baulks the aim and daunts the spirit of the defence. French, by sure and rapid insight, obtained a tactical surprise here, and gained his object. But surprise by an approximately equal force is one thing, and surprise supported by the numbers at French's command another. Most of the Boers present seem to have taken to their horses precipitately before the charge was over—and no wonder! The first brigade was backed by three others; these were backed by a division of Infantry and guns and a quantity of Mounted Infantry. Of the presence of this large force the Boers were perfectly aware. In giving way before the charge, they can scarcely be convicted of the " demoralization " with which some writers charge them.

At Klip Drift, then, the conditions were abnormally favourable to the offence, and when we are seeking evidence concerning the effect of modern rifle-fire upon mounted troops in rapid movement, we must be careful to have these conditions in mind. Still, the facts are there, to be noted : complete success of the horsemen , practically no loss. If Klip Drift stood alone, we should at least be justified in assuming that, under certain circumstances, a large body of troops on horseback, boldly and skilfully led, could face rifle-fire with impunity. But Klip Drift does not stand alone. It is only one—and by no means the most interesting—of a great number of episodes illustrating the same problem, and proving that, under far less favourable conditions—whether of numbers, ground, dust, or surprise, and without support from Artillery—mounted men not only can pass a fire-zone unscathed, but make genuine destructive assaults upon riflemen and guns. But—and upon this reservation hangs the whole thesis I am upholding—the mounted men who do these things must be mounted riflemen, trained to rely on rifle and horse combined, and purged of all leanings towards shock. Otherwise they will not get their opportunities, or, if they accidentally get them, will not be able to use them.

This revolution in mounted tactics was not to come from the Cavalry. It should have come from them. With the exception of our raw Mounted Infantry, the Boer Police, and the small permanent corps maintained by the South African Colonies, they were the only professional mounted troops in the field of war. In them alone lay the tradition of the mounted charge in any shape or form. They alone had, in fact, put the mounted charge into practice. Theories apart, they alone were endowed by years of training with the drill and discipline requisite for that orderly deployment and swift united movement which were exhibited at Klip Drift, and which are the essential characteristics of any charge, under fire or not under fire, by whomsoever made, with whatsoever weapon, and for whatsoever purpose. Unique as the conditions were at Klip Drift, it seems strange that the true lesson did not enter the minds of French and the other Cavalry officers present. They cannot have imagined that shock had anything to do with success. The widely extended formation deliberately adopted was not peculiar to Cavalry, nor was speed peculiar to Cavalry : both were the natural attributes of all mounted troops. They must have realized, one would have thought, that the rifle was dominating the battle-field, causing those extended formations on both sides, preventing shock, and—because it was united with the horse—enabling the enemy to get away, alarmed, but without pursuit or appreciable loss, and ready to return shortly afterwards and to put up a good fight on the following day, again against superior numbers.

The bewildering paradox is that at bottom they did realize these things, though they did not reach the point of drawing the logical inference. Otherwise it is impossible to explain either Cavalry action up to this point or the general impression prevalent at the time of this charge, that it was an extraordinarily perilous and daring performance. Why perilous and daring if the Cavalry, with their steel weapon, are superior to mounted riflemen ? If these Boer mounted riflemen had been represented by an equal or even a much greater number of Continental Cavalry, armed with short carbines like our own Cavalry, and relying mainly on the sword, would the performance have been then considered extraordinarily perilous and daring ?

Questions of this sort ought, I submit, to expose to any unprejudiced mind the fallacies underlying the *arme blanche* theory. But what does the old school say ? Let us turn to the German official critic's remarks on Klip Drift, remembering the praise which has been showered upon his work, and that it is Germany which, even at this hour, inspires our Cavalry ideas. I quote the paragraph in full, as an example of the workings of the Cavalry mind and of its blindness to realities :

" This charge of French's Cavalry division was one of the most remarkable phenomena of the war ; it was the first and last occasion during the entire campaign that Infantry was attacked by so large a body of Cavalry, and its staggering success shows that, in future wars, the charge of great masses of Cavalry will be by no means a hopeless undertaking, even against troops armed with modern rifles, although it must not be forgotten that there is a difference between charging strong Infantry in front and breaking through small and isolated groups of skirmishers."*

* German Official Account of the South African War, vol. i., p. 147.

It will be seen that the writer's method of evading the true moral is to call the Boers "Infantry." In other words, he shuts his eyes to the whole point at issue. The Boers were not Infantry. They were mounted riflemen corresponding to German Cavalry, but with many added functions, and possessing the offensive and defensive power of Infantry. They had reached the field on horses —it might well have been that they could not have reached it in time without horses—they were acting in defence, dismounted, against crushing odds ; but their horses were not far behind them, available for retreat, vulnerable also to attack. They left the field safely on these horses, and a number of them soon returned on these same horses to fulfil the vitally important function of masking the flank march of their own main body. Meanwhile, few as they were, they had compelled the Cavalry to conform to conditions imposed by the rifle and to take the line of least, not of most, resistance. If they had been German Cavalry of that date, trained primarily for shock, with poor firearms and little practice in skirmishing, they would not, in the first place, have had the confidence to take up the extended position which these men took up, unsupported and facing an army. And if they had taken it up, they could not possibly have rendered even a direct frontal attack, however conducted, in any degree dangerous except to Cavalry of exactly their own stamp. If, on the other hand, they had been Infantry, nothing but a miracle could have saved them from complete destruction without any charging at all. The most indifferent operations on their rear and flanks, either by our Cavalry or Mounted Infantry or Colonials, would have sufficed to pin them to their ground, while the Infantry, six times their strength, disposed of them. But, of course, the whole supposition is visionary. If they had been Infantry, they would not have been there at all.

In any case, had they been either Infantry or Cavalry, no critic would permit himself to speak of the " staggering success " of the day's operations. But what becomes of sanity when that unfashionable type, the mounted rifleman, is in question, particularly if he is an " irregular " ? Let the reader only take the trouble to substitute the words " mounted riflemen " for the word " Infantry " wherever it occurs in the German paragraph, and note the disastrous effect upon the Cavalry theories of the writer. It is like finding the key-word to a cipher.

But I may be misleading the reader by taking advantage of the German writer's unconsciously ambiguous use of the word " Cavalry." To him, as to all Germans, that word means mounted troops whose distinguishing feature is a steel weapon and the capacity for shock. As I have already explained, French's troops were not acting as " Cavalry " in this sense. If they had been, there might be some ground for the tameness and caution of the German inference—namely, that in future wars such charges will be " by no means a hopeless undertaking " ; an inference further qualified by the remark (perfectly true) that this was only a case of " breaking through small and isolated groups of skirmishers," by a whole division, be it remembered. Surely a most damaging admission for an upholder of shock ! We may wonder what the critic would have thought if he had stopped to the end of the war, and had seen the situation at Klip Drift reversed—800 Boers making a direct frontal charge upon three thousand stationary troops and several batteries of guns, and coming within measurable distance of success.

Such is Cavalry comment on Cavalry action. It is typical and authoritative, or I should not spend so much space on it. Mr. Goldman * speaks of the " madness " of the charge " according to all military rules," of the " climax of daring " which prompted it, and of the

* " With French in South Africa," pp. 83, 84, and Appendix A., p. 411.

justification it gave to " the advocates of bold *Cavalry* action." Note the implied syllogism : Cavalry carry the *arme blanche* ; this was a successful charge by Cavalry ; therefore the *arme blanche* is justified. This is not to misinterpret Mr. Goldman, for in a special appendix devoted to proving the superiority of Cavalry over mounted riflemen, and under the heading " Shock Action," he expressly instances this charge as testimony. The " Official History " is scarcely less misleading.* Without any instructional analysis of the physical and moral factors, it describes the charge as the most " brilliant stroke of the whole war." Such indiscriminating extravagance of praise does a world of harm. The critic, in his hazy enthusiasm, mixes up two distinct aspects of the attack—its strategical and its tactical aspects. On the assumption, upon which French acted and was compelled to act, that Kimberley needed relief, and that it was worth while to wreck the Cavalry horses and neglect Cronje's main force in order to effect this relief, he may truly be said to have carried out his strategical task brilliantly, even with allowance for the numbers under his control and for the co-operation of the Infantry. Tactically, too, upon the same assumption, he did the right thing promptly and well, and deserves all the higher credit because he was a pioneer in the experiment of subjecting horses to modern rifle-fire. But in a serious history uncoloured by the emotions of the day, to call the charge, regarded as a tactical feat, the most brilliant stroke in the war is an abuse of language which would not be tolerated for an instant if any other class of troops but Cavalry were in question. Judged by a reasonable standard of risks, numbers, and achievements, either set of combatants in any one of the bloody and stubborn fights at this date just beginning in Natal for the final relief of Ladysmith deserved more praise. Among mounted operations the

* Vol. ii., p. 36.

attack at Bothaville (October, 1900), many other British attacks, and many Boer attacks, were more admirable.

What must follow logically from such exaggerated laudation ? That it takes a division of Cavalry to pierce merely—not to roll up or shatter—a thin skirmishing line, and even then it is a brilliant feat. What, then, of future wars—Continental wars ? At Klip Drift we can scarcely dissociate the leading brigade from the three following brigades. Practically the whole division was acting as a unit for one purpose. In the whole of the Crimean, Franco-Prussian, and Austro-Prussian Wars of the last century, there is not, so far as I am aware, a single instance of a division of Cavalry charging as one homogeneous unit. Rare were the charges of more than one regiment ; rarer still those of more than one brigade.* In these wars large armies, approximately equal, were arrayed against one another. And the method was shock —exerted upon substantial bodies of men—true physical shock, for which mass cannot be too dense or coherence too close. Even if we cling to shock, and persuade our- selves that Klip Drift was an example of it, where are our standards ?

What, we may ask lastly, is the explanation of all this confused reasoning, and the strange conclusions to which it leads ? Nothing but the fascination of the *arme blanche.* While giving unstinted admiration to the brave men who faced unknown dangers so steadily and resolutely in this ride at Klip Drift, we must look here for the comparative failure of their branch of the service during the war. They had felt what the training-book calls the " magnetism of the charge," the exhilaration of swift, victorious onset under fire—sensations which they had always been taught to associate solely with the steel weapon and solely with the arm of the service to which they were proud to belong—the Cavalry. The old tradi-

* See Henderson's " Science of War," pp. 53, 54.

tion, somewhat shaken by months of bickering with fire-arms and for the most part on foot, seemed at last to have been triumphantly justified. It was an error. They mistook both the causes and the extent of the triumph, and remained in the old groove of thought, which this charge, properly construed, should have taught them to discard. In reality the best part of their tradition lived in all its pristine splendour ; the rest was obsolete. Clinging to the obsolete, they missed the vital part.

From this time onwards they were to do much hard and good work, not, in the Cavalry sense, as Cavalry, save on a few insignificant occasions, but as mounted carbineers, and, in the last phase, as fully developed mounted riflemen. But their hearts were never wholly in it. There were *arrières - pensées ;* vain longings for situations which obstinately refused to recur ; a tendency to throw the blame on the horses, on the higher command, on any-thing but their own inability to read the signs of the times and vitalize their own traditions by recognizing the uselessness of the steel weapon and the predominance of the rifle.

CHAPTER VII

PAARDEBERG AND POPLAR GROVE

FEBRUARY TO MARCH, 1900.

I.—KIMBERLEY TO PAARDEBERG.

THE true factors of success in mounted warfare received the most convincing illustration in the events immediately following the relief of Kimberley.

The baneful influence of this town continued to react on British strategy. French, in an ardent mood, and with some justification from his original orders, resolved to pursue the investing commandos north with three brigades, two of Cavalry, one of Mounted Infantry and Colonials, and some of the Kimberley mounted troops, altogether something over 4,000 men and five batteries. Ferreira, with most of the Free Staters, had retreated east the night before, and was wholly out of reach. There remained on the route due north, and with eleven miles start, from 1,500 to 2,000 burghers under the Transvaaler, Du Toit, and a heavy convoy. It soon became evident that, in the weak condition of French's horses, the capture of this convoy was the only feasible object, and to this object French eventually confined himself. But an extraordinary hitch arose. One small body of 150 * Griqualand West rebels, with one gun, instead of evacuating the lines of investment during the night, had quietly remained at its post on the Dronfield ridge, seven miles

* *Times* History gives " 150-200 "; " Official History," " 200 " ; German History, " 100."

　　　　　　　　　　

north of Kimberley, and now acted as a sort of improvised rear-guard. One of the Cavalry brigades, about 1,200 strong, with three batteries, in the course of a sweep north-west in order to envelop the convoy from that side, stumbled upon the Griqualand men, and wasted several hours in a vain endeavour to dislodge them by fire-action. The delay destroyed whatever chance there had been of succeeding against Du Toit, and the Brigadier was blamed for the delay. But what followed'? On his way back to Kimberley French attacked the Lilliputian force, now separated by nine or ten miles from its nearest supports, with all three brigades, several hundred Kimberley mounted troops, and all five batteries. Still no result. French gave it up, and under cover of a dust-storm the Griqualanders rode away safely, abandoning their gun and some killed and wounded.

This incident occurred on the day after the charge at Klip Drift, and it shows how completely the real significance of that episode had been lost upon the Cavalry. At Klip Drift there was no chance of testing weapons ; it was a case of riding through fire for an ulterior end. Here was a real chance of testing the value of weapons. Where was the steel ? Where, more pregnant question still, was the horse ? What is the tactical purpose of a horse in attack if not to accelerate aggression and precipitate a crisis, using mobility to overcome vulnerability ? The Boers, it is true, were entrenched, but from what we know now of the physical factors in mounted attacks we can say with tolerable certainty that even the single brigade in the morning, properly disposed and extended, might have ridden, even at a moderate canter, into close quarters with the enemy with less loss than that involved in a lengthy dismounted attack. In the evening, with exhausted horses, but with a thirty-to-one superiority in men and guns, the smallest exertion of aggressive mobility would have made an end of the impertinent handful on the ridge.   Now, the Cavalry were as brave soldiers as ever stepped.   What they lacked was imagination to connect together the horse and the firearm as joint constituents of aggressive mobility, a defect aggravated by the possession of an inferior firearm, and by inexperience in the use of it.   The crack of a rifle transformed the action into what their training-book called a " dismounted·" action, and converted them into indifferent Infantry.   At whose compulsion ?   That of a few mounted riflemen, acting in defence, dismounted, virtually as a rear-guard for the main Boer force ; but with their horses at hand, available for escape, counted upon for escape (for otherwise their owners would not have been there), and eventually used for escape.

Dronfield was an extreme case, and I do not wish to use it further than as a peg on which to hang an argument. With infinite variation of circumstance, the same root principles applied in every action of the war.   Let me make one more point clear before leaving the episode, and passing to another equally interesting and far more creditable to the Cavalry.   When I suggest a more rapid mounted advance, I do not, of course, mean that the horsemen should remain on horseback up to, during and after contact.   That was the old Cavalry view, based on the use of a steel weapon, and its strength accounts for the extraordinary reluctance of the Cavalry to contemplate any other form of aggressive mobility. They could never get shock, because their adversaries willed otherwise, and could always impose their will ; without shock they themselves were rightly conscious that a man on horseback with a sword or lance is not, except under very rare conditions, a match for a man on foot with a magazine rifle.   But why, save for a valueless shibboleth, remain persistently on horseback ?   At Dronfield, though the maps and narratives do not warrant the supposition, the summit of the ridge may, for all I

8—2

know, have been unsuitable for rapid movement on a horse. But, as I pointed out in Chapter II., physical contact is not necessary for a charge by mounted riflemen. A charge is just as much a charge—in the sense of a killing, winning advance—if its mounted phase ends within point-blank, or even within " decisive " range of the enemy. Each and every acceleration in the net rapidity of the whole movement makes it nearer to being worthy of the name of charge. Finally, if actual contact is both practicable and desirable, if the horsemen can ride right home, they *must* dismount when they get there. If they do not, they will lose two-thirds of their killing power. Their horses for the moment will be vulnerable encumbrances, but the men are better off dismounted than mounted, because they can use their rifles. I am premature now in discussing this point, but have thought it best to sketch the idea in advance. Illustration will come later.

To continue. That same evening (February 16, 1900) French received written orders from Roberts to march thirty miles to Koodoos Drift and cut off Cronje's retreat.

On the night of the 15th the old Boer General, alarmed by the news of Klip Drift, had at last awakened to the fact that his 5,500 men and his cumbrous laager were on the point of being surrounded by an army of between 30,000 and 40,000 men. Resolving to retire along the Modder towards Bloemfontein, he called up his men from the Magersfontein trenches, and trekked in bright moonlight across the front of the sixth division at Klip Drift without being discovered by the Mounted Infantry. On the 16th, while French was riding north from Kimberley, Cronje held the sixth division at bay, and secured his next strategic point east, the passage of the Modder at Drieputs Drift. In the action of this day we may note that the Mounted Infantry tried to do what the Cavalry had done so successfully at Klip Drift—to ride in force through a fire-zone in order to pierce the enemy's line. Through no fault of their own, but simply through lack of that drill and horsemanship which the Cavalry possessed, they failed badly, and were thrown into great disorder. After dusk, again unobserved, Cronje continued his retreat, and at 4.30 a.m. on the 17th his main body and convoy were halted within a few miles of Vendutie Drift, with an advance-guard as far east as Koodoos Drift.

It was at this moment that French, in accordance with orders, was leaving Kimberley to head off Cronje. His division as a fighting unit had practically ceased to exist. Horses had died in hundreds ; whole regiments were demobilized. Of the three brigades engaged in the northward sweep from Kimberley, only one regiment— the Carabineers—was fit to march. This and Broadwood's brigade, which had not been engaged, gave French 1,500 men and 12 guns. Ardent as ever, notwithstanding, he started off, and in six hours reached Vendutie Drift in time to head off Cronje. Midway he had passed within two or three miles of Ferreira's force, about his equal in strength. Ferreira, though he appears to have been but dimly aware of the course of events, should undoubtedly have thrown himself across the path of the Cavalry. He missed the opportunity, and French rode on.

The mission of the Cavalry was to hold Cronje until the main army should come up and attack his rear. They performed this mission with skill, tenacity, and complete success, using fire-tactics and bluff to impose upon a force nearly four times their superior. Once more, in short, they were doing what they and the Colonials had done so well in the Colesberg operations two months earlier. Tactically, they stood in much the same position as the 900 Boers at Klip Drift, and if Cronje had come to the point even of contemplating the abandonment of his transport and dismounted burghers, he would have had, theoretically, the opportunity of bursting through the British containing line and making his point on Bloemfontein, just as French had burst through the Boer line and gained Kimberley. Knowing what we know now, we can see that this was what Cronje should have done or tried to do, though we can understand why he still declined to take this sort of action. His was not an independent mounted force, backed by an army. Not only in his instinctive perception, but in fact, it was an army in itself, the reverse of mobile, badly horsed, but, on the other hand, supported by small outlying detachments (under Ferreira, De Wet, etc.), from whom he expected vigorous co-operation. His transport represented not only public commissariat, but the private property of his burghers. Meanwhile his men carried the same rifles which had wrought such terrible havoc at Magersfontein. Slow-witted as he was, we must make allowance for this point of view throughout the operations of which the climax was now approaching, and indeed throughout the whole war. It was a standing weakness of the Boer organization that their transport was as ponderous as their fighting men were mobile. The ox governed net speed, not the horse.

These considerations do not detract in any way from the credit due to French and the Cavalry for their ride from Kimberley to the Drifts, and for pinning Cronje to his ground at this critical moment. During the night two Infantry divisions and the Mounted Infantry division, by dint of severe forced marching, were placed within striking distance of Cronje's laager at Paardeberg. Then came the battle, the week's investment, the surrender.

Unquestionably this day—February 17, 1900—was the great day of the Cavalry in the South African War. But, alas for the tyranny of names! Here is the Official Historian's comment : " Yet that night was a memorable one for French's troops ; for they had accomplished the mission assigned to them by Lord Roberts, and had demonstrated that the conditions of modern fighting still permit Cavalry and Horse Artillery to play a rôle of supreme importance in war." Here is what I may call the inverted moral over again. " Still permit !" What a pitifully cautious conclusion ! Is it for that that we maintain enormously expensive mounted corps and entrust them with vitally important duties ?

The real truth is that it was *in spite* of being " Cavalry," not *because* they were " Cavalry," that French's troops had succeeded in the mission assigned to them by Roberts. Throughout the operations the characteristics, inborn or acquired, which distinguished them from mounted riflemen, had been their bane, not their blessing. Their steel weapons had been so much dead weight, their carbines poor substitutes for rifles, while faulty horsemastership, which we cannot dissociate from the artificialities of their peace training, is admitted to have been one of the causes of the appalling mortality in horses. French, as a spirited leader of horsemen, not as a leader of steel-armed, shock-trained horsemen, by pure force of will had overcome these obstacles and performed his allotted rôle. But without these obstacles, and leading a division of highly-trained mounted riflemen, what might he have done ? Unquestionably, his powerful division would have been employed at the outset to aid in crushing by normal tactical means Cronje's small force where it originally stood. But, apart from that fundamental difference, he might probably have dispensed with men numerous enough and efficient enough to act as eyes for the main army, a function which was in complete abeyance during these operations, with disastrous results at Waterval Drift, where De Wet raided a supply column. He might, perhaps, in the course of his independent rôle, have ridden at, instead of through, the Boers at Klip Drift, with far more demoralizing after-effects upon the enemy. He might have discovered and snapped up in his stride, as it were, Cronje's defenceless laager, then lying so near to him, and still have obeyed his orders to reach Kimberley that night. He might, perhaps, have converted the northerly sweep from Kimberley into a fruitful operation, by eliminating the absurd delay occasioned by the Dronfield detachment. Probably he would have reached the Drifts with a larger and fresher force, able to regard what had been achieved rather as a prelude to still greater things than as the climax of a supreme effort. Climax, in fact, it was. When Roberts, a week later, called upon the Cavalry for another divisional enterprise, French was unable to respond. This sort of thing will not do in any future war ; let us be clear about that. We cannot afford to use up Cavalry at this exorbitant rate. They are far too few and valuable, and will have far more varied and difficult duties to perform than French's division performed.

There is no need, for our purpose, to describe the battle of Paardeberg at any length, or to enter deeply into the controversy which has raged around the question of storming versus investment. Time, I think, will confirm the view expressed in the *Times* and German Histories that Kitchener, in spite of his ambiguous personal position on the battle-field of the 18th, and in spite of his faulty and disjointed tactical methods, was right in his endeavour to storm the laager at all costs there and then, and that he should have received more whole-hearted co-operation from the subordinate commanders. Time, perhaps, may have already convinced Lord Roberts that the subsequent policy of investment, with its far-reaching moral and material consequences, was a mistake. But however this may be, the outstanding technical lesson is the same —the extraordinary power possessed by mounted riflemen, trained to entrench and shoot straight, even when they have lost their mobility, even when they suffer from flagrant defects of organization, morale, and discipline, in holding at bay vastly superior regular forces of all arms.

Directly Cronje accepted envelopment, his force lost its last resemblance to a mounted force.   He was assailed mainly by Infantry and Artillery.   But two incidents, which have a strong mounted interest, if the expression is permissible, deserve brief notice.

1. The pathetic little charge of Hannay and fifty or sixty of his Mounted Infantry towards the end of the day. Kitchener, burning to get into the laager in spite of many a bloody repulse, realizing that an irruption even at one point in the front of two and a half miles would lead to the collapse of the defence, and that such an irruption was beyond the power of the slow-moving Infantry under the deadly Boer fire, sent the following message to Hannay at 3.30 p.m. :

" The time has now come for a final effort.   All troops have been warned that the laager must be rushed at all costs.   Try and carry Stephenson's brigade on with you.   But if they cannot go, the Mounted Infantry should do it.   Gallop up, if necessary, and fire into the laager."

In the existing state of affairs it is difficult to defend the terms of this message.   All the troops had not been warned.   There was no proper provision for a supreme concerted assault.   Stephenson, who was Hannay's senior, received no message till much later.   The Mounted Infantry were much scattered, and the spirit of breathless urgency conveyed by the message was inconsistent with the delay involved in co-ordinating their efforts with those of Stephenson's brigade, which was two miles from Hannay on the opposite side of the Modder.

Hannay's mood at the moment was one of despairing exasperation, after several previous failures to act up to what he considered the unreasonable expectations of his Chief.   He now sent some hasty messages to outlying detachments of Mounted Infantry, and without wasting another moment, collected fifty or sixty of the men with him, and, longing for death, rode straight for the laager. He and many others were shot down, and the little charge flickered out, though a few men actually got into the laager.   Nevertheless, even this tiny mounted effort had disproportionately great results, for under its cover the main firing-line dashed forward, and a part reached a good position within 350 yards of the Boer rifles.   From this we can judge of the effects which might have attended a coherent, well-planned charge on a substantial scale. It was the old question of mobility versus vulnerability, illustrated in a very pointed way.   The Infantryman, a small but a slow and steady target ; the horseman, a large but a rapid and unsteady target, necessitating the spasmodic resighting of rifles on the part of the defence, and, by his very impetus, exercising a coercive moral effect upon their minds.   When to use the aggressive power residing in the horse and rifle combined must be determined in every particular case by local circumstances. No rules can be laid down.   But few can doubt that on this occasion, apart from executive methods, Kitchener's instinct was sound.   " Gallop up if necessary, and fire into the laager."   Substitute some more general word for " laager," and there you have embodied in a few pregnant syllables the true spirit of the modern mounted charge. Nobody on the field would have dreamed of giving the same order to Cavalry, because of the manifest absurdity of demanding this kind of work from troops whose charging efficiency was supposed to depend on remaining in the saddle from first to last and wielding a steel weapon. These limitations, if adhered to, especially with the logical corollary of shock formation, albeit there was nothing to shock, would have rendered the charge a fiasco.   If not adhered to, the Cavalry would have been in no better position than unskilled and ill-armed mounted riflemen. That, in fact, is exactly what they were, technically, plus the soldierly virtues and acquirements common to all professional troops of their race. But the fact was not yet realized.

Neither was the converse realized, except intuitively by Kitchener, that under modern conditions the real power to charge resides in well-armed mounted riflemen, not in the troops conventionally known as Cavalry. Circumstances had conspired to obscure this truth. The very name " Mounted Infantry " was a source of error, and the corps so labelled was a young corps, without a charging tradition, and only at the beginning of its education in the efficient use of the horse.

2. The intervention, first, of Commandant Steyn, then of Christian de Wet, with small mounted forces, coming from outside the battle area.

Steyn, with two guns and the Bethlehem commando " a few hundred " strong (I can get no more specific details), represented the first of the reinforcements which had been summoned away from Ladysmith to assist in succouring Cronje. He came up at 9 a.m., occupied a hill in rear of our eastern attack, delayed that attack for some two hours, and retained his position during the day. How far he had ridden before entering the action I do not know, but certainly a long distance.

Christian de Wet with a small force had, like French, been working independently since the operations began. On the 15th, with 350 men, he had attacked the army's supply column at Waterval, and destroyed or captured a third of it. On the 18th, having heard of Cronje's peril, he rode north from Koffyfontein to the Paardeberg battle-field, a distance of thirty miles (just equal to French's ride from Kimberley to the Drifts), with 600 men and 2 guns, and at 5 p.m., by a rapid *coup de main*, seized the cardinal point in our enveloping line—Kitchener's Kopje—overlooking the rear of our central attack. The hill, with its neighbour Stinkfontein, also seized by De Wet, formed part of a chain, running north and south, of which Steyn already held the northern part.   Firing in concert upon the batteries and troops below them, the two leaders developed a counter-attack, which not only put an immediate end to the British assaults upon the laager, but by the confusion which it caused, brought about the abandonment at nightfall of hardly-won positions.   Whether, under any circumstances, Kitchener could have induced the troops to rush the laager that evening is very doubtful, but it is agreed on all hands that the immediate cause of failure was De Wet's masterly intervention at the right place and the right moment.   The indirect after-effects were still more important.   Though a disinclination to incur further heavy losses was, no doubt, the determining factor in the decision of Lord Roberts not to renew the assault, the marked change for the worse in the tactical situation must have influenced his mind considerably.   And if we follow the chain of causation backward, we shall find, in the heavy blow struck at his transport three days earlier by the same master-hand, an additional reason for postponing what the strategical situation so urgently needed —a rapid and uninterrupted advance on Bloemfontein, before Boer reinforcements had time to arrive from other quarters of the theatre of war.   The Cavalry, for their part, were on starvation rations for two or three days after the 18th, owing to the loss of forage-waggons.

Now let the reader compare the work done by French and De Wet respectively in this third week of February, with a special view to the controversy which this book deals with, remembering the relative size of the armies for which each worked and the relative independent strength with which each operated.   The analogy in regard to work done is in many respects close and obvious, the disparity in force equally striking.   Both men alike were actuated by the Cavalry spirit in its truly wide sense of the mounted spirit : both were dashing leaders of Horse, linked in sentiment by the horse. But what could De Wet have done if he, an uneducated farmer, and his men, a rude militia, unaccustomed to drill together except at rare intervals, had been burdened with the disqualifications under which the Cavalry laboured ?

There are no abnormalities here which in the least degree discount the plain lesson for future wars. But, as usual, the official critics, in discussing the Paardeberg campaign, resolutely ignore its plainest lesson. Our own Official Historian pays ample tribute to De Wet's skill and dash, but refrains from any comparison of methods and armaments which might raise the thorny issue. The German historian (vol. i., p. 187) introduces De Wet with the observation that he " arrived from the south " with 500 men. How very simple it sounds to arrive from the south ! Later on (p. 227), the Boer General is criticized for not having done more, the suggestion apparently being that he might have brought about the rout, or partial rout, of the British forces on the south side of the Modder, and have extricated Cronje there and then. I need not investigate the grounds of this hypothesis, which I take to be far-fetched, to say the least. Certainly, if De Wet had produced these results, he would have performed one of the most extraordinary feats in the history of war. My point is that the suggestion is complacently advanced without a word of explanation, express or implied, as to why such an exacting standard should be applied to Boer troops and such a relatively mild standard to British troops. If the critic were to try and equalize his standards, he would find himself writing of the previous day's operations, that French " arrived from the west " with 1,500 men, and blocked Cronje's advance, but that if he had shown proper resolution, he should have routed Cronje there and then. Or, to take an example from the day of the battle itself : Gordon's brigade of Cavalry, something over 800 strong and 12 guns, arrived from Kimberley at about the same time as De Wet from Koffyfontein, and did useful work in seizing the Koodoos Heights to the north-east of the battle-field ; but why not suggest that it should have intervened with crushing effect in the main battle, or that French himself, who, with Broadwood's brigade and the Carbineers, also performed useful work in watching Cronje's line of retreat, should have assisted actively in the assault ?

To those who imagine that the relative merits of Cavalry and the pure type of mounted riflemen have been judicially weighed, or even consciously contrasted, by Germans, and that we can safely fortify ourselves with their opinion in favour of the retention of the steel as the superior weapon, I commend the study of these chapters on the Kimberley and Paardeberg operations, and especially of the passage dealing in detail with the work of the British Cavalry (pp. 163-165, 176-178). Abounding in wise and true criticism, containing scarcely a sentence which can be challenged in any direct, positive way, they constitute a perfect masterpiece in the art of begging the one really fundamental question. What is the use of demonstrating that Roberts's strategy from the outset bore the character rather of an attempt to manœuvre Cronje away from Kimberley than of an effort to defeat him where he stood, and that it was mainly through Cronje's own errors that his envelopment was accomplished, if no clue is given as to the underlying motives of the British General's cautious policy ? Political motives apart, the dominating military fact was the extremely formidable character of the Boers as mounted riflemen—a known, proved fact, which rightly and naturally exercised a profound influence on Roberts's plans. Without a recognition of this fact the whole operations are unintelligible. It is impossible to understand why it was necessary to employ an Army Corps whose mounted troops alone exceeded the enemy's main force, and to use most of these mounted troops not tactically but strategically. Nor can we understand why the operations ended so successfully as they did, unless we realize that of the two constituents of the Boer fighting strength, the horse and the rifle, Cronje, encumbered by his precious waggons and by his helpless non-combatants, persisted in relying almost wholly on the rifle, to the neglect of the horse. On the other hand, a recognition of that dominant military fact explains most of the minor shortcomings and errors upon which the German critic comments adversely. One fault only it does not explain, the imperfect system of command, but that was far worse in the Boer army than in our own. It explains why Methuen's division was not used for a containing attack upon the Magersfontein trenches, so as to pin down Cronje at an earlier stage ; why the whole of the Cavalry were used for the raid on Kimberley, to the neglect of other important duties ; and it throws into vivid light the detailed criticisms passed upon the Cavalry themselves. As to these latter criticisms, one can only admire the unerring dexterity with which the critic skates over the thinnest of thin ice in avoiding even the most distant allusion to the distinguishing features of Cavalry as the standard European arm. On armament and equipment he is silent. No one could gather that the Cavalry carried steel weapons and were equipped and trained primarily for shock. In commenting on the destruction of horse-flesh (p. 176), he notices several preventable causes, but associates none with the conventional systems of peace training. He is severe on the failure in reconnaissance, and attributes it principally to the effect of the modern long-range rifle in keeping scouts and patrols at a distance, but he does not suggest that the Cavalry carbine was an inadequate weapon, or that the lack of individual skill and initiative was connected in any way with the traditional training of Cavalry.

On the fire-action of Cavalry, as at the Drifts on February 17, he would do well to study his compatriot Bernhardi. Like our own Official Historian, he regards such action as an interesting and important modern discovery, and descants sapiently on the additional value it will give to Cavalry in future wars. No writer on any other arm but Cavalry would dare to show such ignorance. As though, nearly forty years earlier and five years before his own great war against the French, the American Cavalry leaders had not in scores of similar combats proved the value of fire-action ! Surely he must have heard of Sheridan's brilliant interception of Lee's army in April, 1865 ?

On Cavalry in offence he is enigmatically reticent. The strange comment on the Klip Drift charge I have noticed. Equally strange are the comments on subsequent actions. Much impressed, apparently (pp. 159 and 166), by the failure of French's division to dislodge the little Dronfield detachment on February 16, as compared with their success in containing Cronje on the 17th, he seems to be on the very verge of embracing the obvious rational conclusion. The two combats he describes as being of " quite extraordinary value " for instructional purposes. We wait breathlessly for the inference. But there is none, except, so far as I understand him, the depressingly lame conclusion that no more *can* be done by Cavalry than was done at Dronfield. And yet a few pages earlier (p. 150) we find him accepting De Wet's destructive attack on the army's supply column as the most natural thing in the world ; while a few pages later he is actually blaming the same leader for not converting his intervention at Paardeberg (smart enough in itself, in all conscience) into a decisive attack against immensely superior forces.

The exasperating feature of all this is that for a controversialist like myself, who is trying to make a point good, there is never anything quite concrete enough to grapple with closely. It is not as if, in his remarks on the Klip Drift charge, the critic ever even alluded to the conventional function of Cavalry in offence, shock with the *arme blanche*, and endeavoured to explain why it was in abeyance in all this fighting against the Boers, and why we may expect that in future wars it will resume its old sway. If he were to take that course, issue could be joined frankly and fairly. But, as I have said, he is absolutely silent on this crucial point, just as he is absolutely silent on the comparative merits of the Boer type. The two themes, so patently and intimately intertwined, are kept rigorously distinct, shut off from one another by a kind of thought-tight bulkhead which divides his mind into two hermetically-sealed compartments, in one of which, I suppose, is enshrined the *arme blanche* dogma, inviolate, inviolable, not to be sullied by the least intrusion of polemical argument.

It is strange enough to find Germans accepting this class of criticism. It is barely credible that we, whose war this was, should, in our turn, accept it at second-hand from Germans and hail it as oracular. That seems to be the situation. But the paradox does not end there. As I shall show at the proper time, Bernhardi's work, the bible of our own Cavalry school, contains within itself the most crushing refutation of the *arme blanche* theory, simply because his special purpose and special environment permitted him to descant more freely and enthusiastically on the virtues of the rifle. He, too, kept the rifle and the steel in carefully separated compartments, but the arrangement is so transparent that it cannot deceive. Experience of his own in South Africa, confirming in every particular those fire-lessons which he drew from the American Civil War, would have saved him from many palpable inconsistencies. However that may be, let the reader clearly understand this, that what I have quoted from the official critic is the kind of evidence on which German practice is founded. If he thinks it convincing and satisfactory, well and good. But let him not be deluded into thinking that the Germans have honestly assimilated and co-ordinated the lessons of the South African War. The contrary can be proved to demonstration out of their own mouths.

It must be added that, besides these comments on the Kimberley operations, scarcely any attention is paid in the German Official History to the mounted question. The war may be truly said to have been studied by Germans from a purely Infantry standpoint. That the mounted factor was dominant throughout is a fact they disregard, even if they perceive it.

II.—POPLAR GROVE.

MARCH 7, 1900.

I have now to record the progress of events up to the capture of Bloemfontein. The investment of Cronje's laager lasted nine days. De Wet reinforced the key position at Kitchener's Kopje, and implored Cronje to break out. Cronje could not induce his men, whose horses were gradually destroyed by Artillery fire, to try. De Wet, who was driven off his kopje by an enveloping movement in which the Cavalry took the principal part, tried to regain it two days later and failed. Meanwhile reinforcements from other parts of the theatre of war gradually brought the total of Boers outside the lines and between Paardeberg and Bloemfontein up to something between 5,000 and 6,000. Aware of the process of reinforcement, and fully alive to the ill-effects of delay, Roberts tried to arrange for a raid by the Cavalry on

Bloemfontein.   By the 24th transport had been collected, the brigades reorganized, and all was ready for a start. But at the last moment French was compelled reluctantly to state that the horses were not in a fit state for the expedition.   De Wet might possibly have made some more effective diversion with the newly-arrived troops, had not the moral decay which made such havoc in the Boer forces after the date of Cronje's capture begun even before that capture was consummated.

Cronje surrendered with 4,000 men on February 29. Vastly more important as the results might have been, had it been possible to storm the laager and accelerate the advance on the Free State capital, Paardeberg was, nevertheless, the turning-point in the war.   Roberts's broad scheme of strategy was signally justified.   Many days before the actual surrender pressure had been relieved at every threatened point in the theatre of war, Mafeking alone excepted—at Kimberley, at Colesberg, Dordrecht, and other points along the frontier of Central Cape Colony, and at the Tugela heights and Ladysmith. Buller fought the successful battle of Pieter's Hill on the day Cronje surrendered, and on the next day Ladysmith was relieved.

Another week's delay followed Cronje's surrender, a delay attributed by our Official Historian mainly to the need of still further recuperating the Cavalry and Artillery horses, partly also to the necessity of increasing the general supplies for the army, in view of the contemplated change of base to the Free State railway.   Behind all we see the far-reaching effects of De Wet's raid on the supply column on the 15th of the month.

Methuen's division had been sent north by way of Kimberley.   With the other three Infantry divisions, 4,900 mounted riflemen (including some recent additions), and 2,800 regular Cavalry, Roberts, on March 6, had an

9—2

army with an effective strength in round numbers of 30,000 men and 116 guns. Facing him, on the Poplar Grove position, a few miles east, and barring the road to Bloemfontein, were between 5,000 and 6,000 Boers and 8 guns under De Wet. These are the figures supplied at the time by the Intelligence, and apparently accepted by the Official Historian, though Villebois de Mareuil is quoted as having estimated them at 9,000. But the Frenchman appears to have reckoned in the forces at Petrusberg and elsewhere, which did not take part in the coming battle. Roberts, giving the outside estimate of 14,000 men and 20 guns in his Instructions of March 6, evidently included, in order to be on the safe side, all the commandos which were known to have left Colesberg, Stormberg, and Ladysmith, but which the Intelligence mentioned as " not since located."

The Boers occupied a crescent of heights no less than twenty-five miles in extent astride of the Modder River. The ford at Poplar Grove Drift formed the communicating link between the commandos on the left or southern bank, which were the most numerous, and the commandos on the right or northern bank. The natural line of retreat to Bloemfontein lay by roads on the left bank, and in particular by the road crossing the river at Poplar Grove Drift, and thence following its course closely eastward. The only alternative, or rather additional route, on this side of the river, that via Petrusberg, took a much more southerly sweep, and, since it skirted the extreme Boer left, which rested on the hills known as the Seven Kopjes, could only be regarded as a perilous flank line of retreat, which any threat of envelopment on the left would suffice instantly to close.

The plan of Lord Roberts was that French, with all the Cavalry, half the Mounted Infantry, and six batteries, should sweep round the Boer left by a détour of some seventeen miles, get in rear of their centre, and block their line of retreat by the Poplar Grove Road.   To this road, and somewhere in the neighbourhood of the Drift, he foresaw that the greater part of the Boer force, threatened in front by three divisions of Infantry and 70 guns, and in rear by the mounted troops and 42 guns, must converge.   Here, then, he hoped to bring about a second Paardeberg, once more in the bed of the Modder River.

The scheme in general character was what the situation demanded.   After what had happened, and in view of the disparity of forces, there could have been no question here of manœuvring De Wet from his positions.   The marvel was that he dared to risk (and there is no doubt that he intended to risk) a battle against such odds and in the existing moral condition of the burghers.   To aim at his complete destruction was the only course worthy of Lord Roberts and his army.   The tactical method proposed, that of using the bulk of the mounted troops as a distinct tactical unit, was equally sound.   Numerically, our mounted troops exceeded the whole Boer army as estimated by the Intelligence.   The force allotted to French—approximately 5,000 troopers and 42 guns was five times superior in Artillery to the whole Boer force, not far short of equality in horsemen, and was certainly superior to the commandos on the south bank, with which he was specially concerned.   This force, moreover, had the immense advantage of possessing complete independent mobility, whereas the Boers, if they wished to maintain the semblance of an organized army, had to preserve their heavy transport and conform their speed to it.   I have often alluded to the importance of this governing factor, and at Poplar Grove, in particular, it must be borne in mind if we are to gain any instruction from what happened.   For the rest, the function designed by Roberts for French was the same as that performed by him so admirably, albeit with a weak force, at the Drifts on February 17—that is, to contain the Boer force until the rest of our army should have time to come up and crush it.

I have only sketched the plan of operations, and I can only sketch what actually happened. I must assume that the reader has before him the map and the narratives of the Official and *Times* Histories.

There is no dispute as to the facts, and both accounts in this respect are substantially the same, but that of the *Times*, for a reason to which I shall have to refer later, is more lucid. There has been much controversy over the day's work and over the cause which led to an almost painful fiasco. Some of this controversy is not strictly relevant to our inquiry, and I shall refer to it as briefly as possible. The point I have to make is absolutely simple and unmistakable.

Let the reader first read the Instructions issued by Roberts on March 6, and grasp their spirit. Their details are not, and could not have been, cut and dried. Battles never follow the course of cut-and-dried instructions. One point needs special notice, that Roberts expected the Cavalry to be well *behind* the Boer positions and somewhere near the Modder before the Infantry began direct attacks, and before the enemy began any general retreat. The sixth division, which was to follow the track of the Cavalry for several miles, and was then to capture Seven Kopjes, on which the Boer left rested, would find the enemy " shaken by the knowledge that the Cavalry had passed their rear." The movements of the other three Infantry divisions were, it is implied, to conform to the course of events in this quarter. On the other hand, the Cavalry division is regarded as wholly independent of the other arms. It was to set the pace, so to speak, and govern the course of events.

Now, it is quite clear from the narrative that from the very first there was no chance of realizing the Commander-in-Chief's idea in its fulness. To have done that it would have been necessary for French either to make so wide a détour as to pass outside the range of vision of the Boers on Seven Kopjes, or, describing a shorter curve, to circle unobserved round Seven Kopjes before daylight, and thence to make for the Modder. To be seen was to precipitate the Boer retreat. Roberts seems scarcely to have realized this, and I think he is fairly open to the criticism that he might have rested his whole plan more boldly on the specific Intelligence report that there were only 6,000 Boers opposed to him, who must, however good or bad their *morale*, begin an immediate retreat directly they realized that the road to Bloemfontein was threatened by so large and mobile a force as that of French. On this basis he would have altered the tone of his instructions to the Infantry, omitted references to preliminary bombardments, and enjoined speed as the all-important requisite.

French appears from the first to have treated the conception of getting round the Boer rear *unobserved* as hopeless, on the ground of time and the condition of his horses. He himself, with good reason, suggested starting overnight. Roberts rejected this proposal, and named the hour of 2 a.m. Owing to an unfortunate misunderstanding, French did not start till 3 a.m. He marched very slowly, halted at 5 a.m. expressly in order to " wait for daylight," which came at 5.45, and reached the farm Kalkfontein, three miles south-east of Seven Kopjes, at about 6.45 a.m., having covered twelve miles in three and three-quarter hours. He had been observed and, at 6.30, fired at from Seven Kopjes, and so far from circling north-east round that hill in order to make for the Modder, he had inclined, after passing it, slightly to the south, and now, as the official map shows, could not be said to be thoroughly " in rear " even of Seven Kopjes. This inclination was made partly with the object of watering his horses at Kalkfontein dam, a step which he considered essential. The halt at the dam seems to have lasted about three-quarters of an hour for the bulk of the division, though detachments continued to push on north and north-east. In the meantime French rode out to reconnoitre.

Let us pause here for a minute. It must be clear that, whatever the justification, French's action was altogether inconsistent with the idea of a rapid sweep of an independent mounted force round the enemy's rear. He has been criticized for not furthering that idea, and the Official Historian, in the course of his rather rambling and obscure comments upon the day's work, meets the point by replying that if French, owing to the condition of his horses, thought the task impossible, " it is safe to say that there is in the world no living authority who can pronounce a decision against him." Let us accept that conclusion unreservedly, adding, however, that French, under the circumstances, should have frankly told his Chief that he could not attempt to carry out the full design, instead of leaving him and the whole army to understand that an effort, at any rate, would be made. Roberts would certainly have altered his plan, on the assumption that French, although he could turn the Boer left, could not within the time allotted him compass the complete half-circle which would bring him to the Modder before the enemy fully realized the threat to their communications.

Apart from that criticism, let us agree that French was free from blame in not being in a position to move in force from Kalkfontein before 7.30 a.m. or thereabouts. Was the game up ? It had scarcely begun. The Cavalry advance had been a complete surprise to the Boers. Their gun-fire from Seven Kopjes at 6.30 appears to have coincided with their first discovery of the turning movement. At seven they realized that their position was turned, though not enveloped, and between seven and eight they began the only course open to them—a retreat, both from the Seven Kopjes and from Table Mountain, the next position northward, towards the Poplar Grove Road, just as Roberts had foreseen. French in person witnessed the beginning of this retreat, and reported it to Roberts in two successive messages, at 7.30 and 8 a.m., noting in the second instance the presence of a long line of waggons, and adding in both cases that he was " following the pursuit with Artillery fire." But how was he to use his 5,000 horsemen ? There were two alternatives : one, to make a direct pursuit ; the other, to resume the thread of Roberts's original idea, and endeavour to intercept the Boer retreat at the river. The first meant less distance for his horses and a strong offensive rôle over an ideal terrain on the lines traditionally reserved for Cavalry; the second meant a détour involving more strain to his horses, though on equally good terrain, and culminating in a semi-defensive containing rôle like that which he had played on February 17. French rejected the first alternative, because, in the words of his second message, the enemy were " too well protected by riflemen on neighbouring kopjes and positions to enable me to attack them, mounted or dismounted." But, while rejecting this aim, he did not resolutely embrace the other,* which was still undoubtedly practicable, in view of the fact that the Boer retreat, though it was covered by mounted skirmishers, was maintained throughout at the rate of ox-waggons, not of unhampered horsemen. The division was sent to the low ridge of Middlepunt, some five miles north-east of Kalkfontein, where one brigade at least was actually nearer to the river than a considerable part of the

* I follow the account of French's motives given by the " Official History." Both the *Times* History and Mr. Goldman represent him as having decided from the first against interception, and regard the next move, to Middelpunt Ridge, as the first stage in an indirect or semi-direct pursuit. The point is not material. It was either irresolute interception or indirect pursuit.

Boer retreating forces ; but here, again, it was brought
to a standstill by "small groups" of Boer riflemen.
From this time (8.30 a.m.) until the evening, the story is
one of impotence on the part of the division, in the face
of mere handfuls, relatively, of these riflemen, who
represented the only stout-hearted element in a thoroughly
disorganized force. It was the story of Dronfield over
again : the failure of Cavalry, armed and equipped as the
Cavalry were, to develop *offensive* power against mounted
riflemen.

There need be no doubt as to the nature of the Boer
retreat. The "Official History," indeed, speaks of "panic"
(p. 201), and De Wet, when he appeared on the scene,
seems to have regarded the flight as a disgraceful surrender to unreasoning fear. But the evidence does not
support this extreme view. De Wet was not present
on the Boer left when the Cavalry made its appearance,
and did not realize that retreat was imperative. The
fact that every gun and waggon was eventually saved,
and that no prisoners were taken, is inconsistent with the
full meaning of the word " panic." On the other hand,
it is quite certain that the greater part of the Boer force
was thoroughly demoralized, determined not to fight, and
deaf to the entreaties and threats of Kruger, who met
them on the Poplar Grove Road, and that it was only by
the valour and self-sacrifice of a very small minority,
spurred on by the fiery energy of De Wet, that a thin rear-
guard was formed and maintained throughout the morning
and afternoon. A resolute stroke would have broken
down this flimsy screen, and turned what was already a
defeat into a rout.

In the efforts that have been made to explain the
ineffective action of the Cavalry, much stress is laid
on the condition of the horses. But the irony of the
matter is that weak tactics brought their own punishment, and produced far greater exhaustion in the horses

than a policy of strong offence.   At 8.30, Broadwood's brigade, on the extreme right of the division, as it deployed on the Middelpunt ridge facing north, was only seven miles from the river.   French, however, contracting his front, ordered Broadwood to close in westward.   Immediately a party of Boers seized some farm-buildings which Broadwood evacuated, and began to enfilade our line. Broadwood was then sent back, with an additional brigade of Mounted Infantry and a battery, and it took these troops two hours (until 11.30) to dislodge the audacious Boer detachment.   Broadwood now asked for permission to pursue immediately, but French allowed another hour to elapse.*   Then an advance to the river was begun, and even now such an advance offered great possibilities of success.   But again De Wet interposed a screen which checked the whole division.

The principal opposition came from a group of only forty men (" Official History," p. 202) at Bosch Kopjes, on our extreme right.   Broadwood was sent back (about 2 p.m.) by a long détour to envelop this point, while the batteries and a brigade of Mounted Infantry attacked it in front.   Two hours were spent in formally carrying the position.   By this time (4 p.m.) all the commandos, with their guns and waggons, had escaped.   A last rearguard was driven in at 5 p.m. by the Cavalry brigades of Gordon and Porter.   What the average distance covered by the division in the course of the day amounted to it is difficult to say, but Broadwood's brigade, as the *Times* History points out, must certainly have covered at least forty miles, or nearly double the distance which would have sufficed originally to place it astride the Modder. The division had suffered some fifty casualties, and the

---

* Broadwood's request, and the delay, are not expressly noted in the " Official History."   In fairness to Broadwood, I take them from the *Times* History.   But it is quite clear from the official narrative that there must have been a considerable delay.

loss of 213 horses.   These were almost the only casualties to the army during the day.

What of the Infantry? Here the original idea, deeply implanted on the minds of all concerned, that the Cavalry would succeed at an early hour in placing itself directly in rear of the Boer centre, produced strange results. Nobody was prepared for a premature Boer flight, and few could take it in.   It will be remembered that movements were to conform to the right, where the sixth division, acting in concert with the Cavalry, was to storm Seven Kopjes.   The halt of the Cavalry at Kalkfontein caused a corresponding halt of the sixth division.   Repeated messages from headquarters (based on French's reports) could not persuade the divisional Commander that the position was untenanted. It was formally attacked and occupied near noon, four hours after its evacuation.   Hesitation and delay were communicated all down the line, each brigade waiting for the next.

All this indicates an atmosphere, common to the whole army, of excessive caution.   The *Times* Historian suggests that a more resolute advance on the part of the Infantry, and especially on the part of the sixth division, might have turned the scale in promoting more vigorous action by the Cavalry. No doubt it would have had this effect.   But it is surely a very poor compliment to the Cavalry arm to suggest, as Mr. Goldman does, that it is not their business to push home an active pursuit unless the enemy's retreat has been originally brought about by Infantry and guns. The fact is, of course, that the Cavalry controlled the course of events. They had been expressly entrusted with this duty from the first, and nothing could lighten the responsibility, least of all a premature flight on the part of the enemy. They alone were in touch with what was actually happening, and in them alone lay the power to infuse vitality into the action.

What are we to conclude ?   First, that French, apart altogether from the capacity of his men, was below his usual form on this day, otherwise he would have risked more and tried harder, even against his own judgment, for a more energetic officer never lived.   Second, that his men, in training and armament, were unequal to their work, and that at the bottom of his heart he knew it.   I speak with especial reference to the regular Cavalry.   The half-trained Mounted Infantry who worked with them had been brought up to believe that they lacked that highest sort of offensive power which was held to reside in Cavalry. Who can fail to detect the paralyzing influence of the *arme blanche* at Poplar Grove ?   When I suggest that French himself must have felt it, I only make the plain inference from his message to Roberts at 8 a.m.   Who were these " riflemen " whose protective action forbade a direct pursuit, mounted or dismounted ?   Cavalry under another name, performing one of the elementary functions of Cavalry—the shielding of a retreat.   Assuredly, if the steel weapon had any merit at all, then was the time to show it.   Where is the " future war " against a white race, in which, all the circumstances considered, better opportunities are going to present themselves ?   No such war can be conceived unless, indeed, accepting the *reductio ad absurdum* in its entirety, we reckon *arme blanche* training as a disadvantage, and count on meeting mounted troops destitute of the very qualities which enabled the scanty Boer rear-guard to stave off destruction from its main body.

The Official commentary upon Poplar Grove is not well-conceived.   It is difficult to reconcile with the plain narrative of facts, which is evidently written by a different hand, and in lucidity suffers only from not being constructed with a view to the obvious conclusions and from the absence of a map showing times and movements. The map shows none of the original Boer positions on the south bank—only some arrows marked "Boers retreating." The British dispositions are those at 11.30 a.m. As a guide to the action, the map is useless, and the *Times* map, though topographically less perfect, must be consulted. In the text there is no practical instruction—not a hint that there was anything wrong with the equipment, armament, or tactics of the Cavalry. Overlaid with irrelevant invectives against the British public for expecting too much of its troops, and with vague moralization on the psychology of the war, we find two definite propositions recurring : that the initial failure of the Cavalry to work round the enemy's rear before the Boers took alarm necessarily and immediately involved the failure of the whole operation, and that the root-cause lay in the condition of the Cavalry horses, which is written of here and elsewhere as though it were a circumstance attributable to an " act of God " wholly out of control of the Cavalry themselves. The narrative itself refutes both propositions.* They are unfair to everybody concerned— to Lord Roberts in particular, to the Infantry, to the Cavalry themselves, and to French. It is difficult to believe that brave men find any satisfaction in hearing themselves defended in this fashion. That is the vice of worshipping a fetish. A purely technical question is converted into a question personal to a branch of the service. And he who attacks the fetish is forced to risk the odious imputation of attacking persons and regiments.

I allude with some reluctance to Mr. Goldman's commentary on Poplar Grove. His enthusiasm for the fetish, always in excess of his discretion, here leads him into confusions and contradictions which, to an unbiassed mind, effectually destroy the case he is endeavouring to build

---

* See p. 201, line 22, where the Cavalry narrative, broken off at p. 197, is resumed (8 or 8.30 a.m.) " On the left " (*i.e.*, on the south of the Modder) " disaster was only warded off by the gallantry of small groups of the bolder burghers," etc., down to p. 203.

up. His narrative, unintentionally, is not always accurate. At page 132 he represents French, soon after 7.30 a.m., when he first saw the Boer retreat, as " straining every nerve to overtake " a disorganized enemy only three miles ahead, but " crippled by broken-down animals," failing " to bring his brigades up in time to throw them on the close ranks of the enemy." No such scene took place. French, as his own messages and the known facts show, refrained from this sort of direct pursuit on the express ground that the enemy's skirmishers were too strong. In any case, the suggestion is untenable. The Boer retreat was regulated by the speed of their transport. The horses, unquestionably, were in bad condition, but to paint them as too " crippled " to overtake waggons, is not only exaggerated but inconsistent with what followed. To do Mr. Goldman justice, it is also inconsistent with his own subsequent commentary ; for on page 137 he restates the facts, without any criticism, but correctly.

Then he proceeds. Admitting that the occasion was one for the Cavalry arm to " turn a defeat into a rout, and capture guns and waggons," he nevertheless fathers on French (without any authority that I can discover) the idea that such action should rightly be preceded by the enemy's defeat at the hands of Infantry and guns. Then, combating the suggestion that the Cavalry should have charged through the enemy's screen at Middelpunt, as they charged at Klip Drift, he reminds us that the Klip Drift charge was " mainly through flank-fire, while here the Boers were in front," and a charge must have meant " certain destruction and probable annihilation." After reading the Official and *Times* narratives, one can afford to smile at this hysterical exaggeration, but that is a small matter. What does this comment, as a whole, imply ? Once more, a crushing condemnation of the steel weapon. The Boers were just as much " Cavalry," in the broad sense of armed horsemen, as French's troops themselves. Can a frontal charge never be made by Cavalry, in the narrow sense, upon mounted riflemen ? Here, if ever, was the opportunity. It is the old *reductio ad absurdum*—an unconscious but unreserved admission that the rifle dictates mounted tactics, not the steel. For, of course, Mr. Goldman means by " charge " a charge with the steel weapon. No other charge is recognized by him, and I hope the reader will note the tardy but instructive side-light on the Klip Drift episode, where, as I showed, the steel weapon was not in question at all.

Still, Mr. Goldman is always candid, and, in spite of his hypothesis of "certain destruction," we find him admitting in the next breath that French was unduly delayed by a small number of audacious skirmishers. Immediately after he is qualifying this admission by attributing failure mainly to the condition of the horses. Finally, he concludes that " failure was clearly attributable, not in any degree to defects in executive operations on the field, but to the details of the plan as a whole not having been evolved in the first instance with sufficient precise-ness of calculation." Of all lessons to be drawn from Poplar Grove this is the least helpful, and, if only Mr. Goldman knew it, the most damaging to the arm whose interests he has so warmly and genuinely at heart. Of all arms in the service it least becomes the Cavalry to complain of lack of precision in a Commander-in-Chief's calculations. Their mobility invests them with the duty and privilege of correcting and turning to advantage errors in calculation, especially when the error arises in the first instance from an overestimate of the strength and morale of the enemy.

Before leaving Poplar Grove, I wish to make an additional reference to two points :

1. *Condition of Horses.* It must strike any impartial student of these operations that the argument from the

condition of French's horses, weak as they certainly were from unpreventable causes, is subjected to an intolerable strain. I do not wish to lay any undue stress on horse management, though we miss the acknowledgment that the horse is a possession whose good condition is one of the supreme tests of regimental efficiency. Gunners, from the Colonel to the driver, hold it a point of honour not to blame their horses as long as there is anything else left to blame, and the Cavalry have the same high ideal. It is only when the *arme blanche* is in danger of discredit that we find its advocates, official and unofficial, laying excessive stress on the condition of the horses, without even a suggestion that the Cavalry may have been partly to blame for it. But I want the reader to go beyond these operations, and inquire, What standard of speed and endurance have advocates of the *arme blanche* in mind when they represent the arm as tactically unfit? It must be inferred that the standard consists in ability *at any moment* to gallop a considerable distance at high speed—" everlastingly to gallop," as Count Wrangel, the Austrian authority, frankly puts it.* This standard is the logical result of the shock theory of which Wrangel is an uncompromising exponent; for, as I have pointed out, one of the four indispensable conditions of shock is capacity to gallop fast, partly because of the highly vulnerable target presented by mounted troops in mass, and partly because heavy impact is the essence of shock. If, as in our own present peace training, we reduce the standard of speed, in contradiction of our own Manual, we compromise fatally on shock. In South Africa, shock being already obsolete, the steel weapon was in reality obsolete too. This the Cavalry could not make up their minds to recognize, and, among other hampering associations, the idea of capacity for high speed as an ever-present essential for strong tactical offence lived on in a

* " Cavalry in the Russo-Japanese War," Eng. Translation, p. 32.

good many minds. We find it in correspondence and
despatches ; we can trace it constantly in field-tactics, and
it was probably in the back of French's mind during the
whole of the Poplar Grove action, though it must have
been clear that in order to overcome the sporadic opposition of the Boer rear-guard no such efforts were necessary.
There is no question that the Boer horses were far fresher
and stouter than ours. If the Boers to a man had fled
from the field, we could not have caught them. But we
should have captured their guns and transport.

The galloping idea in its extreme form is wholly foreign
to the tactical action of mounted riflemen, for whom the
" charge " is a relative term, denoting the climax of
aggressive mobility, not an isolated exotic flowering in
the midst of a dull waste known as " dismounted action."
If we consider mere physical effects, which are all that
matter, the few mounted riflemen who snapped at Broadwood's flanks as he marched towards the Modder, and
afterwards held up two brigades and twelve guns for
two hours, did just as much for their side as the Scots
Greys at Waterloo, and, when they first made their
attack, " charged " in as real and substantial a sense as
the Cavalry at Klip Drift.

It is tolerably certain that the exaggerated claim for
speed as a tactical *sine qua non* at all moments will do
more in future wars to eliminate shock, and enthrone
the rifle in its true position, than any other factor, even
although the opposing Cavalries enter the war with the
fixed conviction that they must join issue in terms of
shock. The side which first breaks that compact will
win. In future wars Cavalry will have far harder work
to do than they have ever had before. In the thick of
a hard-fought war the galloping horse will be a rarity,
the regiment of galloping horses still rarer, the brigade
or division a nine days' wonder. Any unit whose power
to deal decisive strokes in action can be exercised only

by means of really high speed will be of little service. Manchurian evidence confirms this truth.

2. *Horse Artillery acting with Cavalry.*—This is a new point in our discussion, and I ask the reader to watch it carefully throughout the war. He will have been struck already by the large number of guns which accompanied the Cavalry in these operations, and the disproportionately small results which ensued. French had forty-two guns at Poplar Grove, and was never opposed by more than two at a time, and altogether, I think, by six. The question is, To what extent should mounted troops, acting independently, rely on the support of Artillery ? The war proves, I think, that they should rely as little as possible on that form of aid. When, for strategical purposes, high mobility is required, the strain on the gun-teams is great, and may—though this rarely happened in South Africa—limit the strategical mobility of the mounted troops. But I am thinking more of field-tactics. Here the ill-effects of excessive reliance on Artillery were often visible, particularly in offence. The preliminary bombardment, a serious drag upon all offensive action in South Africa, was the curse of mounted action. Generally ineffective in its physical and moral results upon the enemy, it weakened the spirit of offence by weakening surprise, which, in one form or another, is the soul of aggressive mounted action. As events turned out, French would have done better, I believe, at Poplar Drift if he had had no guns at all. The problem which confronted him when he first sighted the Boer retreat could not then have been solved by a compromise in which a " pursuit with Artillery fire " figured as a prominent element. Such pursuits are useless ; the Artillery fire during the whole day caused, I suppose, scarcely a dozen casualties, while a whole brigade of Mounted Infantry had to be told off as escort to the seven batteries. At every turn the possession of

10—2

guns was a temptation to employ slow, formal methods, where rude, overmastering vigour was requisite.   At Dronfield we can detect the same source of weakness. And at Klip Drift, would French have charged at all without the support of an enormous weight of Artillery ?

The Boers, always weak in Artillery, do not seem at any time to have placed much moral reliance on guns as a support for aggressive action.   Their weakness in aggression came from other causes.   It was only when they had lost all their Artillery that they carried aggressive mounted action to its highest point.

It is true that in defence guns are often valuable to mounted troops.   Since leaving Ramdam, the one occasion on which French's guns were useful to him was on February 17, when he headed and contained Cronje, pending the arrival of the Infantry.   The two batteries which he had succeeded in bringing with him, besides assisting to repel attacks on the Cavalry, covered the drift which Cronje's transport had to pass, and made the crossing impossible.   Later experience, however, proved with increasing force that, even in defence, guns, however well fought—and they were always magnificently fought—were often productive of more embarrassment than advantage to a mounted force.   For the moment I am speaking of offence and defence as though they were distinct functions.   Of course, they are not.   They melt into one another, and may alternate half a dozen times in one day.   The best defence is always tinged by offence. An independent mounted force must be equipped to meet all contingencies.   Nevertheless, all things considered, I suggest that the mounted troops who rely least on Artillery at any rate, when they are given a distinctly aggressive task, will achieve most.

The reason, I think, is this : that their mobility and the surprise which is its fruit make the personal factor paramount.   The rifle is eminently a personal weapon, the gun essentially an impersonal weapon. In that respect, let us note in passing, the gun bears a distant analogy to the sword. For the denser the mass of swordsmen and the greater the shock sought to be produced, the less personal is the weapon.

III.—THE FINAL ADVANCE TO BLOEMFONTEIN.

MARCH 10 TO 13, 1900.

There is little that need detain us in the further advance to Bloemfontein. It began on March 10, in three parallel columns under French, Tucker, and the Commander-in-Chief, and ended in the occupation of the capital on the 13th. Demoralization turned to genuine despair in most of the burghers who fled from Poplar Grove. Whole commandos melted to a shadow through desertion. It was only through the agency of reinforcements brought up by De la Rey, notably the Transvaal Police (Zarps), that a show of resolute opposition could be organized by De Wet. At Abraham's Kraal (or Driefontein), eighteen miles east, where, on March 10, the next stand was made, and where French commanded, the principal interest lies in the fine Infantry attack of the sixth division towards the evening, and the stubborn defence made by the small body of Zarps on the Driefontein Kopjes. An attempt by the Cavalry a little earlier in the day to turn the enemy's left was unsuccessful, and the final pursuit came to nothing.

In the last stage of the march the Cavalry were handled vigorously and did well, though the opposition was slight. The best minor tactical stroke during the month's operations was that delivered by Major Scobell's squadron of the Scots Greys late in the evening of the 12th.* On the 13th Bloemfontein was occupied.

* "Official History," vol. ii., p. 235 ; *Times* History, vol. iii., p. 588. There was no question of using the *arme blanche*.

CHAPTER VIII

THE RELIEF OF LADYSMITH

DECEMBER, 1899, TO MARCH, 1900.

I INTERPOSE a chapter here in order to carry events in other parts of the theatre of war up to the date of the capture of Bloemfontein.

A sketch will suffice, since specifically mounted operations were few. No body, either of mixed mounted troops or of regular Cavalry reckoned separately, comparable in size to that formed by Roberts in the main theatre, existed anywhere else. The largest homogeneous mounted force outside this area was Brabant's newly raised Colonial division, nominally 3,000 strong, which, in conjunction with Gatacre's troops, had been deputed to push back the invaders of Eastern Cape Colony from Dordrecht and Stormberg, while Clements, succeeding French in the positions opposite Colesberg, checked the menace to Central Cape Colony. Brabant, however, seems not to have been able to muster an effective strength of more than 2,000 during the period under review. That fine permanent corps, the Cape Mounted Rifles, was a strong, stiffening element in an otherwise raw force of Cape Colony volunteers. Fortunately, the work before them was not severe, for the success of Roberts in the north threw the Boers into a strictly defensive attitude from the middle of February onwards, and in the early days of March caused

150

a general retreat. A successful attack upon Labuschagne's Nek, between Dordrecht and Jamestown, on March 4, gave the recruits confidence.

Clements had had a much harder task than Gatacre and Brabant. Stronger forces opposed him, and the Boer retreat set in later. Early in February all the regular Cavalry, save two squadrons of Inniskilling Dragoons, had been diverted to Roberts's command. There remained, besides these squadrons, 500 Australian horsemen, together with Infantry and Artillery which made up the force to a total strength of about 5,000 men and 14 guns. Against Clements—if the official estimate is correct—the forces at one time were as great as 11,000. Clements, fighting stubbornly, was forced back south of Rensburg, and, in the course of the retreat, all his mounted troops, and particularly the Australians, did excellent service—fire-tactics, of course, being the universal rule. The danger was soon over. On February 21 Clements was reinforced with 900 mounted men and two batteries, and at about the same period the tide of invasion slackened. A week later, on the news of Paardeberg, the Boers were in full retreat for the north. By the middle of March—two days after the fall of Bloemfontein —Clements, Gatacre, and Brabant were all within the Free State borders.

We need not enter at any length either into the siege of Ladysmith or into the long series of operations which ended in its relief. The numerical facts, broadly speaking, were that White, with 13,000 men and 51 guns, was invested by a force under Joubert which originally numbered 23,000 men and 17 guns, but which dwindled gradually by abstractions to the Tugela, to Cronje, and to Colesberg, and finally fell to a strength of about 5,000 ; while, on the line of the Tugela, Buller, reinforced in the period following Colenso to a strength of 30,000 men and 73 guns, faced Louis Botha and Lukas Meyer with a strength which varied in round numbers from 7,000 to 9,000 men and about 18 guns.

As in the western theatre and in every other part of the field of war, the rifle, whether in the hands of mounted men or Infantry, was the decisive weapon. Artillery, as a mere statement of the relative strengths in that arm shows, was comparatively negligible. Sword and lance were out of court. Every responsible person at the time realized this fact. Short as we were of mounted troops, nobody would have dreamed of asking for more troops trained to shock on the ground that shock was either requisite or possible.

The most striking circumstance about the mounted troops in Natal—upwards of 5,000 in number—was the fact that rather more than half were locked up in Lady-smith during the whole four months of the sieges. Four Cavalry regiments, besides the Natal Carbineers, other Natal Volunteers, and the greater part of the Imperial Light Horse—2,800 men in all—were demobilized in this way. The mistake, no doubt, was serious, and White has been freely blamed for it. At the same time, it is only fair to White to put ourselves in his position, and recognize that the question of retaining or parting with his mounted troops was subsidiary to the much larger problem which originally faced him in deciding what was to be the rôle of the Natal army after the battle of Ladysmith on October 30, 1899. Had he possessed, in his force of professional mounted regiments, troops really capable, in conjunction with the volunteers, of tackling the Boer mounted riflemen, it is difficult to believe that, in spite of the moral and material value of Ladysmith, he would have accepted investment there as an alternative to the maintenance of his army as an active field-force. But the battle of the 30th, revealing a deficiency in the striking-power of the army as a whole, had revealed a weakness in the Cavalry which was in no way attributable to moral causes, but simply to armament and training. This circumstance must have influenced him powerfully in resolving to accept investment, a resolve which it is exceedingly difficult to impugn. A retreat to the Tugela, harassed by a greatly superior Boer force, whose temper was exhilarated by the success at Nicholson's Nek, would have been a hazardous operation. It is no reflection on the regular Cavalry, but the simple truth, to say that they had not as yet shown the capacity to act as rear-guard for such a retreat.

But what kind of investment was White to accept ? Here, no doubt, he is open to the charge of compromising between two logical alternatives, the one being to send away instantly the bulk of his mounted troops and Field Artillery, and with the rest of his force to accept a formal siege, with the purely passive object of detaining as many Boers as he could ; the other, to keep his force intact, and maintain a defence so active and supple in character as to enable him to cut loose at any moment and co-operate with the relieving force. Although something like this latter course was evidently in his mind, as it would naturally be in the mind of any spirited Field Commander, he did not clearly grasp the determining factors and act accordingly. He did not foresee the initial impotence of Buller before the Colenso position, also largely attributable to a deficiency in efficient mounted troops. He occupied too small a perimeter to permit of elastic offence, and he forgot that the tactical weakness of his Cavalry was an obstacle even more serious to the kind of operations he had in his mind than it was to the larger plan of complete freedom which he had rejected. This weakness again became manifest in the small offensive operations of November 14 and December 7-8. Then came Buller's failure at Colenso, and henceforth White's attitude, though courageous and unyielding, was strictly passive. This was all the more to be regretted because the Boer attitude, save for the one big attack of January 5 on Cæsar's Camp and Wagon Hill, and for the minor attack on November 9, was equally passive, while their numbers sank to a point well below the strength of the garrison.

White's mounted troops were reduced by degrees to the rôle of foot-soldiers, and in that capacity took their share in the defence.   The part played by the regular Cavalry, gallant as it was, could not have been, and was not, so important as that played by the irregulars, who were genuine, though improvised riflemen.   All alike took part in the great fight of January 5, and by common consent the chief honours belong to the Imperial Light Horse, whose heroic defence of Wagon Point, the key to the threatened position, at a cost of 25 per cent. of the numbers engaged, was as fine a feat of arms as their final attack at Elandslaagte.   It was by a detachment of the same regiment, in conjunction with a body of Natal Mounted Volunteers, that the brilliant little sortie of December 7-8 was carried out and the two heavy guns on Pepworth Hill destroyed.

During the last month of the siege, when forage became scarce, and 75 per cent. of the Cavalry horses had to be turned adrift or converted into food, the troopers returned their lances, swords, and carbines to store, received rifles instead, and took regular posts in the defence.   That change of weapons once made, it is almost inconceivable that it should not have been adhered to when horses were once more available.   Why deliberately revert to an inferior firearm ?   Why deliberately resume steel weapons whose futility was manifest ?   Tradition—nothing more: the ineradicable habit of associating together the horse and the steel weapon as complementary elements of the highest mounted efficiency ; the same habit which induces General French, in defending the *arme blanche*, to say that " nothing is gained by ignoring the horse, the sword, and the lance," as though these weapons were inseparable adjuncts of the horse, and as though South African experience were not one long and costly proof of the contrary.

Buller's mounted force, about 2,600 strong during the period following Colenso, was composed mainly of South African irregulars,* with two and a half Cavalry regiments, and a few regular Mounted Infantry. It played a creditable, though not a distinguished, part in the operations. The battles, from the British point of view, were all preeminently Infantry battles. In one instance only, so far as I am aware, was a mounted corps employed in conjunction with Infantry in a really critical and desperate fight, and that was the detachment of Thorneycroft's Mounted Infantry at Spion Kop. For the rest, we find them operating on the wings, seizing advanced positions, and guarding the flanks of the main attack. Fire-tactics are the invariable rule, and efficiency in fire-tactics the test of general utility.

There is reason to believe that the mounted troops might have been employed to greater advantage had the higher command of the army been in stronger hands. Though they were less than half as numerous as the mounted force at the disposal of Lord Roberts, they were on the average more than a quarter, and sometimes not far from a third, the strength of the whole Boer force opposed to them—a tolerably high proportion, if we reflect that the Boers, immensely strong though their position was, had to sustain the attacks of 20,000 Infantry, to say nothing of an overwhelming number of guns.

The most hopeful enterprise in which the mounted troops were ever actually engaged was in the opening

* South African Light Horse, Thorneycroft's Mounted Infantry, Bethune's Mounted Infantry, Imperial Light Horse (1 squadron), Natal Carbineers (1 squadron), a few Natal Mounted Police.

operations of the Spion Kop campaign (January 18 to 20), when Dundonald's brigade of 1,500 men, including one Cavalry regiment, acted as advance-guard to Sir Charles Warren, who, with the greater part of the army, was deputed by Buller to turn the Boer right, while Lyttelton threatened the centre.* One of the most disappointing features of a painful story was the waste of a golden opportunity for utilizing mounted strength against an enemy whose high tactical mobility rendered surprise exceedingly difficult. Dundonald, a Cavalry man, certainly did his utmost, and, as far as he was allowed, did well. Unnecessary delays had attended the turning movement from the first, but a considerable measure of surprise was, in fact, obtained. Few Boers had rallied to the threatened flank ; none were entrenched. Dundonald, operating boldly in advance, gained on the evening of the 18th a position, overlooking Acton Homes, which might, under vigorous generalship, have been turned to great strategical advantage. His men were in high fettle owing to the skilful surprise and defeat of a Boer detachment which rode out to check them. But Warren seems to have regarded his mounted troops wholly in a protective light, and to have resented anything approaching independent action. The chance was thrown away† and

---

* " Official History," vol. ii., chaps. xx-xxii. ; *Times* History, vol. iii., chaps. ix. and x.

† It is just possible, no doubt, to take a different view of the affair. The German critic, who is always indifferent to mounted questions, thinks the whole turning movement was a mistake, and that, therefore, the question of supporting Dundonald was not of much consequence. The facts of the wretched friction between Warren and Dundonald are set forth exhaustively in our own " Official History " (pp. 362, 363, and Appendix 9 [c]), and a reader can form his own opinion. The comment affords an example of that criticism by innuendo which so often mars the careful and conscientious narrative of facts, and which generally defeats its own object—that of avoiding direct censure on individuals. The result frequently is to censure the wrong individual. In this case,

the operations never recovered from the initial sluggishness of movement.

Another opportunity for a vigorous use of mounted troops came after the great fight at Pieter's Hill (February 27), which led to the relief of Ladysmith and to a general retreat of the Boer forces both from the beleaguered town and from the Tugela heights. If we regard all Buller's previous operations as one long-drawn battle—and in a sense they may so be regarded—now, it would seem, was the time for pursuit. The two leaders of horse were undoubtedly anxious to pursue. Men and horses were alike fresh. Buller refrained. There is a

---

reading between the lines, one is led to infer that Dundonald was wholly to blame in not sending sufficiently explicit messages to Warren. This interpretation of what happened leaves out of account all the larger aspects of the case, and the chapters are so written as to obscure these larger aspects. Buller's original orders to Warren (p. 347) " embodied," we are told, a " broad and bold conception." So they undoubtedly did. Here is outspoken praise, well deserved. Whence came the failure, then ? No one could guess from comments in the text, although, by exercising common sense on a study of the facts, two explanations stand out plainly : (1) That Buller, having framed his plan in outline, divested himself of responsibility for its execution, and remained a passive, though not an uncritical, spectator of events. (2) That speed in the turning movement was the essence of the plan, but that Warren never realized this, and was too slow, his mind perpetually fixed on his heavy transport and oblivious to the offensive possibilities of his advance. Ignoring these broad considerations, which have an obvious and direct bearing on the Dundonald-Warren friction, the Official Historian takes care to investigate and print every message bearing on that topic, and to justify, at any rate by implication, Warren's caution. Could there be a worse moral, above all, for mounted troops ? Overcurt as Dundonald's messages were, they struck a note which would have elicited the right response from a mind tuned to the right key. One must make some allowance, too, for human nature. Imagine the feelings of a leader of horse who, at such a time and with such an opening before him, had been compelled at the outset to send back a regiment of regular Cavalry " to prevent the grazing oxen being swept away " from the main body ! (Appendix 9 [c]).

general agreement that he was wrong. Whatever the prospects of success, he should unquestionably have tried, for instinctive and habitual mounted energy was the vital need in South Africa if a mounted enemy was to be not only defeated, but conquered.

At the same time, a close examination of the facts does not appear to justify the assumption of the *Times* historian that a pursuit would have involved the Boers in utter destruction and defeat. The critic lays excessive and indiscriminating stress on the demoralization of the enemy. He forgets that Botha's troops and the investing force combined numbered in all about 13,000 men, as against 2,600 of our mounted troops ; that there was not much question of further co-operation by our Infantry, who were exhausted by ten days of continuous fighting, and that the encounters which actually did take place between our mounted troops (regulars and irregulars alike) and the Boer rear-guard were not of such a character as to warrant a belief that a general pursuit, begun at the earliest possible moment, would have led to the destruction of the Boer army.

Both the German and British Official Historians correctly point out that, in order to have been really effective, the intervention of the mounted troops should have begun at, or immediately after, the climax of the great Infantry fight on the 27th. Here was just the difficulty : The British attack, delivered on a front of about three miles, was threefold—upon Railway Hill, Inniskilling Hill and Pieter's Hill, the latter representing the extreme Boer left, the only quarter at which the mounted troops could possibly have intervened. The two first positions were stormed in magnificent style by the Infantry, supported by a tremendous fire of Artillery, and were won at about 5 p.m. and 5.30 p.m. respectively—that is, very late in the afternoon. On the left, at Pieter's Hill, the Boers still stood desperately at bay. It was not till 6.30, in the growing dusk, that the southern, or nearest, crest of the hill, held by the Standerton and Heidelberg commandos, was carried by a final charge of 300 Irish Fusiliers, who lost a third of their strength engaged and had all their officers killed or wounded. The northern part of the hill was still obstinately held when the battle came to an end, and was evacuated only during the night.

According to the " Official History," the same unyielding attitude was shown by the most valiant among the defenders of the other two hills, who " clung most stubbornly to the broken ground behind these kopjes," after their trenches had been carried, and it was in view, we are told, of these signs of dangerous resistance that Buller abandoned the idea of a mounted pursuit. He was wrong, it must be concluded, even at this late hour, when darkness and the Boer rear-guards must have severely limited effective action ; but his real fault lay farther back, in retaining the mounted brigades well in the rear and out of sight all day instead of planting them opposite the Boer left flank, where they would have acted at least as a passive menace to the enemy, and might have caused a premature retirement during daylight. We may speculate at will on what might have happened. All we can say with confidence is that the Boers were never more formidable than on this culminating day of four months' strenuous resistance, and that only by using their own fire methods with the utmost energy and determination could our troopers have turned a defeat into a rout.

On that night a general Boer retreat set in. Among the besiegers of Ladysmith, who had not fired a shot, something in the nature of a genuine panic reigned, but the great majority of these had a long start in respect both of time and distance. Botha's commandos, too, gained fully twelve hours' start, for, in spite of a strong appeal from Barton on Pieter's Hill for a prompt advance by a flying column of all arms, Buller made no preparation for a swift movement by the mounted troops. On the morning of the 28th they were still behind the Tugela. A block on the pontoon-bridge delayed the irregular brigade under Dundonald till 8 a.m., and the regular Cavalry brigade under Burn-Murdoch till 9 a.m. Their orders were to work north-west and north-east respectively, not to " pursue." Still, limited as their orders were, they experienced considerable difficulty in carrying them out. Botha had organized adequate rear-guards to protect his retreat. Dundonald was checked twice within two miles of Pieter's Station, and, on the second occasion, had to send for the assistance of Burn-Murdoch, who, by a later order of Buller's, and against his own repeated requests, had been kept inactive in the gorge between Pieter's Hill and the Station. The combined brigades having eventually driven off this detachment of the enemy, Burn-Murdoch moved on to the north-east, but in his turn was brought to a complete standstill at the Klip River by the rifle and Artillery fire of another Boer rear-guard, which was covering the withdrawal of guns and waggons from Umbulwana Mountain. He held his ground till dusk, prevented the destruction of the wooden bridge which spanned the Klip at this point, and informed Buller that he intended to remain where he was for the night, and to pursue on the morrow. Buller, for in-adequate reasons, recalled him. Dundonald, meanwhile, still meeting with sporadic opposition, pushed on slowly in the late afternoon towards Ladysmith, finally sending in two squadrons, whose arrival denoted the definite relief of the town.

Buller had now, definitely and finally, set his face against pursuit. Yet even on the morning of March 1 the chances of success, which had steadily diminished, were still considerable. Although most of the Free State forces and a substantial part of the Transvaal forces were out of danger, the plain east of Ladysmith was still thronged with waggons and guns, the last of which did not reach Elandslaagte till nightfall. Even as near as Modder Spruit Station siege-guns were entrained as late as 11 a.m. Despair reigned in the Boer army as a whole. A resolute pursuit must, we can fairly surmise, have led to the capture of a considerable quantity of material and many guns. But we are bound equally to affirm that here, as at every previous stage of these operations, and according to our invariable experience through nearly three years of war in South Africa, the measure of success would have been the measure of our ability to overcome defensive fire-tactics with yet more vigorous offensive fire-tactics. That Botha, who had effectually covered his retreat on the 28th with parties of the same men who had gone through the nerve-shattering experiences of the previous ten days, culminating in the desperate struggle overnight, would have subsequently allowed his transport and guns to be captured without an effort for their defence, is a tempting, but an altogether illusory, hypothesis. Analogy points the other way. It was one of the most striking characteristics of the war that, however great the depression of the undisciplined mass, there were always to be found a few indomitable spirits who were prepared to sell their lives dearly to avert disgrace. We saw this at Poplar Grove, when the opportunity for our mounted troops, if we consider the relative numbers engaged, while making full allowance for the relative condition of the horses, was far better than at Ladysmith. Botha himself, the ablest of all the Boer leaders, had again and again in the last few months proved his power to restore discipline and nerve among his burghers. His rear-guard tactics, whatever the strength he might have managed to raise, would in form have been those of Poplar Grove and of his own resistance to Burn-Murdoch and

Dundonald on the 28th. Something more effective than French's action at Poplar Grove, and more effective than the action of Dundonald and Burn-Murdoch on the 28th, would have been needed to secure results of really supreme importance. As for the *arme blanche*, we need not regard it seriously as a contingent factor. If it possessed any utility, it had in the course of the war innumerable opportunities of proving the fact—above all, in cases of pursuit against Boer rear-guards. We can scarcely draw negative evidence from occasions where the opportunity was denied.*

Buller has placed on record his reasons for not undertaking a pursuit.† The only one that need concern us is, curiously enough, his insistence on this very point—Boer skill in rear-guard actions—a skill which he considered it so futile to combat, that, on this occasion, he thought it not even advisable to try. And he bases his view on his own experience in the first Boer War, twenty years before. The admission throws much light on his handling of the mounted troops under his command during the South African campaign, and, in particular, on his dispositions during the battle of Pieter's Hill. He had calculated rightly on a victory that day, and, departing from the usual practice, deliberately kept his

---

* This, nevertheless, is precisely what Mr. Goldman does in a passage of his book, " With French in South Africa," p. 422. His proposition, sufficiently bold in itself, is that the regular Cavalry were not given sufficient chances in South Africa, and he instances particularly Buller's failure to use his Cavalry in pursuit at this period. By the use of the vague word " Cavalry " to cover all Buller's mounted troops, the majority of whom were irregular mounted riflemen, Mr. Goldman introduces into a correct statement of fact the unwarrantable suggestion that the steel weapon, the distinguishing feature of Cavalry, was deprived of a chance of inflicting a " crushing defeat " on the enemy. It must be understood that Mr. Goldman, in the essay I am referring to, is engaged in an express effort to prove the superiority of Cavalry over mounted riflemen.

† War Commission Evidence, vol. ii., pp. 182, 183.

mounted men fresh and concentrated in rear of the army, in order to complete the victory by a pursuit. But the kind of victory he hoped for was one which excluded the possibility of rear-guard actions. In other words, he was a prey to that antiquated habit of thought which was an inheritance from the days prior to the magazine rifle, and which took shape in dreams of massed Cavalry on fresh mounts, whirling, sabre in hand, at the psychological moment, through hordes of helpless fugitives. Even in 1866 this habit of mind was antiquated. It does not seem to have occurred to him, nor does it seem to occur to some of the present advocates of the *arme blanche*, that skill in rear-guard actions, often sneeringly alluded to as skill in " evasion," and always spoken of as if it were some miraculous attribute of the Boers, was, in reality, the simple exercise, by the use of horse and rifle combined, of one of the most important of the functions of any corps of mounted troops, Cavalry included, especially in the case of the numerically weaker side; and that its counterpart—power to pierce a rear-guard, and drive home a victory, a power correspondingly dependent on the use of horse and rifle combined—is a no less crucial test of mounted efficiency. By these tests, among others, Cavalry in future wars will be judged.

Defensive skill in the Boers suggests the allied question : Had they, in the course of the long struggle for Ladysmith, shown any new development of offensive power ? That is a question we must always be asking, as we contrast the merits of the steel weapon and the fire-arm in war. As I have often before remarked, there can be no sharp distinction between defensive and offensive action : excellence in the one is wrapped up with excellence in the other. The British seizure of Spion Kop, for example, was an aggressive stroke ; the Boer counter-attack was a measure of defensive necessity. Regarded in this light, Botha's defence of the line of the Tugela merits the highest praise. Make what allowance we will for defects in British generalship, for the ever-present prejudice against incurring heavy loss of life, and for the extraordinary natural strength of the Tugela heights, the fact stands out plainly that no class of troops but mounted riflemen, experts in horse, rifle, and spade alike—and first-class men at that—could, with numbers comparatively so small, have held for so long a position whose extent for purposes of defence cannot be estimated at less than thirty miles. Neither European Cavalry nor European Infantry of that date could have held it for a week against a European force of all arms and of the given superiority—the former from lack of spade and rifle power, the latter from lack of mobility. But measuring the Boers by their own standard, did they fully develop their own offensive potentialities ?

The answer must be, I think, in the negative. But we cannot in this case afford to be too sweeping or positive. We must remember, here as elsewhere, that the dead-weight of numerical superiority, especially in Artillery, gives a force of low mobility, like the British force, a defensive power disproportionately greater than its offensive power. Still, there were undoubtedly a few occasions when the Boers missed opportunities for counter-strokes. By common consent, I think, the best opportunity of all was on February 23 and 24, when the position of Buller's army, huddled together in Hart's Hollow and other parts of the Colenso basin, after the magnificent but unavailing assaults of the 23rd, was in the highest degree dangerous.* A casual outburst of Boer fire on the night of the 24th actually caused a partial panic among the troops in Hart's Hollow. According to the German historian, who quotes a German officer present with Botha at the time, Botha's reason for not ordering a counter-

---

* "Official History," vol. ii., chaps. xxvi. and xxvii. ; *Times* History, chap. xvi.

stroke on the 24th was that it would "cost too many lives." If so, it was a costly error, an irreparable error. But there was much excuse for it. Moral administrative weaknesses, from which we were free, had sapped their strength from the first, and among these troops on the Tugela at this latter end of February, in spite of Botha's untiring efforts, the tension was becoming unbearable. We have only to contrast the same man, leading tried veterans of the same commandos in latter phases of the war, to understand the full aggressive power that mounted riflemen can develop. Nevertheless, we must, as far as we can, disentangle technical from moral causes, and it remains true that up to this point the Boers had not brought into line the horse and the rifle as the twin factors of aggressive mobility.

The offensive honours rested with the British Infantry. I hope by this time that the reader is beginning to realize how indefinable is the border-line between mounted and dismounted attacks, both of which equally draw their power from that master of modern battle-fields, the rifle. Look at Wagon Hill, where soldiers classed as mounted riflemen were engaged against soldiers classed as Infantry, mounted riflemen, and Cavalry. Here is a case where one almost forgets which class had horses and which had not. When we read of the memorable charge of the Devons, we care very little whether they were Infantry or Mounted Infantry, recognizing, as we must, that, in the given conditions, such efforts are within the power of both classes alike. Our ambition should be to discover how and when the horse may be made to serve as an engine of still more formidable tactics. Look, too, at the Infantry charges on February 23 and at the battle of Pieter's Hill. Watch the old problem of mobility versus vulnerability being worked out in terms of foot-soldiers, and, without rushing to the impracticable extreme of demanding that all riflemen should be provided with horses, observe how close is the analogy when the same problem is worked out in terms of horse-soldiers. Note how the German historian, from whom nothing will force any compromising allusion to shock as a function of Cavalry, lest the whole edifice of Cavalry theory should tumble about his ears, slips unconsciously into the deprecation of " shock " in Infantry, without sufficient fire-preparation.* But for those separate mental compartments, would not some glimmering of the analogy have occurred to him ? Observe, on the other hand, the fundamental differences between the steel weapon of the foot-soldier and the steel weapon of the Cavalry, the efficacy of the former being conditional, not only on the vigour and skill of the previous fire-fight, but on being used at the climax of the fire-fight, still in association with the rifle, and still on foot; the efficacy of the latter a minus quantity, and, for the same reason, everywhere and always, because it was not only incompatible with, but by the habits of mind it engendered, and by the nature of equipment it involved, actively prejudicial to the vigorous offensive use of the firearm.

Grasp now the nature of the problem which confronted us in this war. Our foes were not only riflemen, but mounted riflemen, comparatively few in numbers, but able both to fight stoutly and to retreat safely when overcome in combat. Infantry, though they possess the power to overcome and eject mounted riflemen, have not the power to catch and destroy them, simply because Infantry move too slowly. The responsibility for securing complete victory lay with our mounted troops acting as mounted riflemen.

Widening our horizon to include the whole area of the war at this period, we perceive that the Cavalry theory, so far as it was based on the *arme blanche*, had collapsed.

* Vol. ii., p. 270.

The only and not especially remarkable achievement of that weapon is the pursuit at Elandslaagte on the second day of hostilities. Everywhere else we have seen it directly or indirectly crippling the Cavalry, and the greater the numbers employed and the larger the measure of independence permitted, the more unmistakable is the cause. When the Cavalry succeed strategically, as in the ride to Kimberley and back to Paardeberg, they succeed in spite of disabilities traceable to *arme blanche* doctrine. When they succeed tactically, as in the Colesberg operations and in containing Cronje's force on the eve of Paardeberg, they succeed through the carbine, in spite of its inferiority as a weapon of precision. In tactical offence, the paramount *raison d'être* of the *arme blanche*, and in reconnaissance, they show marked weakness.

CHAPTER IX

BLOEMFONTEIN TO KOMATI POORT

I.—THE TRANSITION.

FROM the capture of Bloemfontein onwards, the nomenclature of mounted troops in South Africa, except as a clue to their race, origin, and professional or unprofessional character, ceases to possess practical significance. There emerges a single military type—the mounted rifleman—the man, that is, who can ride and shoot. Whether in reconnaissance, tactics, or strategy, in defence or offence, in any combination from a patrol to a commando, squadron, brigade, or division, or as a single scout ; be he Boer or Briton, the better he can ride, and the better he can shoot, the better soldier he is.

In the British Army this unity of type soon becomes definitely recognized in practice. Textbook regulations as to the duties appropriate to different categories of mounted troops vanish like smoke under the irresistible logic of experience. There soon ceases to be any practical field distinction between regular Cavalry and regular Mounted Infantry. Both alike must do the same duties, alike relying on the union of firearm and the horse, and judged invariably by the same inexorable and unvarying tests. So with the numerous other categories of mounted corps, Home and Colonial, which from this time forward begin to exceed in number the horsemen drawn from professional sources. Wide distinctions, indeed, are constantly visible, and are constantly recognized between the capacities of different corps according to their country of origin, social class, length of experience, and physical and moral characteristics, and, above all, according to the stamp of officer they possess. But these are distinctions of degree, not of kind. The ideal type never varies— that of the mounted rifleman.

But the practical recognition of an ideal is one thing, and its whole-hearted assimilation another. For the bulk of the mounted troops, given the will, the way was now plain. They had nothing positively to unlearn if they had an infinite amount to learn. The regular Mounted Infantry, indeed, and to a certain extent other classes, had still to rid their minds of an idea that they were a tactical appanage of Cavalry, but the possession of a firearm superior to that of Cavalry, and the absence of any other weapon to confuse their tactical ideas, made the path easy. The regular Cavalry, on the other hand, had still something very substantial to unlearn, and that something was the immemorial tradition of their branch of the service, the theory and practice of the *arme blanche*. It would be idle to underrate the magnitude of the requisite revolution, which primarily was one of thought, rather than of action. Still, five months of fighting had taught a lesson which could scarcely be mistaken, a lesson which at this period of the war would have amply justified, if it did not render imperative, the systematic and universal re-arming of the Cavalry with the magazine rifle, and the return of all steel weapons to store. These changes could not have been imposed upon the Cavalry from without, they must have proceeded from within by the initiative of Cavalry leaders. French alone, perhaps, had the authority and prestige to secure their general adoption at this time; but in French the revolution of thought had not taken place, indeed, never wholly took place, even at a later period, when the necessary changes had been carried through. His very strength and vitality tend, as always, to obscure the issue. He continues to do much valuable and responsible work, and is always the keenest of the keen for ambitious enterprises. But he cannot impress the true Cavalry stamp upon the British operations, in the broadest sense of the word "Cavalry." Big strategical conceptions are useless without high combative capacity in the troops employed, and that treasured tradition of the arm had been weakened because it was not founded on the right weapon.

Without any strong new lead from above, conservatism naturally exerted its full sway over the minds of the elder Brigadiers and regimental officers. It was among some of the younger men, where habit was weaker and enthusiasm stronger, that the new régime was warmly and sincerely welcomed. These men were now finding their most fruitful sphere in the leadership of irregular corps, where there was no tradition to combat, and no weapon but the rifle.

The Cavalry, in spite of their unsuitable armament, continued to conform to the new type—no other course was possible—but as a body they conformed reluctantly and with a lack of imaginative zeal, thereby gravely imperilling their chance of guiding and inspiring progressive mounted action. In common with all other corps they improved greatly as time went on, and always, as befitted their standing in the professional army, set a good example of the prime soldierly virtues. Their staff work, too, was a model to the rest of the army. But when we consider the unique initial advantage they possessed in building on a broad and solid foundation of drill, discipline, and *esprit de corps*, we are bound to admit that the results are disappointing.

The need for vigorous mounted action, always urgent, was becoming daily more urgent. With the relief of Ladysmith and the capture of Bloemfontein, the march of conquest definitely begins. With it the elements of strength and weakness in the Boer character and organization begin to assume clearer shape. Two contrary streams of tendency declare themselves : on the one hand, a progressive decline in corporate strength ; on the other, new and marked symptoms of individual vitality, erratic, spasmodic, ephemeral, but of incalculable significance in determining the nature and length of the struggle, the character of the conquest, and the future political relations of the two belligerent races.

Of these two streams of tendency, the former, now and for six months to come, was the stronger and more rapid. It was hastened naturally by the overwhelming numerical superiority of the invaders at every threatened point. What to defend ? where concentrate ? was the distracted cry. Under this strain the old national fabric crumbled visibly, and although, by a process which was scarcely perceptible to the superficial view, the corrupt and diseased elements of the old body politic perished with it, the immediate military results were fatal. It became increasingly difficult for the Boers to maintain organized forces of any size in the field. Only one so considerable even as Cronje's at Magersfontein ever appeared again. The opposition to our central march up the railway to Pretoria, to Buller's advance through Natal, and to the other parallel movements, was made with miserably small forces. In the centre, before Pretoria was reached, the Free Staters had parted from their comrades of the sister State, and taken to local warfare. In June the Transvaalers rallied well at the battle of Diamond Hill outside Pretoria ; then there was a reaction ; then a revival, ending, after a creditable display of resistance along the line of the Delagoa Railway, in the sudden and apparently complete dissolution of the organized burgher forces on the Portuguese border in mid-September.

Such, in a few words, is the main course of events. But in the vast and thinly-peopled rural areas which constitute the great bulk of the republican territories periodical disturbances delay the main British advance. Amid the general wreck one Boer institution survives in its integrity, the territorial military system, based on the obligation of every individual citizen to serve in arms when called upon as a member of his ward and commando.   Centralized forces melt, only to reappear as local bands inspired by a local patriotism, and summoned into sudden activity at the call of some trusted leader.   Through the chequered drama flits the restless figure of Christian de Wet, the first Boer leader to teach his countrymen the real meaning and potency of aggressive mobility.   Behind him is the sombre, passionate Steyn, and together these two men are the incarnation of that stubborn national purpose which often seemed to sleep, but which never died.   All their efforts, nevertheless, are apparently unavailing.   Wherever bands, by accretion or coalition, exceed a certain size, they succumb to the law of decay.   The great machine of invasion and occupation rolls slowly but irresistibly forward.

Plainly, each fresh exhibition of weakness, and, *a fortiori*, each fresh spasm of activity, on the part of the defence, should have been an incentive to redoubled efforts on the part of the attack.   I do not refer so much to our national efforts in the shape of reinforcements, horses, and the material of war ; these flowed uninterruptedly and in enormous volume from the home country and the Empire at large.   I refer to field efforts, and here again not so much to the higher strategy, which was uniformly worthy of the great soldier who conceived and directed it, as to that tactical fire and energy which alone could give us really substantial victories over the men opposed to us, instead of such limited successes as resulted in the occupation of towns, positions, and railways, but left the heart and will of the foe daunted, indeed, and depressed, but unsubdued. These crushing blows we

never succeeded in attaining. Paardeberg, the nearest
approach to such a victory, was robbed by the nine days'
investment of much of its moral value. Prinsloo's surrender in the Brandwater basin in July of the same year
produced as many prisoners as Paardeberg, but was
marred by the escape of De Wet and Steyn, with the
most resolute elements of the Boer forces present. Reviewing the combats of the period, we see one pattern
of action recurring again and again with monotonous
regularity, although with innumerable variations of local
circumstance and personal performance. A very inferior
Boer force defends an immensely extensive position ; there
are proportionately wide turning movements by our
mounted troops, which fall short in vigour and complete-
ness ; frontal attacks by our Infantry ; an action more or
less prolonged ; a Boer retreat covered by a small, but
extraordinarily efficient, rear-guard ; an ineffectual pursuit. The position is won, but the enemy has suffered
physically very little. A time comes later when positions
count for nothing, and men count for everything. Then
earlier shortcomings bear bitter fruit.

If I were to enter deeply into the psychological causes
of this instinctive relaxation of effort—for it was not a
conscious process traceable in orders and despatches—
I should travel far beyond the limits of my subject. In
absolute strictness the psychology of the war is not
relevant to that subject. If the student were to observe
an ideal sense of mental proportion, distinguishing between the ardour inspired by a particular weapon and
the ardour inspired by racial and national ambitions, there
would be no need to stray beyond the purely technical
aspects of the subject with which I am dealing. I have
recognized from the beginning, however, that there are
three objections to taking this course : first, that the line
in question is often exceedingly difficult to draw ; second,
that in tracing and illustrating the development of

mounted tactics some reference to the deeper moral causes at work tends greatly to elucidation'; third, and most decisive reason, that one of the most subtle and insidious methods of discrediting the rifle and investing the *arme blanche* with a kind of posthumous distinction, has been to smother plain technical issues under hazy moralization. "Thought waves" are in fashion. Now, let us insist by all means on the old Napoleonic axiom that the moral forces in war count in the proportion of three to one to the physical ; but when we see one weapon palpably outmatched by another let us recognize the fact as a fact. When we call the war "peculiar," from the peculiar moral factors underlying it, let us not erase its technical lessons from our memory on the same ground. I remarked an example of this perverse tendency in the official comments on Poplar Grove, but Mr. Goldman is its most outspoken and sincere exponent. He has honestly convinced himself that the Cavalry never had any real chance of grappling with the enemy, and, consequently, no chance of proving the pre-eminent value of the *arme blanche*.* The picture he suggests is one of the Boers continually on the run, and running so fast that the exhausted troopers can never catch them. Their oxen, it would seem, run equally fast, or else take the most unsportsmanlike course of beginning to retreat prematurely. These are rear-guard actions, it is true, but these do not count. In some mysterious way they "make pursuit all but impracticable." The Boers, in short, who "had no Cavalry in the proper and technical sense of the word," by their aggravating pusillanimity did not supply the "primary conditions" for the "discharge (that is, on our side) of Cavalry duties." That we had an enormous preponderance of force, and that it is the business of Cavalry to take advantage both of numerical and moral weakness in the enemy, Mr. Goldman does not recognize. He altogether ignores, too, that

* See "With French in South Africa," pp. 420-423, and 426, 427.

counter-current of offensive Boer activity which, throughout the war, supplies us with the most interesting and instructive examples of mounted tactics. But for the moment I need dwell no longer on this version of a war which lasted for two and a half years, cost us a heavy list of casualties and prisoners, and not a few very sad disasters. It is an unconscious insult, not merely to the army as a whole, but to the Cavalry, who did much excellent work as mounted riflemen, and to the great body of irregular mounted troops, whose existence Mr. Goldman appears to forget, and the best of whom surpassed the Cavalry in aggressive action. That a serious writer can commit to print, without qualification or reservation, the statement that the Boers " invariably beat a hasty retreat when confronted by Cavalry that could fight on horseback with carbine, lance, and sabre," shows the fantastic lengths to which the *arme blanche* bias can carry those who submit to it.

Faced, however, with the fact that such travesties are extant, a writer on the *arme blanche* is compelled to take at least a passing account of moral factors. I need not spend any more words in proving that there was, in fact, on our side a general mildness of effort. Nearly all critics have agreed upon the fact. What were the causes ?

1. About the deepest of all there is no dispute. Long years of peace and civil prosperity had softened the national fibre. We were not only unprepared for war, but forgetful of the grim meaning of war. In a general reluctance to incur heavy losses the commanders only reflected the national and social sentiment behind them.

2. Unfamiliar with wars in general, we were blind, above all, to the meaning of this particular war, whose object was not only to defeat, but to conquer, annex, and absorb a free white race. Since we became a nation, we had never before attempted to achieve such an object,

and we did not realize its inherent difficulties. Signs of weakness in the enemy encouraged the delusion that the war was an ordinary war, whose events were to be estimated by ordinary standards. Signs of strength were undervalued and misinterpreted. Lord Roberts, the soul of generosity and humanity, after the fall of Bloemfontein, initiates an exceedingly indulgent civil policy which defeats its own end. He is compelled as time goes on to pass from the extreme of indulgence to the extreme of severity. But in spite of this disagreeable necessity he is always inclined to believe—and the whole army shares the feeling—that a collapse is imminent, and that no absolutely supreme and sustained efforts are required to hasten the end and seal the definitive triumph.

And what sort of triumph.? The philosophic historian will discern that momentous problem already formulating itself, not merely in the minds of statesmen, but, dimly and inarticulately, in the minds of the army, which embodied in an extraordinarily representative manner the civic instincts of the British race. Did we really in our hearts desire such crushing victories as would shatter the spirit of our opponents and lay the foundation for a racial ascendancy, as opposed to a racial fusion, in South Africa? The question becomes of absorbing practical interest in later phases of the war, when the antagonistic schools of thought find expression in two equally able and determined men. For the present it is only a matter of conjecture how far a latent instinct of fraternity with our foes and future fellow-citizens, now that Majuba was at last avenged by Paardeberg and Pieter's Hill, reacted on the vigour with which hostilities were pressed.

3. A more simple and prosaic motive for caution was the very well-founded respect entertained for the military capacity of the Boers. The sense of some absolutely overwhelming necessity for decisive blows would, doubtless, have gone far to neutralize caution, but this con-

viction was not present.   The reverses of the early months
had left an impression both on the popular mind and on
the leaders in the field which subsequent successes could
not wholly obliterate.   Fresh reverses, on a smaller scale,
were soon to mar the onward progress of success.   From
this time forward every action, however feebly or strongly
contested, shows the Boers still highly formidable.   Until
the actual *débâcle* on the Portuguese frontier, there are no
panics.   Retreats are orderly, transport and guns are
preserved almost intact. However dispirited the majority,
there invariably reappears that manful minority of
stalwarts upon whose conduct, at one or another point,
the difference between repulse and defeat hangs. Numbers, indeed, almost cease to count; quality is everything.

This resisting power, with its offensive counterpart, was
derived, on its military side, solely from skill and audacity
in practice of the mounted rifleman's art.   And here we
return again to the solid ground of our inquiry. Giving
their due weight and proportion to the broader moral
factors which affected both sets of belligerents and, in
our own army, all branches of the service alike, we can
see our technical issue sharply and vividly defined in
every phase and detail of hostilities.

Against a mounted enemy, even if his strategical
mobility is conditioned by heavy transport, in the last
resort it is always to vigorous mounted action that we
must look both for the power to give effect to the attacks
of Infantry and Artillery and for retaliation against those
stinging little raids and counter-strokes which so often at
critical times turned the scale in the higher Boer counsels.
Foot-riflemen will never develop their full aggressive
power against mounted riflemen unless they are conscious
that their efforts will lead to a decisive issue through the
correspondingly indispensable agency of mounted riflemen.

II.—THE HALT AT BLOEMFONTEIN.

There was a pause of seven weeks in the British advance after the capture of Bloemfontein. Reinforcements of all arms, remounts, transport, supplies, were collected in great volume. The supply system and hospital system were reformed, communications strengthened, garrisons organized. During a large part of this period the mounted troops in the central theatre were at little more than half their effective strength from lack of horses.

One small forward movement only was made : that to Karee Siding, twenty-seven miles north of Bloemfontein, a movement deemed necessary for the purpose of safe-guarding the passage over the Modder at Glen. Three thousand five hundred or 4,000 Boers with 8 guns held a line of low hills astride of the railway, with a level plain behind them. French and Tucker, who seem to have held a joint command, attacked with 9,000 men and 32 guns. Of the mounted troops present, 650 were regular Cavalry, 880 regular Mounted Infantry and Colonials, numbers which should have been sufficient to turn and hold the enemy effectually enough to give the Infantry their full chance. In principle the Poplar Grove tactics were employed, with variations of detail. The mounted troops, riding well in advance, were to turn both hostile flanks, and, when the Infantry attacks had been driven home, cut in upon the retreat. The engagement was a dull example of the now too common type. Both flanks were duly turned without opposition, and in good time (10 a.m.), by the mounted troops, but then a sort of paralysis set in. The Cavalry brigade, which was now somewhat behind the Boer right flank and within eight miles of the railway, was inactive from 10 a.m. to 3 p.m., though still unopposed, while the Mounted Infantry on the Boer left were held up by a small outlying detach-ment. Meanwhile the Infantry attacks, spirited enough, though not very well directed, ran their course, the Boers making a fairly steady stand, and yielding only between 3 p.m. and 4 p.m. to threats of the bayonet. But there was nothing to intercept or hamper their retreat. Both mounted corps had eventually begun to move on, but were checked by slight flank guards. Our casualties were 189, almost entirely in the Infantry ; those of the enemy 34.

This was emphatically a case where the professional mounted arm, which was separately brigaded, should have set an example of vigour to the younger and improvised corps. There seems, from the official and other narratives, to have been no valid reason against attempting an interception, though we must make allowance for the division in the higher command which may have had ill-effects. Such inaction was very unlike either French or Tucker. The poor condition of the horses is no explanation.

From Karee Siding (March 29) we turn to its anti-type, Sannah's Post (March 30). With the exception of De Wet's raid on the main army's transport at Waterval, this was the first genuine feat of independent aggression on the part of the Boers which the war had as yet produced. The same leader was again the guiding spirit, and he began a career of aggression just when most of his countrymen were thinking more of surrender than resistance, and in several districts were actually handing in their arms.

De Wet, with 1,500 men and 7 guns, made a swift and secret expedition against the Waterworks, twenty-one miles due east of Bloemfontein, and then in British hands. Arriving within striking distance on the evening of March 29, he learnt that there was bigger game afoot, in the shape of an independent British force under Broadwood, who was retiring westward before a greatly superior force of Free Staters under Olivier and others. Broadwood was safely ahead, however, and his pursuers do not come into the story. De Wet resolved to ambush him and to that end posted 400 men in the bed of the Korn Spruit, which Broadwood would have to cross, and the rest, under his brother Piet, three miles away behind the British camp, on the high ground bordering the Modder River.

Broadwood's was an exclusively mounted force, numbering 1,700, with 12 Horse Artillery guns. There were two regiments of regular Cavalry, together only 330 strong, and Alderson's brigade of mounted riflemen, 850 strong, and composed of regular Mounted Infantry and Colonial riflemen. In fact, it was a typical mixed force of all the various classes of mounted troops then in the field. The gist of the story is well known. Breaking camp early on the 30th, without prior reconnaissance of the ground before them, the head of the transport and one of the two batteries marched into the ambush, and were captured. " Q " battery managed to escape, with the loss of a gun and many men. Piet de Wet meanwhile began his attack upon the rear, though as yet only with stationary fire upon the troops holding the Modder drifts. Broadwood acted with coolness and resolution. While the greater part of Alderson's brigade kept Piet de Wet in check, the regular Cavalry and two companies of Mounted Infantry were sent across the Korn Spruit to take the 400 Boers who lined it in reverse. Dangerous as Broadwood's own position was, the position of those Boers was for some little time almost equally dangerous. They were separated by three miles and by the Modder River from their main body, which, moreover, was being briskly engaged by the Mounted Infantry. Cramped in their narrow gully, they were being attacked in front by the five guns of " Q " battery, and threatened in flank and rear from rising ground which overlooked the spruit by the superior force of Cavalry and Mounted Infantry. They had no guns, and were much weakened in numbers by the detachment of the necessary guards for the captured British guns and waggons.

As the Official Historian remarks, everything depended on the execution of the Cavalry turning movement. But again the paralysis sets in, as at Dronfield, Poplar Grove, and Karee Siding—a paralysis not due in the remotest degree to moral weakness, and certainly not in this case to weak horseflesh. There is nothing that we need talk about with bated breath or tactful reticence : neither our men nor their officers were to blame—only the habits and disabilities imposed by an obsolete weapon. A party of riflemen thrown out by De Wet from the spruit brought the attack to a standstill.

Disappointed on this side, Broadwood had no other course than to order a retreat of Alderson's Mounted Infantry and the guns from the other side of the spruit (10.30 a.m.). As in so many similar actions in South Africa, everything hinged on the extrication of a badly crippled battery. The rescue of " Q " by the heroism of its own gunners and its mounted escort forms a brilliant little episode by itself. When the guns were out of immediate danger, the general retreat began. Piet de Wet's men instantly poured across the Modder drifts and pursued hotly. The behaviour of Alderson's brigade— Colonials and Englishmen alike — in this their first defensive engagement was very steady, though they suffered greatly from inexperience in manœuvre and fire. The retirement, conducted by successive movements of units, was orderly and cool, New Zealanders and Englishmen in combination having the honour of constituting the ultimate rear-guard. Eventually Broadwood's force was concentrated safely on the farther side of the Spruit, having lost seven guns, most of its transport, and a third of its strength in casualties and prisoners.

Broadwood should have received help from other forces in the neighbourhood, including some Mounted Infantry, who were very feebly handled ; but there is no need to enter into that lengthy and controversial topic.

We have to note certain points of interest :

1. *The Boer Pursuit.*—Except for the Stormberg case three months back, this was the first example of a Boer mounted pursuit. All narratives agree in saying that it frequently took the form of charging on horseback up to close quarters, accompanied in some instances by a wholly new practice—*fire from the saddle.* Sometimes the burghers dismounted, and, with the rein over the arm, fired. Here we see the germ of important later developments. A year afterwards De la Rey or Kemp in similar circumstances would have used the same methods with more system and audacity.

2. Conversely, and again with the exception of Stormberg, this was the first example of a really critical rearguard action for British mounted troops. We note remarkable proofs of improvement in general efficiency, together with several faults : indifferent marksmanship ; lack of adroitness in the handling of led horses ; lack of judgment in deciding upon the right moment to retire (several detachments were cut off through holding on too long) ; and a general insufficiency of that individual skirmishing capacity which enabled the Boers in similar predicaments to make one skilled man go as far as five unskilled men.

3. The contrast between the *arme blanche* and the rifle is unusually marked. Nomenclature is immaterial. All the work on the field was Cavalry work, not only in the broad sense of the term, but by the regular Cavalry's standards. In essence, De Wet's intercepting ambush in the Korn Spruit was the same kind of work as that done by the Cavalry themselves on the day before Paardeberg, and the same as that which they should have tried to do at Karee Siding. The projected, but abortive, counterstroke upon the ambuscaders was Cavalry work. Piet de Wet's rear attack and pursuit, and Alderson's resistance to them, were both Cavalry work. The terrain was open.

We may add that De Wet's whole enterprise and the rapidity, secrecy, and nerve with which he carried it out were a good example of the true Cavalry spirit. Whether we call De Wet a " partisan " or not makes no difference. If his good qualities constitute partisanship, every Cavalry officer, from the highest to the lowest, should be a partisan.

4. The absence of reconnaissance on the morning of the battle needs no comment. There were some exceptional reasons, which I need not go into, for a relaxation of normal precautions, but no valid excuse.

De Wet, in his characteristically impulsive style, wasted no time after his victory, but dashed off south, and on April 4 snapped up a post of 600 men at Reddersburg. Then, instead of raiding the communications of the main army, which would undoubtedly have been his best course, he succumbed to the Boer craving for sieges, and wasted more than a fortnight in investing Wepener with a force which increased to more than 7,000 men. Wepener, defended by 1,900 men, who were mainly mounted troops belonging to Brabant's Colonial Force, made an excellent and successful defence until relieved by Hart and Brabant himself.

De Wet's activity, however, had changed the whole military situation. The south-eastern Free Staters were up in arms to the estimated number of 10,000, and Roberts was compelled before proceeding farther to clear this flank. His design, however, was not merely to clear it, but to make the relief of Wepener the starting-point for an enveloping movement of great magnitude, and with overwhelming force. Three Infantry divisions joined directly or indirectly in the operations and large numbers of mounted men of all classes. First came some ill-knit and overcautious preliminary operations, which I need not describe ; then French, with an Infantry division and two Cavalry brigades immediately under his hand, assumed general control over the British forces from April 22 onwards.

The critical day was April 24, when he endeavoured to surround and crush a force of 6,000 Boers posted near Dewetsdorp. The scheme on that day, as French planned it, was in general form a repetition of the Poplar Grove and Karee Siding schemes, and was made to hinge on the intercepting action of the two Cavalry brigades upon the Boer line of retreat. Inevitably, and from the same unvarying cause, the intercepting movement came to nothing, the Cavalry being easily checked by small Boer parties. Again and again, in reading of such incidents, we feel how unfair it was to brave men to have given them an armament and training which prevented them from showing their best qualities.

In the course of the earlier operations detachments of the newly-raised Yeomanry, brigaded under Rundle, were for the first time in action. They did tolerably well, considering their rawness and inexperience, and I think it is generally agreed that Rundle, in his original attack upon Dewetsdorp on April 20, with a greatly superior force, might have relied somewhat more on their aid, in association with his other mounted troops.

De Wet now ordered a general retreat north of all the south-eastern Free Staters. By the end of April that portion of the country was wholly in British hands, and on May 3 Roberts was able to begin the grand advance for which he had been so long preparing.

III.—The Advance to Pretoria.

When that advance began there were in round numbers 200,000 British troops in South Africa, of whom 50,000 were on the lines of communications. With a moderate allowance for absenteeism, there were 30,000 Boers in the field, including the 2,000 besiegers of Mafeking.

Our particular concern is with the British mounted troops, which had been remounted, reorganized, and largely increased in number. An additional regular Cavalry brigade joined the central army under Roberts; fresh battalions of regular Mounted Infantry, suffering from a serious scarcity of officers, were hastily formed, and fresh contingents of Colonial troops, both from overseas and within South Africa, continued to come into line. Half the Imperial Yeomanry—between 4,000 and 5,000 men, that is—were available at the beginning of May, and the whole force of 10,000 was before very long in the field.

For administrative purposes, Cavalry and mounted riflemen, hitherto associated together, were now separated. For the central army a division of four brigades of regular Cavalry, about 5,000 sabres strong (without counting Horse Artillery) was formed ;* and at the same time the mounted riflemen were organized anew in one big division, 11,000 strong, divided into two brigades of four corps each, each corps being composed jointly of regular Mounted Infantry and Colonial mounted riflemen. Neither of these organizations proved to be permanent. The latter was from the first little more than nominal. In order to supply the mounted needs of the army at large, as time went on units had to be broken up and distributed where they were most required. The Yeomanry, similarly, were never employed as a divisional unit, but only in detachments.

Brabant's Colonial Defence Force was now at its full strength of 3,000, and Buller, in Natal, though he had had to part with the Imperial Light Horse, who were sent round with Hunter's Division to Kimberley, possessed, owing to the union of the Tugela and Ladysmith armies, between 5,000 and 6,000 mounted men, divided into three brigades, two of them homogeneous Cavalry units of

* Two Australian detachments were included in one of the brigades.

three regiments apiece, the third composed of South
African mounted riflemen.

In the far west of the theatre of war the Kimberley
mounted troops were now available for active work, and
in the north-west Plumer, with some 750 mounted
Colonials, was still conducting his clever and plucky
operations for the assistance of Mafeking and the security
of the Rhodesian border. In the far north the Rhodesian Field Force, some 4,000 strong, mainly consisting
of Australasian mounted riflemen and partly of Yeomanry, was on its way westward from Beira, under
Carrington. Strathcona's Horse, a new Canadian corps,
500 strong, had been detached on an abortive scheme
for raiding the Delagoa Bay Railway via Lourenço
Marques.

To sum up, if we compute the Yeomanry at their full
strength, but exclude from the calculation the garrison
of Mafeking and various small detachments doing duty
on the communications or in process of formation into
regiments, there were at this period in the field nearly
40,000 mounted men, of whom about 8,300 were Cavalry,
still armed with carbine and lance or sword, and the
rest, in the generic sense, mounted riflemen. Numerically,
therefore, our mounted strength, viewed apart from the
great masses of Infantry and Artillery, was greater by
several thousand than the Boer strength actually in the
field, even if we deduct half the Yeomanry as not yet fully
available. But I need scarcely again warn the reader
that such comparisons, for many obvious reasons, must
be used with caution. In one quarter, however—the
centre—our preponderance in mounted strength alone
over the Boers opposed to us was very remarkable.

The Commander-in-Chief's strategical scheme was of
great simplicity and enormous magnitude. On a front of
300 miles, 109,000 men (I am using round numbers), with
350 guns, were to execute converging marches northward,

with Pretoria as the central objective. On the extreme right, Buller, with 45,000 men, was to march through Natal ; on the extreme left, Hunter, starting from Kimberley with 10,000 men, was to penetrate the Western Transvaal, and, incidentally, to relieve Mafeking. Methuen, starting with another 10,000 from the same point, was to march through the Western Free State. Lord Roberts, in the centre, with 25,000 men, was to move directly up the railway from Bloemfontein ; while immediately on his right flank Ian Hamilton, with 14,500 men, supported by Colvile with 4,000 men, moved through the Eastern Free State.

Such was the plan of the grand advance. The principal subsidiary field-force was that of Rundle and Brabant, who were to follow slowly through the Eastern Free State, which was the most formidable region of all, sweeping up arrears, and making good the ground won. Warren, with 2,000 men, was to quell the rebellion in Bechuanaland ; and Carrington was designed to co-operate from the far north, moving through Rhodesia upon the Northern Transvaal.

The distribution of mounted troops was as follows : Exclusive of Artillery corps, troops, etc., there were with Roberts and the central army four and a half corps, in all 3,600 strong, of mounted riflemen, and three brigades of Cavalry under French, also 3,600 strong. These three brigades, however, did not come into line until May 8, five days after the beginning of the advance. Having been employed almost continuously since the capture of Bloemfontein, and having received only small instalments of fresh horses, they had to spend the first days of May in a thorough refit. Their Horse Artillery had been wisely reduced to one battery for each brigade. The remaining brigade of Cavalry, under Broadwood, and the four remaining corps of mounted riflemen—1,400 and 4,300 strong respectively—were with

Ian Hamilton. Buller's mounted troops I have mentioned. Hunter's were the Imperial Light Horse and the Kimberley corps. The Yeomanry were distributed between Methuen, Warren, Carrington, and Rundle, with the latter of whom Brabant's Colonial division was acting.

There is no need, even if my space permitted, to follow with any closeness the fortunes of the grand advance. I have now reached a point in the war where it is necessary only to summarize events, to select from a vast number of operations conducted over a vast expanse of territory, typically interesting examples of mounted action, and along with the process of selection to trace the growth of principles.

The most interesting, naturally, of all the operations of that period were those of the two central columns under Roberts and Ian Hamilton, which from May 3 onwards* worked in close combination, and may be regarded as one force, nearly 40,000 strong, with 119 guns, exclusive of Colvile's supporting column. It will have been noticed that they were far stronger in mounted troops than any other portion of the army. Indeed, at the lowest computation of their effective mounted strengths, and at the highest estimate of the Boer effectives from time to time opposed to them, it appears that Roberts and Hamilton together must at every stage in the advance have had a decisive superiority in mounted troops alone over the whole force of their opponents. Until May 8, when French's three brigades of Cavalry came up, not more than 5,500 Boers in all opposed both columns, which at that time had 9,200 mounted men between them. At the Zand River fight on May 9 and 10 the Boers, reinforced by 3,000 Transvaalers under Botha, who thenceforth took over the supreme control from De

---

* Hamilton had begun his fighting on April 30, at Houtnek, where he dislodged Philip Botha from a strong position, though without inflicting any appreciable loss.

la Rey, reached their highest numerical fighting strength
of about 8,000. At the same moment, reinforced by
French's Cavalry, our own mounted strength also reached
its highest point of nearly 13,000.* After this, and until
the fall of Pretoria, the enemy never appear to have
mustered more than 5,000 men in opposition to the combined columns ; for the Free State forces withdrew altogether before crossing the Vaal, and betook themselves
to local warfare. At Diamond Hill four fresh Transvaal
commandos from Natal counterbalanced other defections,
and enabled Botha to put 6,000 men into the field.
Here, for the first time, our mounted strength in action
(a little below 5,000) was below the total Boer strength.
This was partly the result of wastage in horses. All
along our mounted troops suffered heavily from this
cause, and the same cause affected the Boers also, though
not in anything like an equal degree. Botha, in his
despatches at this time, used habitually to refer to his
" Infantry," meaning the burghers who had lost their
mounts.†

I need not dwell on the significance of these figures.
If we dismiss from our minds the existence of an irresistible backing of Infantry and Artillery on our side, it
is quite possible, and from an instructional standpoint
very interesting, to contemplate *in vacuo* the conflict of
the two opposed mounted forces, supposing them, if we
will, to have been the mounted screens of two great
European armies. Even on that restricted plane the
inquiry teems with absorbing practical interest for future
wars, and abounds in illustration of the functions of the
mounted arm. But I need not remind the reader that in

---

* I am reckoning French's three brigades at the figure of 3,600 given
in the Appendix to the " Official History." In the text they are said
to have numbered 4,500 " sabres," plus Artillery. This would make
the total nearly 14,000.

† " Official History," vol. iii., p. 72.

actual fact here was no matter of screens. The Boer troops were small armies in themselves, depending on and limited strategically by the speed of heavy transport, for which they were the sole protection. Our own mounted troops—or, at least, the bulk of them—cannot be regarded otherwise than as an independent mobile weapon of high general utility, whose mission it was in concert with the other arms to secure the destruction, not merely the repulse, of the enemy.

This is how Lord Roberts had always regarded his mounted troops. Ever since the middle of February he had called upon them, and particularly upon the Cavalry, for decisive efforts, but only once with decisive results. Disillusioned gradually, he continued, nevertheless, to pursue the same policy wherever, during the long march to Pretoria, opportunity offered. He inculcated the right spirit. So did Ian Hamilton, so did French ; and both these Generals were endowed with a large measure of independence. The trouble was that in actual contact on the field the superiority in fighting power of the individual Boer to the individual Britisher invariably caused the best-laid plans to fall short of the desired achievement. A continual instigation of more dashing, if more costly, tactics might have schooled the troops rapidly to higher efficiency, but, as I indicated in dealing with the moral issue, the supreme stimulus to such a policy was wanting. Victory in the medium degree was only too easy, thanks to weight of numbers. Roberts himself appears gradually to have expected less and asked less of his mounted force.

Let us first of all summarize what happened. Starting on May 3, Roberts took Pretoria on June 5. He had marched 300 miles in thirty-four days, sixteen of which (for the central column) were marching days. Hamilton, who midway made a détour to the east, marched a good deal farther. Let us not forget that, whatever its shortcomings, this march, regarded as a military feat, was a very remarkable and memorable performance, especially for the Infantry.   At Brandfort and the Vet River (May 3 to 5) the Boers made but a very slight stand ; at Zand River (May 9 to 10) they offered battle, and were out-manœuvred into retreat.   At Kroonstad, which was not defended, Roberts halted for ten days (May 12 to 22). The Vaal was crossed without opposition on the 24th, and from May 27 to 29 Botha made his most resolute stand on the hills covering Johannesburg—namely, the Klip-riviersberg and Doornkop.   Here on the 29th there was something in the nature of a pitched battle, Doornkop being finally stormed by Infantry.   Hitherto this arm had come into action only at Zand River.   On the 30th Johannesburg fell, and Pretoria, which was not seriously defended, shared the same fate on June 5.

To this record we must add the battle of Diamond Hill, fought sixteen miles from Pretoria on June 11 and 12, with the object of finally driving Botha away from the neighbourhood of the capital.   It was a genuine pitched battle, in which Roberts achieved his object, though he inflicted no loss of any consequence upon the enemy, and suffered little himself.

The Boers had lost their capital and railway, but their losses in men and material were negligible.

Now let us look for mounted lessons.

The first and clearest is that it is useless for a superior force to confine itself to combating the wide extensions of an inferior force by still wider extensions. This is what was constantly happening.   The Boer fronts, in proportion to the numbers employed to defend them, were, as usual, enormously extensive.   At Brandfort, for example, De la Rey occupied a front of some fifteen miles with 2,500 men ; at Zand River Botha stood on a front of twenty-five miles—half the distance from London to Brighton—with 8,000 men ; at the fighting outside Johannesburg he held eighteen miles of hilly country with about 4,000 men.   Outside Pretoria an equally extensive front was held, though very weakly.   Finally, at Diamond Hill, Botha held thirty miles with only 6,000 men during two days of continuous fighting.   Here, however, the position was unusually strong.   Let us note in passing :

(1) The proof afforded by these greatly extended positions of the revolutionary effect of the modern rifle upon mounted tactics, for it was only by the close union of the rifle and the horse that such dispositions were possible.

(2) That, given this close union, no ordinary skill is required to choose the cardinal points of defence, and maintain the field discipline and field intelligence requisite for the elastic and orderly handling of detachments so widely dispersed.   No narrative that I have seen does full justice to the Boers for their efficiency in these particulars.   In the whole course of these operations, and in the whole course of the subsequent advance from Pretoria to Komati Poort, only one small detachment was cut off and overwhelmed.

(3) That the Boer system admitted of no reserves. Practically every man was in the front fighting-line.

Now, how were these tactics to be met ?   Roberts nearly always endeavoured to meet them by still wider extensions, designed to overlap the enemy's front.   He planned to throw substantial bodies of mounted troops right round one or both of the hostile flanks, with the view (as at Poplar Grove) of intercepting the enemy's retreat.   These movements never led to interception, though they were generally successful as turning movements which led to the enemy's retreat—a very minor object.   On the other hand, they were exhausting to horses and men alike, reducing offensive power when, after long riding, it was at last called for, to a point below the normal, and the normal was not nearly high enough.

Zand River (May 9 and 10) illustrates this class of action. There, 4,000 mounted men under French and Hutton on the left, and 3,000 under Broadwood and De Lisle on the right, were deputed to get round both flanks of a front of twenty-five miles, held by 8,000 Boers. French, having passed six miles outside the last Boer post on the 9th, got well round to the rear on the 10th, with his Cavalry leading and his mounted riflemen in support, but was then held up for several hours by small detachments, and suffered considerable loss. He covered thirty miles on the 10th, and could not, owing to the condition of his horses, respond on the same night to a suggestion by Roberts for raiding Kroonstad. Broadwood's turning movement was abortive, partly through an accidental withdrawal of his horse battery, but mainly through the circumstance that the Boer left (wide as Hamilton's extension was) still overlapped our right, and that the overlapping portion, not content to remain on the defensive, endeavoured during the morning to envelop our extreme right. Botha effected an orderly retreat, his centre maintaining a good show of resistance against the Infantry and Artillery attacks. With our main body there was a brigade of Cavalry and considerable numbers of mounted riflemen.

Diamond Hill, where Botha defended thirty miles of hills, was a still more extreme instance of the same method. French, with 1,400 Cavalry and mounted riflemen, was designed to ride right round the enemy's right, and cut the railway in his rear—a ride of at least thirty-five miles, without any allowance for interruptions or détours. Broadwood, with 3,000 men, was to turn the enemy's left and support our right attack. The centre was to be withheld until one or both of these movements should succeed. Botha had anticipated these tactics and had strengthened his flanks accordingly. Both mounted columns were held up, and stood for a time in considerable danger of envelopment. On the second day the centre was forced by Infantry, aided, and very effectively aided, by mounted riflemen.

It must be remarked that our total strength at Diamond Hill was unusually small—14,000 men in all, of whom 4,800 were mounted, and 64 guns. The Boers had 6,000 men and 20 guns.

Now, there is but one way of looking at situations of this sort. If we are seeking instruction for further wars, we must recognize that the only sound method of combating such prodigiously wide extensions of a numerically weak enemy is to force his line instead of turning it. To devote the major effort to turning it is to play into his hands, to permit him by sheer bluff to impose exhausting tactics which neutralize your own numerical superiority.* The difficulty was to apply forcing tactics against so formidable a foe as the Boers. Our crying need all along was tackling power with the horse and rifle combined— high, mobile tackling power, based on surprise and speed, and taking the form, where need be, of mounted charges into or through the enemy, on the lines afterwards taught us by the Boers, and already exhibited by them at Sannah's Post. Again and again, in reviewing the South African combats, we look back to the Klip Drift charge of February 15, 1900, with profound regret that its true lessons were not laid to heart and its false lessons discarded. There was the germ of success. Add operative tackling power to the nerve required to ride through fire, eliminate the *arme blanche* and every last vestige of tactical theory connected with it ; eliminate as far as possible Artillery preparation and support ; be content with a

* Bernhardi utters a wholesome warning on this subject in his " Cavalry in Future Wars " (p. 54), and advocates direct fire-action. " Cavalry Training," if it could reach the point of regarding mounted riflemen as " Cavalry," would, of course, do the same, and thereby refute the theory of the inevitable " shock duel " between opposing Cavalries.

reasonable superiority of strength, and there you have for future wars the true tactics of mounted offence.

It is impossible to blame Roberts for over-reliance on wide turning tactics.   In the last resort, whatever the scheme employed, whether we rode wide or rode through, success depended on sheer fighting capacity in the ulti-mate fire-fight.   Nothing could replace that.   Roberts could only endeavour to make the best of the material to hand.   His frequent attempts to encircle far-flung fronts were an instinctive recognition of inadequate aggressive power in his mounted troops.   The prejudice, so general in South Africa, against " frontal attacks " by Infantry was often a reflection of the same instinct, that is, of an instinct to avoid heavy losses which could not, unaided, lead to a decisive result.   In point of fact, all attacks eventually become frontal, in the local sense. And, in the case of mounted troops, it was of no avail to send round a large body of men to take the enemy in flank or rear, unless they were able to burst through frontally the detachments sent against them.

Still less tenable is the suggestion that the right course for Roberts was to have projected still vaster and more circuitous mounted operations, designed to cut the enemy's communications far in rear of the zone of imme-diate hostilities.   French is said to have favoured this course more than once, but did he realize what it in-volved ?   If the requisite speed were sustained, the horses, already tried to the limit of endurance, would have suffered from that very over-exhaustion of which there had been so much complaint in the past.   But, in fact, such raids, on the scale of those made by Stuart, Wilson, and the Civil War leaders, entailed complete independence of the main army, an object never attained in South Africa without transport arrangements which reduced speed to too low a level.   The question, of course, was not peculiarly a " Cavalry " question—for raids, American,

South African, or Manchurian, turned exclusively on fire-action. I shall be compelled, nevertheless, to argue the matter again, in Chapter XII., on a " Cavalry " basis, taking Zand River once more as an illustration.

2. It must not be supposed that frontal or semi-frontal attacks were not tried by the mounted troops. Local circumstances often brought them about. Generally, however, they tended, even locally, to take a too circuitous form, the tendency, inevitably, being more noticeable among the Cavalry, with their inferior firearm, than among the mounted riflemen.

These latter troops, now possessing an acknowledged and independent status of their own, and led by some able men like Hutton, Alderson, and De Lisle, did remarkably well in some instances, though poorly in others. The Australians and New Zealanders seem always to have shown the most tactical vigour. Hutton's fight on May 5 to secure the passage of the Vet on the left of the main army was a good performance. The mounted riflemen did well also in the pursuit north of Johannesburg on May 30, in the fighting outside Pretoria on June 5, at Diamond Hill on June 12, and on several other occasions.

French's operations outside Johannesburg on May 28 and 29, when, prior to the arrival of the Infantry, both classes of mounted troops were employed in unison, are interesting. French was in his best mood. There was no lack of vigorous will on the spot, but the turning movements by the Cavalry (except the last, which followed the Infantry assaults), and the frontal attacks by both classes, alike failed. There would seem on this occasion to have been a good opportunity for a rush through the centre on the lines of Klip Drift.

3. *Charges.*—The only actual charge *upon a position*, to which I can find reference, is that of the New Zealand Mounted Rifles on May 24, at the passage of the Vaal (*Times* History, vol. iv., p. 136, footnote).

Two small cases occur of charges in the open with the *arme blanche*—namely, at Diamond Hill, on June 11, where, in some indecisive fighting on the right, sixty men of the 12th Lancers made a gallant charge against some Boers who were threatening two of our guns, and at the same time the Household Cavalry endeavoured to ride down another detachment. The lance disposed of a few Boers in the former case, but the enemy retaliated as successfully with fire. In the latter case the Cavalry drove the Boers away, but caught only one, and lost twenty-one horses from rifle-fire, many burghers dropping down among the mealies and shooting at the troopers as they passed, in the manner recommended in our own handbook, " Infantry Training." The two incidents were momentary episodes in two days of fire-action, and serve merely to emphasize the inferiority of a weapon with a range of two yards to a long-range firearm.

4. *Pursuits.*—There were no really " general " pursuits. The best local pursuit was that of Hutton's Australasians on May 30, at Klipfontein (" Official History," vol. iii., p. 90), where a gun was captured. The Boer talent—not exactly for pursuit, but for pressing hard upon a rear-guard—was strikingly displayed in the course of Ian Hamilton's evacuation of Lindley, whither he had been sent during the general halt at Kroonstad. We may call these guerilla tactics ; but they have not a whit less real tactical interest on that account.

5. *Horse-wastage.*—With full allowance for the poor quality of remounts, this was too extravagant. It seems to have been greatest among the Cavalry, whose average waste between May 19 and June 9 was over 30 per cent., than among the mounted riflemen, whose average, for the same period, was 18 per cent.* Apart from that

* No complete figures exist. The ".Official History" ignores the subject. I take these figures from the *Times* historian, who quotes from calculations made by one of Roberts's staff (see vol. iv., p. 162).

difficult question of overloading, and from defective horse-management, which seems to have been universal among our mounted troops, this difference in loss of horses was probably the result of longer distances ridden by the Cavalry. In the whole of this question we have to recognize, in the case of all mounted troops, the close relation between horse-wastage and deficiency in aggressive tactical power, a deficiency which, as I pointed out above, was the real, though, perhaps, not the consciously thought-out reason for the immense encircling movements which were so often being attempted. It will be the same in future wars. The higher the direct tackling power, the lower the average horse-wastage.

By the middle of June, when Pretoria had fallen to the central armies and Diamond Hill had been fought, every other column composing the grand advance had, to all appearances, successfully accomplished its object. Buller had traversed Natal and entered the Transvaal. Methuen had traversed the Western Free State. Hunter had relieved Mafeking, and had occupied towns in the Western Transvaal as far north as the meridian of Pretoria. Warren, too, had disposed of the rebels in Griqualand West. Both Cape Colony and Natal were cleared of the enemy. The Free State had been annexed.

Buller had scarcely made any use of his six regiments of regular Cavalry, and had even left them at Ladysmith during the first phase of his advance over the Biggarsberg. His action was partly due, no doubt, to that old fatalistic prejudice against pursuits, which, in his mind, we must assume, were associated so closely with the *arme blanche* that he did not think it worth while even to give the Cavalry a fair chance of developing other methods. The error was all the less justifiable in that the Natal army, nearly 45,000 strong, and the largest in the field of war, was disproportionately weak in mounted troops. The irregular mounted brigade, about 3,000 strong, under

Dundonald, together with Bethune's Mounted Infantry, about 600 strong, took a prominent part in all the actions, and did very well.   Eight thousand Boers faced Buller originally on the Biggarsberg, but they must have dwindled to something like half that number in the later stages of the advance.   No especial points of mounted interest, not alluded to already, arose in these operations, which, from a tactical standpoint, were often very cleverly and ably conducted, although from the strategical standpoint they were too slow and unenterprising. I need not enter into the long story of Buller's two months' inaction after the relief of Ladysmith, and of his repeated failures to rise to the height of the Commander-in-Chief's conceptions for the strategic rôle of the powerful Natal army.

In the western sphere of advance, there are two principal points of interest :

1. The good behaviour of the new Yeomanry under both Methuen and Warren ; for example, at Tweefontein (April 5), and, in defence, at Faber's Put (May 29), though on the latter occasion we have to recognize an early instance of that lax and careless outpost work which so often characterized the Yeomanry and other irregular corps.

2. The relief of Mafeking.   This, although not a dramatic, was none the less a very skilful and able performance, carried out by Colonel Mahon, with a small column of 900 mounted irregulars (Imperial Light Horse and Kimberley men), 100 picked Infantry, and 6 guns. Starting from Barkley West on May 4, Mahon marched 251 miles in 14 days (an average of 18 miles a day), through a badly-watered region, with two fairly hot engagements *en route*.   Hunter, with his main body, rendered skilful support by distracting the attention of the Boers in the neighbourhood, and, in the final phase, Plumer, who for many months had been tirelessly worry-

ing the besiegers, co-operated with Mahon. On the penultimate day of the march, May 16, De la Rey and Liebenberg managed to bar the road with 2,000 men, a force about equal to those of Mahon and Plumer together, but were driven off after a spirited action. In expense of horse-flesh, which was small, and in tackling power in proportion to numbers, the whole expedition compared favourably with the relief of Kimberley by the Cavalry. It must be remarked that, mobile as Mahon's force was, it included 100 Infantry and 55 mule-waggons.

In the meantime the guerilla war—and by that expression I mean all hostilities which were not directly connected with the seizure on our side, and the defence on the Boers' side, of railways, capitals, and large towns—had already begun in the Free State, and was eventually to spread to the Transvaal even before the final collapse of that State in September. Rundle, Colvile, and Brabant, acting on the right rear of the central armies, had had to cope with constant opposition in the Eastern Free State. Rundle met with a sharp check at the Biddulphsberg on May 29, and two days later a detached force of Yeomanry, 500 strong, surrendered to Piet de Wet near Lindley, after an investment of some days. This was the first serious reverse which befell a Yeomanry corps. The only moral we need draw from it is the vital importance of spirited leadership for mounted troops, especially for untried irregulars. On this occasion the true " Cavalry spirit " was lacking in the officer in command, who, with a substantial force of mounted men and travelling light, should never have allowed himself to be invested at all.

A few days later, Christian de Wet, with 1,200 men and 5 guns, again took the field, and continued the series of raids which he had initiated at Sannah's Post and Reddersburg. This time he directed his efforts mainly against the weakest British point—the enormously lengthy line of railway communications which linked Roberts to his base. After snapping up a convoy near Heilbron on June 4, he attacked and captured simultaneously three posts on the railway between Kroonstad and Pretoria at daybreak on June 7, and a fortnight later, with varying success, carried out other raids upon the railway or upon convoys. Trivial as the direct military results of these exploits were, their moral effect was enormous, not only in awakening De Wet's compatriots to a lasting sense of their own capacity, but in strengthening the higher Boer counsels at a very critical moment. Roberts and Botha had opened tentative negotiations for peace between June 5 and 11, after the capture of Pretoria. There can be no question that De Wet's successes on June 4 and 7 inclined the scale in favour of war.

The firebrand next appears in July, midway in the drama of the Brandwater Basin. Hunter's envelopment of this, the great mountain fastness of the Eastern Free State, and his capture of over 4,000 men under Prinsloo on July 29, was the most extensive and the most ably conducted of all the subsidiary operations during the year 1900. " Subsidiary," indeed, is the wrong term. It was capital, in the sense that it actually removed from the field a large body of fighting burghers, a result which no other operations, those of Paardeberg alone excepted, had achieved. The mounted interest, however, in the manœuvres which led to the surrender, is small. For us the chief interest lies in the eruption from the death-trap, on July 15, just before it closed, of De Wet, Steyn, and 2,600 of the best Boer troops, with 5 guns and an immense convoy.

Dashing away to the north, flinging off two Cavalry brigades, and capturing a train *en route*, De Wet reached the neighbourhood of Reitzburg, and lay there for twelve days (July 25 to August 6), occupying himself with little raids upon the railway. Roberts, who had just completed his eastward advance to Middelburg, determined to run to earth the irrepressible Boer leader, and for nine days all eyes in South Africa were turned upon the extraordinary spectacle presented by the first of the three great " hunts " with which De Wet's name is associated.

Ten mobile columns, including large numbers of mounted men, took part, at one time or another, in the chase, and in all nearly 30,000 men were engaged directly or indirectly in the enveloping operations. Thrice the net was drawn so closely around the quarry that there seemed to be no hope of escape. But De Wet got through, dodging and doubling over the Vaal, across the Western Transvaal, and through the Magaliesberg Range to the district north of Pretoria, having achieved—with a loss of a gun and some waggons—the only specific object of all this desperate marching ; that, namely, of escorting President Steyn to a point whence he could reach the Transvaal leaders, and concert fresh measures of defence with them.

Perhaps the most striking feature of this and many another similar feat of evasion was that it was performed throughout at the " net " speed of ox-waggons, of which a large number accompanied the Boer column, together with herds of cattle and sheep, an increasing number of dismounted burghers, and, until near the end, a considerable number of British prisoners. De Wet himself, from the beginning to the end of his career, was always dead against taking heavy convoys on independent expeditions of this sort, but his power over his burghers rarely reached the point of persuading them to adopt his view With our vastly superior resources for forming advanced bases we should have been able to make our mounted troops far more independent, but we never succeeded in overcoming the transport difficulty. Our " net " speed was less than De Wet's on this occasion. Mounted interest from the Boer standpoint is confined : (*a*) To their customary skill in handling small protective screens, so as to check pursuit, and compel us to waste time in the preparatory shelling of positions ; (*b*) to the brilliant scouting of Theron's corps of 200 picked scouts. Knowledge of the country had very little to do with the success of these scouts, a considerable proportion of whom were foreigners from Europe. Reconnaissance was our own weakest point. Touch was rarely kept for twenty-four hours together, and we find already growing up that insidious tendency to rely more on centralized intelligence for the blocking of all supposed outlets of escape to the pursued force than on local scouting, backed by universal co-operation in strenuous tackling energy, for running that force to earth wherever and whenever it could be found.

There was plenty of individual British energy displayed in the chase, but very little co - operative energy. Methuen's column, which originally was a mixed force of all arms, bore almost the whole brunt of the direct pursuit, and performed marvels of endurance. During the last three days Methuen dropped his Infantry, and followed the trail with 600 Yeomanry, 600 Colonials, and 11 guns, and with these men on the 12th made the only effective attack in the course of the hunt, capturing a gun and sixteen waggons. The purely mounted columns, of which there were three, two of Cavalry and one of mounted riflemen, never gained fighting contact with the enemy at all.

For the rest, De Wet's own native audacity and ingenuity were his salvation. We deceive ourselves if we imagine that we European peoples, with our " regular " armies and our authorized textbook regulations for " regular " war, can afford to ignore the very least of the elements of success in these feats of evasion. If they seem to be wholly defensive in character, we must remember that they could not have been otherwise. To stand and fight it out meant envelopment by overwhelming numbers, and the loss of men who could never be replaced. And defensive power is only the correlative of offensive power. I need scarcely add that the whole of the work done by both sides in this hunt, and in all similar hunts, was essentially Cavalry work. Every good quality shown by either party was a Cavalry quality.

IV.—THE ADVANCE TO KOMATI POORT.

President Steyn's safe arrival in the north about the middle of August, after this perilous series of adventures, brings us somewhat prematurely to the last scene in the first great phase of the war. He came too late to be of use in averting the final dissolution of the Transvaal forces before the advance of Lord Roberts up the Delagoa Railway to the Portuguese frontier. But we must retrace our steps a little before we reach that point.

Since Diamond Hill (June 12) the Transvaal leaders had gradually abandoned all serious intention of defending the Delagoa line to extremities. Botha soon seems to have resigned himself to the eventual necessity of guerilla warfare, and during June sent off most of his commandos to their own districts, there to fight for their own homes, reserving for the defence of the Delagoa Railway only those burghers through whose districts it passed, together with the Police and most of his Artillery. For a month he held the Tigerpoort range of hills, fifteen to twenty miles east of Pretoria. Meanwhile the south-eastern men opposed Buller's advance from the Natal border to Heidelberg, the northern men prepared to defend the Pietersburg Railway, and De la Rey organized the first of many formidable offensive revivals in his own district, the Western Transvaal, culminating on July 11 in the capture of the post at Zilikat's Nek, in other small attacks, and in a general threat to Pretoria from the west. Botha, who had just been driven off the Tigerpoort range by a well-managed movement of mounted troops under Hutton and French (July 5 to 11), now saw a chance of an effective combination with De la Rey by a counter-attack upon the position just lost. Viljoen, with 2,000 men (against about 4,000 on our side), carried out this enterprise with considerable spirit on July 16, and came dangerously near success on our left at Witpoort. The situation was saved in this quarter by what the Official and *Times* narratives call a " charge " of the Canadian Mounted Rifles, though how near it came to being a mounted charge I am unable to discover.

These events, together with De Wet's escape from the Brandwater Basin, further delayed the eastward British advance, which was eventually begun on July 23. Middelburg was captured with little difficulty on July 27, and then there was a halt of another three weeks, rendered necessary by the hunt of De Wet and many other minor elements of disturbance. During this period French, with several thousand mounted troops (his own Cavalry and Hutton's mounted riflemen), held a semicircular outpost line fifty miles in extent to the eastward of Middelburg, and showed the same kind of skill and activity as he had exhibited at Colesberg in sparring with the Boer forces in front of him.

Buller, in the meantime, was marching northward from the Natal border with 9,000 men (including two mounted brigades) and 42 guns, and effected a junction with French on August 15. Belfast fell to the joint forces a few days later, and on the 27th, reinforced by an Infantry division to a total strength of nearly 19,000 men (of whom 4,800 were mounted), Roberts fought the last pitched battle of the regular war at Bergendal. Strange and characteristic climax it was ! Exceeding all previous records in extension, Botha, with about 7,000 men, on an extreme estimate, and 20 guns, held a line of difficult mountainous country no less than fifty miles in extent from end to end, reaching from the approaches to Lydenburg on the north to the approaches to Barberton on the south. No more than twenty miles of this front, however, held at the most by 5,000 men, was concerned in the action.

Upon the extreme right of this position French, with two Cavalry brigades, together about 1,600 strong, made the normal wide turning movement against strong but lightly-held positions, and made it very vigorously and successfully ; but it took him all day, so that he could not make the further projected sweep round the Boer rear.* Buller meanwhile assaulted the key to the Boer position —Bergendal Hill, on the left centre. This was a truly extraordinary episode in its proof of the terrific power of the modern rifle in the hands of disciplined men. The summit of the hill, about 200 yards by 100 yards in extent, was crowned with boulders, which made it a natural fort. It was bombarded with lyddite and shrapnel for three hours by thirty-eight guns, including heavy naval pieces and howitzers, until, as an historian puts it, it looked like Vesuvius in eruption. Then it was assaulted in the most intrepid style by a brigade of Infantry (1st Inniskilling Fusiliers and 2nd Rifle Brigade), who, before storming the crest, lost 120 officers and men, mainly, but not wholly, from the fire of the Bergendal burghers ; for two or three other small detachments co-operated at long-range from neighbouring hill-tops. When all was over, it was found that the hill had been held by seventy-four men of the

* I have no space for details, but I ask the reader to study either the *Times* or the Official narratives ; and I suggest that it was not worth while to make so great a circuit in order to turn out 500 Boers from distant flank posts. If French, leaving a small containing force, had advanced direct upon Lakenvlei by the road the Infantry took, he would have been in a position to act upon the Boer rear at an early hour.

Johannesburg Police—mounted riflemen, be it noted. Thirty got away on their horses, twenty were captured alive, and the rest were killed or wounded. As an example of the truth that defensive and offensive power are correlatives of one another, it may be remarked that these same " Zarps," under at least one of the same leaders (Pohlmann), had taken a leading part in the assault and capture of Nicholson's Nek ten months earlier. The Police, we must remember, were the only regular disciplined force (gunners excepted) which the Boers possessed.

This cardinal success in the centre brought the battle —if battle it may be called—to an end. French could not pursue, and the pursuit of Buller's Cavalry was ineffective.

This was Botha's last resolute stand. His own and Steyn's efforts together could not prevent the subsequent disintegration. Indeed, it is a remarkable proof of their ability and moral courage that during the next fortnight, with the help of some minor leaders like Kemp and Viljoen, and with the support of the most sturdy and patriotic burghers, they were able to present a decent show of resistance on the immense front from Lydenburg to Barberton and onwards ; to avert anything in the nature of a decisive defeat in the field ; and finally, when the crash came on the Portuguese frontier, to concentrate, and by perilous and exhausting flank marches to save from the wreckage, not only the acting executive Governments of both Republics, but substantial bodies of resolute men—the nucleus, in short, for nearly two more years of strenuous resistance.

It was here that the now inveterate habit on our part of overrating the importance of winning positions and of underrating the importance of defeating the Boers in person led to its most unfortunate results. The Portuguese frontier was the " touch-line." Short of incarceration (and a large number of horseless and destitute men chose this course), there was no alternative but a wide flank march to the north across the British front, at first over the fever-stricken "low veld," then over precipitous mountains whose spurs for a long distance were already held by our troops. Steyn, travelling light with 250 men, and starting on September 11, got through with ease. Botha and Viljoen, with 2,500 men, starting on the 17th, only just rounded Buller's extreme left flank at a point thirty miles from the railway on September 26. All eventually arrived at Pietersburg, which became henceforth a workshop, a recruiting-ground, and an administrative centre whence plans for future hostilities were hatched. One of the young leaders present—Kemp of Krugersdorp—was in later days the first to put in systematic use those formidable charging tactics which did so much to prolong the war.

It is one of the ironies of the campaign that, with all the elaborate and extensive flank movements of mounted troops—often far too extensive and elaborate—which had characterized our operations in the past, we had not ready at this crisis, when its presence was of vital consequence, a compact, independent mounted force for the interception of these important Boer detachments.

But, in truth, in spite of a week's explicit warning of Botha's intended march, his escape and that of Steyn passed almost unnoticed. All eyes were fixed on a spectacle of seemingly irreparable ruin ; of abandoned guns, stores, and rolling-stock ; of burghers flying into foreign territory ; of Kruger and his officials flying to Europe. The army, from Roberts downwards, and the whole outside world, seems to have interpreted these phenomena as signs that the war was practically over. At the time this was very natural, and this we should not forget when criticizing the error of judgment by the light of after-events.

Nor would it have been easy, even had the warning of

our political agents received full attention, to arrange for the interception of Botha in addition to the other pre-occupations of the time.   Buller had two Cavalry brigades on the northern flank, but they were scattered over a long series of posts.   A few hundred mounted riflemen were with the central Infantry column on the railway ; but most of the remaining mounted troops, in two columns composed of 1,000 mounted riflemen under Hutton, and 3,000 Cavalry and mounted riflemen under French, both well supplied with guns and auxiliary troops, had been employed since the 8th in marching on parallel routes through the mountains on the southern flank in order to clear this side for the central advance of the Infantry up the railway.   On September 13 both arrived at their respective goals—Hutton at Kaapsche Hoop, French at Barberton, the terminus of a small branch railway.   Both these marches, but especially the southernmost—that of French—though they met with slight opposition, merit high praise, and were a worthy culmination of the efforts of the mounted troops during the regular war.   It is true that they scarcely raise our special issue, or raise it only to afford us new evidence against the *arme blanche*, for the terrain—steep, wild, and intricate mountains—was as unsuitable for the exercise of that weapon as the hedge-bound plains of England.   But we can afford for a moment to forget our immediate issue in admiring the staunch endurance of all the troops alike, the nerve, energy, and self-reliance of French, and the admirable staff-work which, by assuring supplies and communications, enabled him to give full rein to his soldierly instincts.

CHAPTER X

THE GUERILLA WAR

SEPTEMBER, 1900, TO MAY, 1902.

NOTE.—For actions and operations mentioned in this chapter (part of which covers ground not yet dealt with by our Official Historians), the reader is referred to the *Times* History, vol. v.

So ended what is usually known as the " regular war." In South Africa the expression had no precise significance. Regular war had been melting imperceptibly into guerilla war for some time past. The Boers were not dependent, as thickly peopled industrial communities are dependent, on their railways, capitals, and principal towns. The vast majority lived on the land, and the land was theirs, very little ravaged as yet, and, as to vast areas, still even unvisited. The guerilla war may truly be said to have begun in the Free State in March, 1900, after the capture of Bloemfontein, and in the Transvaal not later, at any rate, than July, when Botha, from necessity rather than from choice, sent most of his burghers to their own districts. Nor was the crash at Komati Poort followed by anything more than a partial lull in hostilities.

Over both the newly annexed Colonies we exercised no authority outside the range of our guns. In the greater part of the Transvaal, it is true, there were two months during which the burghers, like wasps, stung rarely unless they were disturbed ; but in the sister state, De Wet's return at the end of August, after the first " hunt," had roused his countrymen to fresh offensive efforts. After some weeks of propaganda and reorganization he took the field on September 20, just when Roberts was approaching Komati Poort. A month later he was laying formal, though unsuccessful, siege, to a fortified town in the Transvaal—Frederikstad—and in Mid-November, undeterred by a sharp reverse at Bothaville (November 6), he was marching south through the Eastern Free State, besieging and, this time, capturing another fortified town—Dewetsdorp—and endeavouring to invade Cape Colony. By a great concerted effort, organized by Kitchener, and known as the second " De Wet hunt," he was checked, but not before he had succeeded, early in December, in throwing across the border bands under Kritzinger and Hertzog, which lit an inextinguishable flame of rebellion among the Dutch colonists.

Certain incidents in this period (September to November, 1900) call for special notice.

1. The march of 173 miles made by French's Cavalry division, about 3,000 strong, across the Eastern Transvaal in October, with the object of " clearing the country." This march revealed with startling clearness both the nature of the campaign which was beginning, and the incapacity of the Cavalry, armed and equipped as they were, to cope with it. Bands, which never exceeded a third and rarely exceeded a fifth or sixth of French's strength, harassed the column all the way with vicious little attacks, which were repelled, but which met with no punishment, nor with any adequate tactical retaliation. The expedition achieved nothing, encouraged the enemy, and was attended by enormous losses of oxen and horses. It is true that numbers of other columns (the majority composed mainly of Infantry) were tramping about the country at this time with scarcely better results, and nearly all suffering from the disability imposed by heavy ox-transport. It is true also, that the country traversed by French presented peculiar difficulties in its remoteness from railways, and in the pugnacity of

14—2

its burghers. But, with allowance for these considerations, the marked feature of the expedition, from the point of view of our inquiry, was the failure of the Cavalry to reap advantage, tactically, from occasions when the enemy sought a conflict.

2. A more hopeful omen for the future was afforded at about the same time in the Free State, by the action of Bothaville* (November 6, 1900), at the end of a long chase of De Wet by some columns of mounted riflemen under Charles Knox, after the Boer leader's retreat from Frederikstad, and before his attempt to invade Cape Colony. His laager and guns were surprised and attacked at close range in brilliant style by a small advance-guard composed of only sixty-seven regular Mounted Infantry, who held their ground until reinforced, and brought about the capture of several guns, much transport, and 100 men, after a fiercely contested fight of some hours' duration. This exploit was something wholly new. Nothing exactly like it had been done by our mounted troops since the war began. Some excellent work, too, though never quite good enough for the purpose, was done by the same and other mounted columns in the subsequent hunt of De Wet, arising out of his attempted raid on Cape Colony (November 24 to December 13, 1900). Co-operation was far better, and tackling power higher than in the " hunt " of the preceding August.

3. *Charges.*—We note the Boer mounted charge occurring—

(*a*) On at least one small occasion during the march of the Cavalry division, referred to above. I have no details, only a bare mention of the circumstance in the " Official History " (vol. iii., p. 432). The movement was repelled.

(*b*) On November 6, at Komati River, in the course of some operations under Smith-Dorrien, near the Delagoa

* " Official History," vol. iii., pp. 485-488 ; *Times* History, vol. v., pp. 15-20.

Railway, where Boers, firing from the saddle, charged clean through a rear-guard of Canadian mounted troops (*Times* History, vol. v., p. 51; " Official History," vol. iii., p. 442).

(*c*) In the second " De Wet hunt." This, I think, was the first example in the war, on the Boer side, of what I may call the penetrating charge, after the Klip Drift pattern, that is, designed to pierce a screen for ulterior purposes, not to inflict immediate loss on the enemy. It occurred at the close of the hunt, when, at Springhaan's Nek (December 14, 1900), the Boers, accompanied by a mass of waggons, burst through the Thabanchu line of fortified posts, which had been strengthened at the point attacked by small detachments of mounted riflemen. It is worth while, though I have not the space, to examine the incident side by side with the Klip Drift charge, noting relative numbers, size of target, ground, and the effect of fire upon men and animals in rapid movement (*Times* History, vol. v., pp. 40-42. Not mentioned in " Official History ").

(*d*) A successful little charge, this time by Britons, occurred on the same day in another part of the field, at Victoria Nek, where a detached Boer force was attacked and very roughly handled by the Welsh Yeomanry and the 16th Lancers. The " Official History " makes no mention of the episode, and my own information is scanty. Some of the Yeomanry, it is said, used clubbed rifles. Whether the Lancers used their swords I do not know. As to clubbed rifles, contrast the Boer plan of firing from the saddle (*Times* History, vol. v., pp. 41-42).

(*e*) On the British side again, Bothaville (referred to above) was certainly on the border-line of charges. The advance-guard dismounted at something like point-blank range. So few in numbers, they would have gained little by riding home, and might have defeated their own object. As it was, they achieved their object, and that is all that matters, whether it is Infantry, Cavalry, or mounted riflemen who are charging.

My digression has run to greater length than I intended. There was no pause in the current of Boer aggression. No sooner had De Wet turned his back on the Orange River than the long-prepared offensive revival in the Transvaal was carried into effect. Viljoen's enterprises against the Delagoa Railway towards the end of November had heralded the storm, which, during the early part of December, broke with violence in the western district, where the Buffelspoort convoy was destroyed (December 2, 1900), and De la Rey defeated Clements at Nooitgedacht (December 13, 1900). The revival spread to the southeast, where several towns on the Natal border were attacked, and culminated in the north-east, with Viljoen's capture of Helvetia, on December 31, and Botha's simultaneous midnight attacks of January 5 upon the garrisons of the Delagoa Railway, one of which, that on Belfast, came perilously near success.

Kitchener, who had assumed the chief command in South Africa on November 20, 1900, just when the Free State revival was declining, and the Transvaal outbreak was beginning, was faced with an extraordinarily difficult and complicated problem. He had to cope with a new national spirit among the Boers, emanating from men who were wholly unconnected with the old Kruger régime, and gathering strength from the elimination, by surrender or voluntary exile, of the supporters of that régime. The new national spirit took practical shape in a new military spirit, one of vigorous offence, conducted by men who represented what, beyond all question now, was the most formidable type of soldier in the world—the mounted rifleman—men who were equally at home in defending or assaulting entrenched positions, and in attack or defence in the open field.

Our own resources for dealing with the situation were manifestly inadequate. It was not only that there had been visible in some of the recent events disquieting signs of feebleness in defence, leading to unjustifiable surrenders. This evil was largely due to the lassitude and staleness which affected the army in general. The really grave feature was our inability to retaliate effectively against these aggressive enterprises, an inability strikingly illustrated by the long but futile operations which were set on foot in the Western Transvaal after Nooitgedacht. The truth came like a flash, pitilessly illuminating past shortcomings, that all along we had been conquering the country, not the race, winning positions, not battles. Psychological causes apart, our cardinal military weakness had always lain in the mounted arm, not in numbers, except at the very first, but in quality. Unless we carry self-deception so far as either to eliminate from the calculation the great masses of Infantry who had borne the main brunt of the regular campaign and had suffered far the heaviest losses, or, on the other hand, to count the enemy twice over, once as opponents of the Infantry, and again as opponents of our mounted troops ; unless we perpetrate one of these errors, we must candidly admit that we had had our full chance of securing decisive victories through the semi-independent agency of mounted men. The figures and facts to which I drew attention in sketching the main operations from Paardeberg to Komati Poort prove this conclusively. We had missed our chance, and the consequences of missing it, obscured at the time by a long record of successful invasion and occupation, were now apparent. The war, obviously, was to be a mounted war. In the last resort nothing but efficiency in the same formidable type which the Boers represented could enable us to conquer them. Infantry would still perform the task of holding the ground won ; they would also perform many valuable

subsidiary duties in the field, but always of a defensive
or semi-defensive character. For offence, whether for
finding the enemy and forcing him to action, or for beating
him when he sought action himself, mounted riflemen,
good enough and numerous enough, were an indispensable
necessity.   In this respect, what were our prospects ?

We had evolved our type of mounted rifleman, which,
in essentials, followed the Boer type, but in practice
fell short of the ideal. The Cavalry, who from the
first should have inspired and furthered the educational
process, were only just beginning to substitute the
rifle for the carbine, a change which must, I imagine,
have been finally prompted by the experience, alluded
to above, of their divisional march across the Eastern
Transvaal, in October, 1900. So far as I know, the first
occasion on which any considerable force of Cavalry
carried rifles in the field was in the great driving operations which began in that same district, and again under
French, at the end of January, 1901. The lance was
already discarded, and eventually the sword also was
discarded, but not until many months later. There seems
to have been no simultaneous abandonment of swords by
all Cavalry regiments alike. The change was gradual.
In dwelling once again upon the backwardness of Cavalry
training, I must explain once again, for fear of misunderstanding, that I am criticizing them by a standard
special to themselves, the only standard appropriate to
a professional force which had been in the field for more
than a year. I need scarcely say that their record in
the guerilla war, as in all the war, is honourable, and
in many respects admirable ; but by contrast with what
they might have become without the *arme blanche* habit
and training, it is comparatively negative and tame. With
a few trifling exceptions they escape the reverses which
so often befell their less disciplined and less experienced
irregular comrades, but they do not stand out pre-

eminent in that aggressive energy which was the great tradition of their arm. In the matter of leadership we find them supplying many excellent column commanders—men like Byng, Briggs, Scobell, and Rimington, to name only a few—but on the whole they can scarcely be said to have surpassed other arms of the service in the production of good leaders. Needless to say, good leading never came from any other source than oblivion of steel methods and unreserved reliance on the rifle.

The regular Mounted Infantry had made rapid strides in efficiency, in spite of the extraordinary difficulties with which they had to grapple—inexperience in riding and horse-management, dearth of officers, hurried organization, absence of common tradition and *esprit de corps.* But they had been worked with great severity, had shrunk greatly from the ordinary wastage of war, and could only be reinforced by the same unscientific and wasteful methods by which they had been raised—that is, by abstraction from Infantry battalions, which, in their turn, lost in efficiency from the process.

The prospect was even worse with the irregulars, Home and Colonial. All had worked hard, and most had done exceedingly well, considering their inexperience and the faults inseparable from improvised unprofessional corps. In sheer fighting efficiency the best of the seasoned Colonials, South African, Australasian and Canadian, had undoubtedly excelled all other mounted troops. Like the self-made soldiers of the American Civil War, they had seemed by intuition to grasp the possibilities of a union of the rifle with the horse. But the irregular mounted army was dissolving in Kitchener's hands. Enlisted for limited terms, the various corps, Yeomanry included, had reached, or were soon to reach, their limit. It was necessary to forego their accumulated experience, to issue fresh appeals for volunteers, and to reconstruct this part of the army from top to bottom.

The thing was done, but the stamp of new men enlisted (for there were many re-enlistments), whether from Home or the Colonies, and in spite of higher pay, was never again so good as of old. This deterioration was especially noticeable in some of the minor South African corps, whether raised for general purposes, or for the special purpose of acting as a local militia for the defence of Cape Colony. There was one marked exception to the general rule. The South African Constabulary, recruited from all parts of the Empire, and designed to be a permanent force, obtained the cream of the recruits.

Kitchener's first reconstruction of the volunteer mounted army was not final. Limited terms again ran out, as the war dragged on, and fresh contingents replaced time-expired men. But the sources never ran dry, and on balance the strength tended to increase.

The constant changes and fluctuations make it exceedingly difficult to obtain accurate numerical estimates of our total mounted strength (regular and irregular) at any given time during this period. But we may say with approximate accuracy that in June, 1901, when all the volunteer mounted troops first appealed for in December, 1900, were in the field, and when the professional element had been reinforced, the total mounted strength was about 80,000, of whom 14,000 were regular Cavalry, and 12,000 regular Mounted Infantry (now divided into 27 battalions). The new contingent of Yeomanry numbered about 16,000 ; the South African Constabulary 7,500, and the Australasian contingents 5,000. Exclusive of the Cape Colony militia (District Mounted Troops and Town Guards), South Africa itself provided about 24,000 men enrolled in active corps. These are the full nominal figures. The effective fighting strength of the same units, on June 19 (according to an official state), was, within a man or two, 60,000.

The total strength of the whole army at the same

period was about 244,000 ; " effective fighting strength " (according to the same official state), 164,000.

During the last year of the war, from June, 1901, to June, 1902, the regular Cavalry increased, in round numbers, to 16,000 ; the regular Mounted Infantry to 15,000 ; the Australasian and Canadian contingents to 13,000 ; and the South African Constabulary to 9,500 ; while in the last five months a wholly new mounted corps, eventually 2,300 strong, was formed from the personnel of the Royal Artillery. By this time the second contingent of Yeomanry had dwindled considerably, and a third was formed, 7,000 strong, most of whom did not arrive in time to fight. At the end of the war, with the active South African corps and the District Mounted Troops reckoned in, there must have been 100,000 mounted men in the field, without counting the Boer levies, known as National Scouts and Orange River Colony Volunteers. The whole army numbered about a quarter of a million.

While this progressive increase went on in British strength, and predominantly in mounted strength, the Boers steadily diminished. Here, too, periodical estimates are extraordinarily difficult. Within the two annexed states, not only enrolled burghers of fighting age, but every surviving male, except boys below, say, fourteen, and infirm old men, now had to be reckoned as potential enemies. The rebel element in Cape Colony was an indeterminate quantity. The foreign element gradually disappeared. If we accept the calculation of the Official Historians, that from first to last in the whole war, with the inclusion of rebels and foreigners, a grand total of 87,365 persons took arms against us at one time or another ; if, at the other end of the scale, we bear in mind the number of men who laid down their arms at the conclusion of the war—namely, 21,256, and if we examine the intermediate statistics of surrenders, captures, and casualties, the rough conclusion may be drawn that at Christmas, 1900, we had still about 55,000 potential enemies to reckon with, and in June, 1901, about 45,000. During the last year the average monthly reduction was about 2,000.

But, apart from estimates of potential strength, the numbers actually on a war-footing at any given moment were very small—rarely more than 15,000—and sometimes as low probably as 9,000. No single body of men larger than 3,000—and this figure was exceedingly rare—ever again took the field.

The reduction in total numbers was one of quantity, not of quality. The weakest, morally or physically, were weeded out. The fittest survived and became continuously more formidable. That is what gives such extraordinary interest to the mounted operations of the guerilla war. How the small nucleus of veterans with limited resources and without external help managed to hold out for a year and three-quarters after the crash at Komati Poort against an Empire drawing upon inexhaustible resources of men, money, and material, and how, though losing their independence, they succeeded in obtaining terms which ensured to them in the near future political equality with their conquerors, is a story I have endeavoured elsewhere to take my share in telling. In these pages I have to confine myself, as closely as possible, to my own narrow issue. But it is necessary, once more, to say a few words on the larger aspects of the campaign.

First let us rid our minds of the fallacy that guerilla war is a wholly distinct thing in kind from regular war. It is nothing of the sort. War is a science whose fundamental principles are constant, however wide and numerous the variations of circumstance under which it is conducted. Perhaps I may be allowed to quote what I wrote on this point in my preface to vol. v. of the *Times* History :

" Whether the enemy be based on rich and populous towns, linked by a network of railways, or on nomadic knots of waggons, filled from half-ravaged mealy fields, whether he draws ammunition from well-equipped arsenals, or gleans it from deserted camping-grounds, whether he manœuvres in armies 100,000 strong, or in commandos 500 strong, the problem of grappling with that enemy and forcing him to admit defeat is in essentials the same. Moreover, it is the peculiar interest of guerilla war that it illuminates much that is obscure and difficult in regular war. Just as the Röntgen rays obliterate fleshy tissues, and reveal the bony structure, so in the incidents of guerilla war there may be seen, stripped of a mass of secondary detail, the few dominant factors which sway the issue of great battles and great campaigns. Subjected to close analysis, one of Kitchener's combinations may be perceived to have succeeded or failed from the same causes which dictated the success or failure of Marlborough's combinations. It is equally true that in many of the short and sharp actions described in this volume there may be distinguished, following one another with kinematographic rapidity and vividness, the same phases through which long struggles on historic battle-fields have passed."

I repeat these words here because, among the many perversions of history for which the *arme blanche* school is indirectly responsible, none is more widespread than the vague idea, for it cannot be called a reasoned opinion, that the guerilla war may be ignored for instructional purposes. This is only an insidious extension of the proposition that the whole war was so " peculiar " as to afford no condemnation of the *arme blanche ;* but the guerilla war is supposed to lend itself especially well to the propagation of that fallacy. So mercurial and intangible was the enemy (the suggestion is), so incalculable and irresponsible his movements, so numerous and safe the lairs from which he could gather, and to which he could disperse, so complete his independence of bases and communications, that it is useless to look for strategical, much less for tactical and technical lessons. To speak plainly, all this is pernicious nonsense. Every soldier knows in his heart that no success in action was ever gained on either side but by high individual efficiency in the men, by clever and spirited leading, and by putting into practice ordinary military principles. When we compare the Boers, in the way of legitimate metaphor, to wasps or mosquitoes, do not let us vainly imagine that their tactical methods were no more highly developed than those of that class of insect. *A fortiori* let us reject Mr. Goldman's strange delusion that they practised evasion so perpetually and successfully as not to give our Cavalry—to say nothing of our mounted rifle-men—a fair chance for the " discharge of Cavalry duties." Neither sporadic sniping nor persistent evasion would have enabled the Boers to maintain their long resistance. They needed victories, however small, not only to replenish their ammunition, but to sustain their spirit, and they could only obtain them by careful preparation, bold execution, and disciplined tactical methods. In war you can get nothing for nothing. However familiar the ground to you, and however great the disabilities under which your enemy labours, if you are going to do damage of any consequence you must concentrate a disciplined force, however small ; feed it when concentrated ; make plans, often concerted plans needing accurate co-operation ; scout boldly and intelligently ; hold your force well in hand and in close order up to the limit of prudence ; and when the hour for action comes, rely on the valour and skill of your men to execute a definite tactical scheme in a coherent, disciplined fashion. In this way only—a way old as war itself— were actions, small or great, won in South Africa either by ourselves or by the Boers.

As to the *arme blanche*, whatever opportunities, if any, the past had afforded, those opportunities still existed.

If it had been possible to exert shock in the past, it was equally possible now. That the numbers engaged on either side in any given action were on the average smaller made no difference. Nor did the Boer way of fighting, though it improved greatly in vigour, change in any essential particular. They had always fought and still fought in such a way as to make the rifle absolute arbiter of tactics. The secondary characteristics which lend such peculiar difficulties to guerilla war had not the remotest bearing on this question of weapons for horsemen. What bearing could they conceivably have ? The problem still was to thrash the enemy whether he sought action or declined action. If it was a case of finding and forcing to battle an evasive foe, the weapon which inspired most ardour and nerve in the search was the best weapon. If the foe chose to accept action, or himself forced an action, the weapon which decided the issue was the best weapon. Combat is the one and only test, and combats were innumerable. Whether the Boers came to the scene of combat by train, or from some base-town, or whether they had been summoned suddenly from the farms of a certain limited district, was immaterial to the efficacy of weapons. In accepting combat, whether with little or great ardour, they accepted all the risks and penalties of combat. That is the only healthy way to look at the matter if we are to gain true instruction from the war, and not merely to drug our minds with the complacent thought that the difficulties were immense, and that on the whole we did as well as we could be expected to do.

The whole of the South African War, and the guerilla war in particular, was a superb school for mounted troops. It was an exceedingly hard school, but hard schools are the best. Our soldiers, and above all our Cavalrymen, ought to thank Providence on their knees for having given them this unique and unrivalled opportunity for practice in their art within a ring-fence, so to speak, subject to no external disturbance, and against an enemy who, however formidable in quality, could never be reinforced, and were bound to dwindle in numbers.

Did we tackle the guerilla war in such a way as to make the most of our schooling ? I am afraid we did not. I am not at all sure that, by the time we had reached that stage, we had the power to do so ; but however that may be, when we are looking for lessons, let us ruthlessly eliminate bad or doubtful precedents, and fix our eyes on good precedents.

Our principal weakness was not a new one, though it assumed a new shape. We had always aimed too much at the positions and possessions of the enemy, and too little at his personnel. It was the same now. His new base henceforward was the land, and we made it one of our principal endeavours, if not our primary endeavour, to cut off that great and fruitful source of supply. Roberts, as early as September, 1900, had enjoined the destruction of crops, and, under certain conditions, of farms, though comparatively little had been accomplished when he quitted the command. Kitchener initiated a plan of systematic devastation, with its corollary, the systematic deportation of non-combatants to concentration camps. With the ethical and political aspects of this measure we are not now concerned. Its military result was to retard the education and restrict the fighting efficacy of our mounted troops by setting before them two incompatible aims : that of grappling with the enemy, and that of destroying his crops and cattle and deporting his families. The latter aim, which was secondary, too often tended to become primary, simply because it was the easiest to put into practice, and human nature is prone to follow lines of least resistance.

Another doubtful precedent, closely allied with the last, and only to be justified as a *pis aller* to meet an

immensely difficult case, was the system of " drives "—
the system, that is, of sweeping defined tracts of country
with large groups of columns, according to formal
plans worked out in a central staff department, and controlled in execution from that department. This, broadly
speaking, was Kitchener's method of dealing with the
guerilla war. He varied it with other methods, with
concerted movements of a minor and less centralized
character, with the night-raid system, the constabulary
post system, and with the work of independent columns,
while periodical eruptions of spontaneous Boer activity
often compelled him to retaliate with any rough-and-
ready means that came to hand. A vast amount of
good independent or semi-independent work was done in
one way or another by enterprising British leaders, but
on the whole it is true to say that the drive was our
principal weapon. Now, the spirit of the drive was
diametrically opposed to the spirit which should actuate
ardent mounted troops. It sacrificed dash to symmetry,
and it gave no scope for surprise, the soul of mounted
effort. Designed to cope with evasion, it bred habits
which reacted on enterprise just when enterprise had its
best opportunities—that is, when the Boers took the
offensive. Except in weeding out weak-kneed burghers
and in facilitating devastation, it proved sterile until
reinforced by its complement, the block-house system.
This system added physical barriers to human barriers
and provided a far-flung network of communications
and supply centres, by the aid of which, in addition to
the railways and base-towns, enormous numbers of men
could be manœuvred in driving lines, fifty or sixty
miles in length, with mathematical precision and speed.
But the system was not ready for application in its complete form until February, 1902, after sixteen months
of guerilla war, and even this huge and elaborate mechanism, although by a throttling, starving process it

eventually brought the Boers to their knees, failed to achieve the supreme object of war, the defeat of the enemy in the open field.   To the last, veterans who still possessed horses and the will to escape, overleapt the strongest barriers, whether animate or inanimate, and to the last, wherever pressure was relaxed, dealt biting blows at isolated columns.

It is easy to point out the drawbacks of Kitchener's military policy.   But it is difficult to see how, with his professional mounted troops still so backward, and with the raw levies which constituted so large a portion of his mounted army, he could have adopted any other policy. As it was, he took great risks and incurred substantial penalties in throwing prematurely into the field untrained troops.   The fact, about which there can be no question, that during the last year of the war the enemy replenished his ammunition almost entirely from British sources, and at the end had largely re-armed himself with Lee-Enfield rifles, is proof enough by itself of the penalties incurred. The most we can say in criticism of Kitchener is that he might have done more, as the troops gained confidence and efficiency—and they did gain both, rapidly and continuously—to temper the rigidity of his excessively centralized system. Even here we are on debatable ground.   His genius was for organization ; his countrymen profited by that genius, and it ill becomes them to cavil at the defects which were its inevitable accompaniment.   A weaker man, actuated by the theoretically higher aim of educating his mounted troops on ideal lines, at whatever cost, might very well have failed miserably. We can obtain a rough criterion of what this education meant by a study of the guerilla war in Cape Colony, where devastation and deportation were out of the question, where drives were barely feasible, though they were sometimes tried, and where the single object of finding and fighting the rebel bands stood out unobscured.

With full allowance for the immense difficulties of the problem, the results cannot be regarded as satisfactory.

In summing up the whole matter we must remember that two great factors—one military, the other moral—exercised an influence upon events which Kitchener, beyond a certain point, was powerless to modify. The military factor was simply the initial inferiority of our troops to the Boers as mounted riflemen. At bottom, the excessive driving tendency was promoted by the same cause as the tendency during the regular war towards disproportionately wide turning movements, as opposed to direct aggressive tackling. The idea was to circumvent, not to attack ; to trap, not to pierce. Similarly with reconnaissance. This, by the time Kitchener took the command, had become almost a lost art. To revive it, in the exacting conditions, was beyond the power of a Commander-in-Chief. We came to rely almost wholly on outside agencies—natives and Boer spies—for our intelligence, and on central agencies for the diffusion of this intelligence. This was a fatal precedent for our Cavalry in future wars. Naturally, the effect was to favour centrally organized drives and to discourage that highest form of enterprise which inspires men who use their own eyes to secure opportunities for their own weapons. What is the weapon which not only decides the combat but aids the scout to use his eyes ? Everywhere and always, in Manchuria as in South Africa, the rifle.

I touched on the moral factor in my last chapter. The Boers had the highest possible moral stimulus—that of defending their homes and nationalities. We had no motive so stimulating. Racial hatred would have been the only stimulus correspondingly strong, but we had none. The Boers improved on acquaintance. We had taken up arms to secure the political equality of our countrymen, and we had already secured that object beyond question, and annexation as well. To go farther,

15—2

and aim at so cowing the Boer national spirit as to gain a permanent political ascendancy for ourselves was an object beyond our power or will to achieve, and beyond the power or will of any free democracy or confederation of free democracies of the British Imperial type to achieve. Peaceable political fusion under our own flag was the utmost we could secure. That meant a conditional Boer surrender, on a promise of future autonomy. The unconditional surrender which Lord Milner was anxious to obtain, however long and bitter a struggle it entailed, could scarcely have led to peaceable fusion. The only other alternative, feasible possibly, but outside discussion or contemplation, was the permanent expatriation of all the most vigorous elements in the two Boer races. Kitchener grasped the truth as soon as he took command. That his own spontaneous instinct as a soldier was towards sharp, mercilessly decisive blows in the field he had shown clearly enough at Paardeberg. But that opportunity and many others had been lost, never to return. From a soldier's point of view he saw the insuperable difficulties at this hour of attempting, with the material now at his command, to deal blows sharp and heavy enough to destroy the Boer national spirit. Hence his rather mechanical military system, aiming at slow attrition rather than fierce aggression ; hence his schemes for dealing with the civil population ; and hence his political policy, which was to obtain at the earliest moment, but without the least relaxation of strong military effort—indeed, with a daily intensification of those efforts—a settlement on agreed terms. The Boers, clinging desperately to their independence, held out against any settlement whatever, conditional or unconditional, until May, 1902. Meanwhile the task of inducing them to recognize the inevitable was not one which evoked, or could be expected to evoke, any marked degree of military enthusiasm. There was a great deal of very natural caution among commanders in the field, increased by the ever-present impression that the war was on the point of ending and by a well-grounded reluctance to make a bold use of new troops against veterans. It was useless for Kitchener to enjoin daring and enterprise if he could not get his subordinates to accept the necessary responsibility. There is no doubt that some of his genuine efforts in this direction met with inadequate reply. But, again, we cannot blink the fact that the responsibility, as events showed, was very heavy, and from purely military causes. The net result was that the strongest will in South Africa exerted its full and legitimate influence, and produced a military system based mainly on organization and numbers, rather than on expert capacity in normal field operations.

Raids.—It was natural, therefore, that during the guerilla war sound lessons for the future should come mainly from the Boer side. In strategy—so far as the word is applicable to the guerilla war—they had little to teach us ; but that little is not unimportant. Beyond the simple policy of distracting our efforts and alleviating their own distress by outbreaks timed so as to relieve one harassed district at the expense of another less harassed, they had only one consistent strategical object—that, namely, of feeding the rebellion in Cape Colony by successive small invasions. The instinct was sound. Infinite embarrassment came of it and a drain on our mounted troops, which was constant and severe. The principal raids by which this policy was carried out—(1) that of Hertzog and Kritzinger, December, 1900, to January, 1901 ; (2) that of Christian de Wet, January to March, 1901 ; (3) that of Smuts, August to September, 1901—are well worth careful study as examples of what small numbers of determined mounted riflemen can do, even when burdened, as De Wet was, with heavy transport, in traversing great tracts of country through hosts of enemies for a strategical purpose.   No. 2 led to the third and greatest " De Wet hunt "—an episode packed with excitement and dramatic interest from beginning to end.   No. 3—the ride of Smuts with 340 men from the Gatsrand (West Transvaal) to Cape Colony—merits even closer attention.

We must add to the list of raids Botha's attempted invasion of Natal—September to October, 1901—which was also an instructive example for future wars, regular or irregular.   Botha failed in what from the first was a hopeless undertaking, but he showed audacity and nerve, not only in tactical aggression, but in extricating himself from envelopment by immensely superior forces on his return journey.   Both for making and checking such raids—and we must include under the same general heading the previous " hunts " and De Wet's early raids upon the railway — rifle - power is everything.   In Chapter XIV. I shall contrast the abject failure of the Russian Cavalry in similar enterprises owing to lack of rifle-power with the rare but brilliant Japanese successes. Kimberley and the American Civil War drive home the same lesson.

Night Attacks. — These were numerous, and prove conclusively that in this class of enterprise small, thoroughly disciplined forces have good chances of suc- cess against troops who fall short in the slightest degree in vigilance and sound outpost work.   We may divide the attacks roughly into two classes—those against mobile forces encamped for the night, and those against more or less permanently fortified posts or towns.   Of the former class, one of the most brilliant, because it was undertaken against the wariest of wary veterans, was that of Colonel Scobell upon Lotter's rebel commando at Bouwer's Hoek (Cape Colony) on September 4, 1901.   A Cavalry regiment—the 9th Lancers—and the Cape Mounted Rifles shared in the assault, which led to the only complete and unqualified success we ever obtained in Cape Colony. Another plucky exploit was that of Major Shea and a detachment of South Australians, who attacked Smuts at Grootvlei on the night of August 1, 1901, just as that clever young leader (for once caught napping) was beginning his ride to Cape Colony.

The chief Boer successes of the same type were at Wilmansrust (June 12, 1901), Quaggafontein (September 20, 1901), and Tweefontein (December 24-25, 1901). Careless outpost work by irregular troops was responsible for all three reverses. On the first two occasions camps on the level were rushed and overpowered instantaneously ; but Tweefontein, besides illustrating stratagem and stalking skill, is also suggestive of the risks taken by a force which attacks in the dark. De Wet's men scaled a precipitous cliff to storm the British camp, and, in doing so, overlooked a strong picket ensconced below the crest on the opposite side. It is possible that if reinforcements to the hill had come as promptly as they might have come, this picket, which was eventually discovered and overpowered, might have served as a useful *point d'appui* for a counter-stroke. At night, in the confusion of a sudden assault, the slightest stand made by a handful of determined men is likely to bewilder and daunt the enemy.

Lake Chrissie (February 5, 1901) and Moedwil (September 30, 1901) were finely conceived and finely executed night attacks by Botha and De la Rey respectively against columns under Smith-Dorrien in the one case and Kekewich in the other. Both were repelled in the most spirited fashion, but in both there were moments of extreme danger. At Langerwacht (February 23, 1902) there was a very dramatic and exciting night combat, when De Wet, to avoid envelopment in one of our great drives of the latest model type, burst through the cordon of entrenched pickets with a horde of waggons, carts, cattle, and non-combatants. There were several other episodes of the same type at that period.

Nooitgedacht (December 13, 1900) may also be placed in the category of night attacks. De la Rey's first and unsuccessful attack was delivered in pitch darkness ; the subsequent assault of Beyers in the grey of early dawn. All the above night attacks were upon the camps of mobile forces, but there were many others upon fortified posts and towns. Helvetia (December 29, 1900) and the small post at Modderfontein (January 30, 1901) were stormed in darkness. At Vryheid (December 11, 1900) an outlying post and the Mounted Infantry camp were rushed under the same circumstances, though the main position held out gallantly. Belfast (January 7, 1901) had a similar, but a more dangerous, experience, losing a strongly held outlying post and two entrenched posts, all defended with great tenacity, shortly after midnight and in misty weather. But the mist and darkness eventually favoured the defence. Viljoen and Botha, in endeavouring to unite their forces against the inner defences, lost their way, and had to retire baffled. The six other attacks on the garrisons of a section of railway forty miles in extent, made simultaneously on this same night, were carried out with marvellous punctuality, but were all gallantly repulsed. In the Western Transvaal, at a later date, De la Rey's unsuccessful attack on Lichtenburg (March 2, 1901) was begun and carried on for several hours in the dark.

One of the most thrilling episodes of this class was at Itala (September 25, 1901), the frontier post under Colonel Chapman, which Botha struck at when he was trying to raid Natal. An outlying post on the peak of Itala Mountain was taken by a sudden *coup de main* at midnight, and the fight, fiercely contested on both sides, raged round the central position until dawn and throughout the following day. At nightfall there was a lull, during which each side concluded that the other was irresistible, and both retired ! Prospect, a neighbouring frontier fort, was also attacked on the night of the 25th, but held its own with ease.

Columns on the march were very rarely attacked in complete darkness. The only case I know of is that of Yzer Spruit (February 24, 1902), where De la Rey ambushed a convoy, beginning his attack before the dawn. Attacks in twilight were common.

Scrutinizing these incidents with a view to our special inquiry, let us note three points :

1. This is of general application—that is, to day or night attacks. All mounted troops should, in the art of entrenchment, be as nearly as possible the equals of Infantry. Though regular Cavalry were not, I think, concerned in any of the above incidents, the kind of work involved, whether in attack or defence, was work which normally falls to Cavalry in all modern war. Troops who cannot make entrenchments will never be able to storm them.*

At this moment the regular Cavalry are supposed to be able both to attack and defend entrenched positions. " There are certain difficulties in modern war," admits " Cavalry Training " on page 186, " which cannot be overcome by mounted action "—that is, by shock action. This action, it is explained, " is precluded against an enemy posted behind entrenchments or occupying intersected or broken ground," or " an extended position," etc. In other words, the Cavalry are expected to be able to do the same offensive work as Infantry. Can they do it ? How far could they do it in South Africa ? Similarly in defence. They are " to deny important points to the

---

* I am not theorizing. This was the experience both of the Japanese and the Russians, as in South Africa and in the American Civil War. See "Reports of Military Observers (United States) attached to the Armies in Manchuria " (Part V.). Also Chapter XIV., *infra.*

enemy " by fire-action (and presumably to deny them effectively), and on page 215 (" The Defence ") they are " often to be called upon to occupy localities for defence, especially in small bodies. . . . Whenever time and means permit, the position should be put into a state of defence ; the preparations, however, should be *limited to those of the simplest kind.*" The italics are mine. It is thus that, after South Africa and Manchuria, we persist in ruinous error. One thinks of Majuba, of Spion Kop, of Nicholson's Nek, Dewetsdorp, Nooitgedacht, and only too many other examples of the Nemesis which attends " defences of the simplest kind," no matter by what class of troops they are made and used. The compilers of the section entitled " Dismounted Action " should have taken to heart the lesson of Zilikat's Nek (July 11, 1900), where regular Cavalry were concerned, both in defence and in attack. Of course, behind all the compromise which pervades the section there lies the fatal obsession that openings for shock action must at all costs be allowed for, and that, in defence, entrenchments should not be so good as to encourage Cavalry to rely on them, to the prejudice of " mounted action," which in Cavalry language means *shock.* This is to disregard the facts of war. Why did not the Cavalry execute shock charges at or after the Boer assaults on Wagon Hill ? They were there, fighting bravely enough on foot in defence, but the counter-charges were made by Infantry and irregular horsemen acting dismounted.

2. Nothing, not even the strongest entrenchments, can replace vigilance. Here the Cavalry showed an excellent example to their irregular comrades. Cavalry outposts were rarely surprised, and, I think, there was only one case of any consequence of a homogeneous Cavalry force being completely surprised in daylight.

3. Mark the skill and confidence with which the Boers arranged for the disposal of their led horses in their night

attacks, whether on columns or posts. Of the cases I have quoted, in no instance that I can discover did they suffer any appreciable loss in horses, or fail, if repulsed, to get away safely on horseback. One of the many fallacies dissipated by the South African War is the idea that mounted riflemen can never have full confidence in attack, because, if they dismount, they perpetually think too much about the line of retreat to their horses. In darkness, one would think, this feeling, if it existed, would be particularly strong. But whether by day or night, this was neither a Boer nor a British weakness.

Night Raids.—These were a British speciality, and must come under a separate heading, for they were not strictly night attacks, but long nocturnal expeditions designed to culminate in a surprise attack at dawn upon a Boer laager. Fond themselves of night enterprises, the Boers were also very sensitive to attack while in laager. This weakness began to be exploited by some of our mounted leaders in the early part of 1901. The first noteworthy night raid was on April 13 of that year at Goedvooruitzicht, where Sir Henry Rawlinson surprised the laager of Wolmarans at dawn, and captured his transport and a gun, though it is true that the Boers retaliated with some effect later on in the day. Other small raids followed in various quarters, and in August and September Colonel Benson, R.A., with the assistance of Colonel Woolls-Sampson, operating with a single column in the Eastern Transvaal, brought the system to high perfection. After his death in the unhappy reverse of Bakenlaagte, General Bruce Hamilton successfully carried on the same system in the same district, though with very much larger forces.

These raids supply most valuable instruction as to the best way to transport a mounted force with speed and secrecy over long distances of hostile country at night.

Immense distances were sometimes covered with unerring exactitude of direction. Nerve in leadership and the highest standard of discipline among all ranks were required, both for the march across country and for the deployment at dawn for attack. Ability to imitate these marches would be invaluable in any sort of war. But there are reservations to be made. Accurate information and skilled guides were absolutely essential to success. Both, in the case of these raids, came from extraneous sources—namely, Boer spies and native scouts. These are luxuries which we are not likely to get in future wars. We shall have to rely mainly, if not solely, on our own eyes and wits. Nor were the material results of the raids commensurate with the efforts put forth—at any rate, in the later period when very large forces were used. Much transport was captured, but most of the prisoners taken were horseless men, who formed a proportion of every commando in the field. There was rarely any fighting. If a thorough surprise was effected, all who could fly fled ; but it was noticeable that all through the raiding period, and in the raided district, the Boers were a match for us in ordinary daylight actions. On the other hand, the nervous worry and exhaustion caused by the raids had a very powerful moral effect upon the burghers.

Artillery with Mounted Troops. — I pointed out in Chapter VII. the disadvantages of allowing mounted troops of any class, acting independently, to rely too much on the support of Artillery. Guns weaken surprise, which is the soul of mounted effort. This truth came out with increasing clearness during the guerilla war. The Boers, having exhausted all their ammunition and resources for repair and upkeep, learnt, perforce, to do without guns altogether, with immense advantage to their tactics. When they obtained them by capture, they soon abandoned them. We ourselves, in offence, obtained little, if any, value from guns, and were apt to lose in vigour by the ever-present temptation of shelling before attacking. In defence they were often useful, but often, magnificently efficient as the gunners were, a source of tactical embarrassment. How vulnerable guns are to the assaults of bold mounted riflemen the record of losses in South Africa shows with painful clearness. The truth is, that the conditions created by the smokeless magazine rifle are highly unfavourable to the use of artillery in exclusively mounted warfare. When both sides are mounted, and acting freely, the game should be " loose " and " fast," to borrow football metaphors. The battery has no target worth speaking of, and is itself a very substantial and a highly sensitive target, whose mobility is liable to be destroyed in a few moments by rifle-fire. The team is the vital point, and the team alone, in the vulnerable surface it presents, is six times more extensive than a single troop-horse, and twenty times more extensive than a rifleman skirmishing on foot.

As I have already suggested, the gun, while it calls for the skilled co-operation of a number of individuals, is essentially an impersonal weapon. No amount of courage and dexterity in its handling can compensate for this inherent defect. When used with independent mounted troops it should be as small, light, in a word, as " personal " as possible. The bearing of these observations on the *arme blanche* question is obvious. No superficial peculiarities of the guerilla war in any way lessen the force of the physical and moral principles involved. If mounted men, in defiance of physical facts and the inexorable laws of the modern game, use shock formations—and shock is the fundamental condition for the use of the steel—they reduce the personal factor to its lowest point, and play into the hands of the hostile gunners. As a matter of fact, the steel-charge upon guns was never tried in any form, dense or loose, in South Africa, and that, surely, is a sufficiently conclusive circumstance in itself, when we recollect the numerous cases in which guns were successfully attacked by mounted riflemen. If most of these exploits were performed by the Boers, and if they afford undoubted proof of the superior efficiency of the Boers as mounted riflemen, we must, none the less, bear in mind the fact that our men had not the same chance of performing them. The Boers, as they lost both their faith in Artillery and their resources for maintaining it, grew callous to its loss, and were wont to abandon guns without a qualm. With ourselves it is always a point of honour to defend guns *à outrance*. That is an admirable rule, but it carries with it the obligation on the one hand of using Artillery only in strict accordance with its positive tactical utility, and on the other of making sure that its escort is absolutely efficient.

Attack on guns brings me naturally to the consideration of mounted charges, and to that important topic I must devote a separate chapter.

CHAPTER XI

MOUNTED CHARGES IN SOUTH AFRICA

FROM time to time in recent chapters I have noticed cases where the Boers showed unusual boldness in pressing on horseback, where the nature of the ground permitted, into decisive rifle-range, sometimes firing from the saddle as they came, and sometimes actually mingling with our men. I have noted similar cases of bold mounted aggression in our men, though without saddle-fire. I purpose now to treat the subject as a whole, taking the Boers first.

Faint symptoms of this were observable as early as Graspan (November, 1899). Sannah's Post (March, 1900) was the first occasion, I believe, where they rode into close quarters in the course of pressing a rearguard. The same tactics appear again in November of the same year at Komati River and elsewhere in the Eastern Transvaal at the dawn of the Boer renaissance, if we may so term the burst of offensive vigour which signalized the end of 1900. They are not much in evidence in the height of that outbreak, because the Boer offence took the form mainly of attacks (often by night) on fortified posts, where they were neither necessary nor feasible ; but signs of increased boldness in submitting horses to rifle-fire are visible in all the fights of that period. From the middle of 1901 onwards, when combats in the open field were the rule, this tendency took shape in a definite system of tactics. Curiously enough, these tactics, on their aggressive side, were confined mainly, though not wholly, to the Transvaal. The Free Staters used the semi-aggressive or " penetrating " charge freely enough, in order to escape from drives, but rarely in direct offence. This may have been due to the influence of De Wet, who nearly always preferred stalking to rushing. From the point of view of instruction, however, both types are equally interesting. They differed only in object, not in method.

On March 22, 1901, at Geduld, in the Western Transvaal, three squadrons of the Imperial Light Horse, under Colonel Briggs, of the King's Dragoon Guards, were engaged in a reconnaissance, when, with very little warning and to the blank astonishment of all who witnessed the scene, several hundreds of De la Rey's Boers, under the young General Kemp, in good order, and firing from the saddle, galloped down upon the extended skirmishing line of two squadrons. Our men just had time to mount, retire to a flank, and receive the support of the third squadron, when the enemy swept over the vacated position, swerved, and disappeared. This appears to have been a sort of rehearsal for future occasions. The charge inflicted no loss, but it is also significant that it incurred no loss. It was not repeated, though the Imperial Light Horse were followed back for several miles to their camp with vehement attacks, which they repelled with great coolness and gallantry. This may be noted as an excellent example of a steady retirement under difficult circumstances (*Times* History, vol. v., p. 224).

Twice on later occasions, at Reitz (October, 1901) and at Tigerkloof Spruit (December 18, 1901), the Imperial Light Horse had to sustain something in the nature of real mounted charges, in the first case of a serious character. They repelled them well (*Times* History, vol. v., pp. 393 and 428-431).

Two months after Geduld, at Vlakfontein* (May 30, 1901), operating against a column of all arms under General Dixon, Kemp used the same tactics with deadly effect, this time employing stratagem to heighten surprise. A rear-guard of 150 Yeomanry, 100 Infantry, and 2 guns, was beginning a retirement towards camp. While feinting against other portions of the columns, Kemp concentrated several hundred men against this rear-guard. The Boers, having fired the grass to windward, in order to mask their approach and bewilder their foes, burst through and rode down the Yeomanry screen, cut to pieces the company of Infantry, and the gun detachments, and took possession of the guns. No less than 150 of our men fell killed or wounded in a very short space of time, while the Boer losses were slight. There was a prompt and vigorous counter-attack by the rest of the column, which the Boers scarcely waited to receive, and the guns were recaptured. But the balance of success was with Kemp. Our column was crippled and Dixon had to retreat by a forced night march to his base.

Let us note certain points, some of general, some of local interest :

1. The Yeomanry engaged on this occasion were in-experienced troops—the Infantry and gunners, veterans.

2. The Boers, for the most part, remained in the saddle and fired from it, until they reached close quarters. The terrain, which was open and unobstructed, permitted this. After dismounting, some dropped the rein altogether, and some advanced firing, with the rein over the arm. The same plan was adopted in most of the subsequent charges.

3. There was no " shock," nor any idea of shock in this or any other instance of the charge. The lean, undersized Boer ponies were incapable of it. Shock is

* *Times* History, vol. v., pp. 281-284.

16

incompatible with the destructive use of the rifle, and this was a massacre with the rifle, short, sharp, and murderous. Even if it had been possible for a body of steel-armed horsemen using shock formation to reach close quarters under similar circumstances—and such a thing was never done or attempted in the whole course of the war—their destructive power would not be a tithe of that possessed by mounted riflemen, and their exposure to retaliation infinitely greater. Think of the physical incidents of the two types of charge, remembering that shock requires the steel-armed horsemen to remain on horseback, bursting through the enemy at the first onset, and doing what damage they can *en route*, and rallying from their disarray at some more or less distant point for a second charge. Think of the opportunities for retaliation if a spark of spirit lives in the defence : and the Infantry and gunners in this case were as firm as rocks.

But, even in making this imaginary contrast—for neither South Africa nor Manchuria provides any historical contrast—beware of assuming too much. The Boers had first to drive back and overthrow an extended skirmishing screen of mounted troops. They could not have done this in dense formation. Nor could steel-armed Cavalry have done it. Beware, then, of assuming that these latter, in virtue of their hybrid character, could effect a tactical transformation in the midst of a rapid, loose action, where each second was of importance, and close up for shock at the psychological moment. This is not even practised in peace manœuvres. It was never done in war, and never will be done in war, not so much from the purely mechanical difficulties as from the sudden and total change of spirit required. Wrangel, whom I have quoted before on this point, is right.* The modern horseman cannot serve two masters so different

* *Vide supra*, p. 41.

as the rifle and the steel weapon. He must serve one
faithfully or fail towards both. We profess to secure
" thorough efficiency " in both, an unattainable ideal.

4. *Fire from the Saddle.*—This, for the most part, was
unaimed or but roughly aimed, and probably did but
little damage to the stationary part of the defence, though
the Yeomanry, who had 60 casualties out of 150 men,
must have lost appreciably in the course of their rout from
more or less aimed saddle-fire. But the moral effect, in
this case, and in all cases, was the best justification of the
practice. Contrast the " terror " of cold steel, which has
so little reality in actual war. Here was the moral effect
of a really terrible weapon, materializing, before the phase
of contact, in bullets which sang over or impinged among
the defence, confusing aim and sighting.

In regard to the purely physical effect, note, especially
for future reference, the opening for aimed or unaimed
saddle-fire against horses, whether in the course of a
pursuit of mounted men like the pursuit of the screen
at Vlakfontein, or against groups of " held " horses in
rear of a position, when a few chance bullets may cause
a stampede.

5. *Formation.*—We have no special details as to
Vlakfontein, but I infer from the narratives that the Boers
charged in a very rough line with fairly wide intervals.
Second and third lines were a later development. Formations, intervals, speed, points for dismounting, etc.,
were dictated, and always must be dictated, by local
circumstances. They admit of no rigid rules.

To resume our historical survey, we find the Boers of
the Eastern Transvaal charging again under Viljoen at
Mooifontein (May 25, 1901), against a convoy column,
very ably and steadily handled by Colonel Gallwey.
Though Viljoen's attacks failed, it is to be noted that he
suffered little loss.

Then comes a long gap of four months, during which

the drought of the South African winter compelled the
Boers to remain for the most part on the defensive.   At
the end of September, 1901, with the first spring grass,
Botha took the field for the raid on Natal to which I
have already alluded.   His first contact with British
troops came at Blood River Poort (September 17), near
the Natal frontier, and 100 miles from his starting-point
in the Eastern Transvaal.   Here by a skilful stratagem
he decoyed into an exposed position* a body of 300
mounted riflemen, and then, charging down on their flank
in one lightning stroke, put out of action nearly 50 men,
captured 3 guns, and forced a general surrender within
ten minutes.   Curiously enough, our own force, when
the calamity happened, had just attempted something
in the nature of a charge, in order to overwhelm the
small Boer detachment which was acting as decoy—not
a charge " home," but a rapid ride over open ground into
close range.   They had just dismounted to open fire
when Botha fell on them.   The incident shows how useless
mere audacity and dash are, unless founded on careful
reconnaissance.

We paid dearly for the hesitations and delays which
marked our attempts to envelop Botha on his long and
perilous return journey from Natal.   He had held from
the first, and maintained to the last, a moral ascendency
which took effect at the end of October (a fortnight after
his return), in one of the most remarkable Boer successes
of the guerilla war, and in one of the chief examples of
the charge.   This was at Bakenlaagte on October 30,
1901.†   At this time Colonel Benson was operating
independently in the midst of the " high veld " of the
Eastern Transvaal.   His vigorous night raids upon
laagers (alluded to in the previous chapter) had ex-

* This is probably the explanation of what happened. See *Times*
History, vol. v., pp. 339-340.

† *Times* History, vol. v., pp. 360-376.

asperated the burghers to the last degree.   Long on the
look-out for vengeance, they seized upon Botha's return
to make an appeal to him for co-operation.   Botha, at
the moment, was seventy miles away to the east.   By
forced marching, rapid and thoroughly screened, he
appeared on the field of Bakenlaagte at exactly the right
moment, bringing a reinforcement whose strength must
be regarded as doubtful, but which, at the utmost,
did not exceed 500.*   Probably the whole Boer force
on the field was about 1,000.   Benson's total strength
was 1,600 riflemen, of whom 650 were Infantry, and 6
guns.

The tactical and topographical conditions were closely
similar to those of Vlakfontein.   At 2 p.m. a rear-
guard of 380 mounted riflemen (this time seasoned
soldiers of the regular Mounted Infantry, Scottish Horse,
etc.), a company of Infantry, and 2 guns, were retiring
towards camp.   Other mounted detachments and guns
were still out on the flanks.   The main body of Infantry
were either in camp or on their way to it.   The weather
was wet and misty, the terrain open and undulating.
While demonstrating vigorously all round the perimeter
of defence, Botha ordered a charge against the rear-guard.
The Boers, shouting and firing from the saddle, swept over
a mile and a half of ground, overwhelming the company
of Infantry, catching and capturing the rearmost, or
" covering " sections of mounted riflemen, and stopped
just short of the crest of an elevation, afterwards known
as Gun Hill, where the guns and the remainder of the
mounted riflemen had hurriedly taken post.   Here the
Boers flung themselves from their ponies, and engaged
our men at close quarters (barely thirty yards distance)
on foot.   The resistance they met with was magnifi-

* This was our own Intelligence estimate.   General Botha, in a
recent visit to London, informed me that to the best of his recollection
he brought no more than 250.

cent. The defending force had to be almost literally exterminated before the hill was won and the guns captured.

This action reveals in a pointed way the gulf which divides *arme blanche* charges from rifle charges. In the former you must charge *home*, at all costs, and whatever the nature of the ground. There is no place in the *arme blanche* scheme for an assault like that at Bakenlaagte, where the Boers, with instinctive dexterity and rapidity, converted themselves in a flash from horsemen into footmen at the right place and moment, using the dead ground at the foot of Gun Hill for the protection of their horses during the fire-fight. When the charge began I do not suppose that one of them knew under what conditions of ground it would end. The ridge was of gentle gradient and of unobstructed surface, but, supposing that it had been of a sharp gradient and encumbered with boulders, these conditions would have made but little difference to the efficacy of the foot-attack, and might very well have assisted it. To an *arme blanche* charge they would have been fatal. (*Cf.* the Dronfield incident, p. 113.) The same principle will hold good in every sort of future war, and particularly in European wars, where open, undulating plains like those of the " high veld " are extremely rare. To one opportunity for an *arme blanche* charge there will be a hundred for rifle charges.

An intermediate example of charging, which illustrates this point about ground, was given at the small, but sad episode of Tafel Kop in the Free State (December 20, 1901), where the crest of the hill on which our troops (90 men and 3 guns) were posted, was in fact steep, boulder-strewn, and impracticable for horses.*

The Eastern Transvaalers are found charging again with damaging effect in the actions of Holland (December 19, 1901), and Bank Kop (January 4, 1902).† The

---

* *Times* History, vol. v., pp. 423-427.   † *Ibid.*, pp. 455-458.

latter was the case of a counter-charge under circumstances very similar to those of Blood River Poort.   Their last exploit of this nature was on April 1, 1902, at Boschman's Kop, the only occasion, I think, during the guerilla war where regular Cavalry (though unequipped with steel weapons) were concerned.   The regiment, 312 strong, with 40 National Scouts, in the course of a night raid, stumbled upon a concentration of about 800 Boers (I cannot guarantee the numbers, but give the maximum estimate), who had gathered together to discuss the question of peace.   The surprise for the moment was complete, and the Boers scattered in all directions ; but rallied later in considerable force and engaged the Cavalry, who had retired to a position about a mile away.   The attack was vehement, with frequent charges into close range, which were repelled with equal gallantry.   At last the Cavalry flank was turned, and our men had to retire. As long as defensible positions were available the retreat was steady and methodical, but the last few miles to camp were a dead-level plain, over which pursuers and pursued rode as hard as they could, until reinforcements and Artillery fire from the British camp checked the Boers.   In the whole affair, which was galling, but not in the least discreditable to the Cavalry, they had seventy-seven casualties, and there is no question that a considerable number of men succumbed to saddle-fire during the pursuit whom no steel weapon could have reached. The complaint, it is said, was raised by some of those present that they had been crippled by the removal of their swords, and that if they had carried them the result would have been different.   The regiment had only recently arrived in South Africa : otherwise the mere hint of such a complaint would make one despair of reform.   During something like a year and three-quarters of war the Cavalry had had countless opportunities—if they existed—of showing the superior value of the *arme blanche* in first producing and then taking advantage of circumstances tactically similar to these. The point is, that it was impossible to force the Boers to accept combat on the terms required by steel. It was the rifle which settled the nature of combats. The Boers had conducted the original fire-fight in loose formation, and they pursued in loose " swarm " formation. Consider the futility of our endeavouring, at any phase, to mass into shock formation, with nothing whatever upon which to exert shock, only to present a helplessly vulnerable target. If we did not form close shock formation, we abandoned, as I have repeatedly pointed out, the whole *raison d'être* of the steel weapon. Individual swordsmen, separated by wide intervals, are outmatched by capable riflemen, mounted or dismounted. It is a cruel injustice to our Cavalry to teach them otherwise.

De la Rey's district, the Western Transvaal, may be considered as having been the true birthplace of the charge, and it was here, during the last period of the war, that it reached its highest development. At Kleinfontein* (October 24, 1901) Kemp galloped down upon the centre of a column on the march, threw the convoy into confusion, and captured a dozen waggons, then whirled down upon the rear-guard, and inflicted severe loss upon it, taking temporary possession of two guns, which, for lack of teams, the burghers were unable to remove. The remnants of our men made a splendid resistance, and reinforcements eventually drove the Boers off. In this action we find the first mention of the use of successive lines of horsemen for charging.

At Yzer Spruit (February 25, 1902) De la Rey ambuscaded and captured entire a convoy-column, using the mounted charge freely at the crisis of the action ; and ten days later, at the sad disaster of Tweebosch (March 7, 1902), the same General (using three successive charging lines)

* *Times* History, vol. v., pp. 383-384.

routed Methuen's mounted troops, who in this case were of a very heterogeneous and unstable kind, and forced a general surrender of the column.   In the stirring action of Boschbult (March 31, 1902), the defeat of part of our flank screen by a determined Boer charge caused for a short time an exceedingly critical situation.   Later in the day, when Cookson's force was concentrated and entrenched, Liebenberg led a plucky charge against some farm-buildings adequately held by riflemen.   This was a daring departure from the rules governing such attacks, and Liebenberg paid for it in a sharp repulse.*

But the most dramatic and interesting of the Boer charges was reserved for the last important action of the war, that of Roodewal (April 11, 1902).   It failed, but the cause, manner, and results of its failure are full of instruction.   I wish I had space to recount the episode in full ; but I can only sketch what happened, and ask the reader to refer for a full account to chapter xix. (section iv.) of the fifth volume of the *Times* History.

One of our great mobile driving lines of the latest model, organized in three divisions, each about 4,000 strong, under the command of General Ian Hamilton, was sweeping on an immense front across the Western Transvaal.   On the early morning of April 10, the right division, under Colonel Kekewich, about 4,000 strong and composed of two columns under Colonels Grenfell and Von Donop, was changing ground to the right (or west) in accordance with orders to widen the front of the driving line prior to the day's operations.   The columns were still in closed-up route formation, Von Donop's leading, Grenfell's following, with an advanced screen of 280 mounted riflemen thrown out to the front. Terrain, a level, open plain rising almost imperceptibly for

* *Times* History, vol. v. : Yzer Spruit, pp. 498-500 ; Tweebosch, pp. 501-508 ; Boschbult, pp. 520-522.

about two miles to a gentle elevation on the farm-lands
of Roodewal. Kemp had concentrated in the course
of the night behind this elevation, and at about 7.30 a.m.
was sighted, by our foremost scouts, marching parallel.
Whether, when the action first began, he knew of the
massed British columns, is not clear. Probably he did
not. There is ground for the view that he had mistaken
our advanced mounted screen for the flank of a driving
line already fully deployed for the day's drive in the
manner then customary, and had resolved to roll up part
of this supposed line by a flank-charge.

However this may be, he deployed and put into motion
a number of men variously estimated from 1,000 to
1,500, who, in widely extended order, trotted slowly
forward in two very long, arc-shaped lines. As they
approached our advanced scouts, they broke into a
canter, and began to fire from the saddle. Our screen
and the pompom with it retired hastily upon the main
body, some forty men being caught and overpowered.
The crest of Roodewal once topped, the main British
forces, in column of route about a mile and a half away,
became visible to the Boers and the Boers to them.
Grenfell executed a hurried but fairly orderly deployment to meet the attack, which was directed mainly
against his column. The South African Constabulary,
Scottish Horse and Yeomanry—about 1,200 mounted
men in all—were thrown out in a rough defensive line.
Von Donop was slower in deployment, but had to meet
only the northerly part of the Boer line, which split off
and attempted a wider and more normal and deliberate
attack. The centre and right—estimated roughly at
800 men—closed in, corrected the convexity of their
line with wonderful precision, and with the brave Commandant Potgieter at their head, charged straight upon
Grenfell. In an episode lasting so few minutes, and
crammed with such breathless excitement, it is impossible

to ascertain relative strength, positions, and formations with positive accuracy ; but it may be taken as fairly correct to say that when the charge reached a point 600 yards from the British front, it was exposed to the fire of some 1,500 rifles and 6 guns, and that the Boer formation—at any rate, in portions of the line—was now very close—some say almost solid, or " knee to knee "— and from two to four deep.   The pace at this stage, we infer, was the best the small Boer ponies could ever attain to, and that amounted to little more than the canter of a Cavalry horse.   The plain would not have sheltered a mouse, and it was a clear day with a bright sun.   Under these conditions it would have been strange if the charge had not been checked, high and wild as much of our fire was.   It faltered appreciably within 300 yards, and stumbled on in fragments to within 100 yards.   Potgieter was shot dead only 70 yards from our line.

The significant thing was not the failure of this piece of brilliant recklessness, but that it came so near success, and met with so little punishment.   The Boers retired without disorder, carrying some of their wounded with them, and leaving on the field fifty dead and thirty badly wounded men.   Our own losses, besides prisoners taken from the advanced screen, were seven killed and fifty-six wounded, mainly by fire from the saddle, and from those figures the reader may judge of the moral effect of this form of fire, coupled with the spectacle of the charge, in baulking the aim of the defence.   It is safe to say that one casualty inflicted in this way has as much moral effect as three inflicted by men on foot.   But in the physical sphere there was another important effect of saddle-fire.   Grenfell's column lost, partly from this cause, no less than 150 horses. Many more stampeded.   In other words, the column for the time being was demobilized, and deprived of any possibility of a counter-stroke, though a more fruitful opportunity for a counter-stroke can scarcely be imagined.* The weak points in this charge are apparent. The cardinal factor—surprise—high as it was, was not high enough to counteract the vulnerability due to comparatively low speed, in good light, over a bare plain ; and the excessively close formation aggravated this vulnerability. Formation, of course, admits of no dogmatic rules. There is no insuperable objection to a dense line, if the surprise is great enough to justify it, and if, when close quarters are reached, the line is not so dense as to strike too small an area or impede that free use of the rifle on foot which is the object of the charge.

It is never easy to picture an *arme blanche* charge in direct analogy to any given rifle charge, because the *arme blanche* never creates for itself the opportunities which the rifle creates ; but so far as we can picture an analogy at Roodewal, the advantage is overwhelmingly on the side of the rifle. Saddle-fire, with its power of demobilizing the defence long before contact, is a decisive advantage. But would an *arme blanche* charge ever have taken place ? It is very doubtful. " Cavalry Training " appears to make provision for a charge over a distance as great as 1,800 yards, but that is for a shock charge against " Cavalry," who are assumed to be in their saddles (pp. 125-128). What of a charge against Infantry ? In the ten lines devoted to that subject (p. 129) there is a very natural silence on this and many other points. But were these men of Grenfell's to be regarded as Cavalry or Infantry ? They had horses, deployed with them and dismounted from them. Suppose them Cavalry (in the Cavalry sense) who at the last moment declined to engage in the conventional " shock duel," and, having brought the charge to a standstill by rifle-fire, and having retained their full mobility owing to the absence of hostile

* An hour and a half later a general pursuit was begun by all three divisions. It went on for eighteen miles, and resulted in the capture of three guns and thirty burghers.

saddle-fire, retaliated with a counter-stroke ? But that is not the only perplexity. How were the leaders of the shock charge to know in advance which course the defending troops would take ? They must decide before starting, for there is no provision in " Cavalry Training " for changing while in rapid movement from dense shock formation to the " extended formation " recommended for a charge upon " Infantry." If a charge is not a steel-charge they are bound by the rules of " Dismounted Action," under which heading, of course, this rifle charge of the Boers would have to be included. One of these rules is that extra ammunition is to be served out when such action is contemplated. Another point : Whichever formation, dense or extended, was adopted at the outset, Grenfell's advanced scouting screen, whose inrush was accountable for a good deal of wild firing in the defence, would have had little to fear against horsemen using only a steel weapon. They had only to transform themselves into " Infantry," and let the storm blow over. Acting as skilfully as the Boers at Poplar Grove and many other actions, they would have stopped the charge altogether. For the rest, whatever the weapon relied on in the charge, the vulnerability of the surface exposed was the same and the chance of obtaining contact, judged on a purely physical estimate, no better or worse. On possibilities after hypothetical contact I need scarcely again enlarge. There would have been nothing in the firing-line on which to exert true shock, and palpably men who are doomed to stay in the saddle and execute complicated and difficult " rallies " are worse off than riflemen on foot. The latter, taught not to fear cold steel, and acting as directed in " Infantry Training," are in the superior position. My argument is not academical. It is based on the living facts of modern war.

Such were the principal examples on the Boer side of

the mounted charge. But they do not exhaust the list. There were numerous cases—in the Free State especially (as I remarked above)—of charges for the purpose of piercing driving lines or block-house lines, interesting, if only for the light they throw on the effect of fire upon horsemen in rapid movement. Nor must it ever be forgotten that, in the parlance of mounted riflemen, the "charge" is only a relative term, which does not necessarily imply contact. The more rapid the tactical approach, by a more daring use of the horse, the greater the approximation to the fully developed charge.

These incidents have received far too little attention. Cavalry writers have generally ignored them, or alluded to them in terms of indifference, as curious phenomena in a class of war which scarcely concerns Cavalry. Mr. Goldman, in the 1909 edition of his translation of Von Bernhardi's "Cavalry in Future Wars," in the course of a gentle rebuke to his author for venturing to admire these charges, disposes of them in a footnote as the work of mere "Mounted Infantry," and reveals his imperfect acquaintance with the facts by speaking of the "*one or two occasions*" on which Boers "brought about a decision by rifle-fire from their horses" (p. 56). He adds, with unconscious irony, that "he can recall no instance where they actually charged—*i.e.*, endeavoured to decide the action by *shock*." Those few words, embodied in their complacent little footnote, supply a complete revelation of the mental attitude of the *arme blanche* advocates towards the tactics of mounted riflemen. Names are everything, results nothing. Attach the label, "Mounted Infantry," and that disposes of the charges, Boer and British, such as they were, and, since they did not involve "shock," what were they, after all ? It is true that throughout the whole war there was not one solitary instance of "shock" in Mr. Goldman's implied (and, in this single case, perfectly correct) interpretation of that term.   But what matter ?   In his view, the Boers never gave the Cavalry a chance of "discharging Cavalry duties."   Was I wrong in suggesting that the *arme blanche* theory dwells in a mental shrine, sacrosanct, unapproachable by argument ?

Of a diametrically opposite character, and no less harmful than this contemptuous indifference, is the idea— often enough expressed by those who have never studied them—that these charges were non-military exploits, comparable only to the onslaughts of wild dervishes, a blend of fanaticism and luck, and no model for sensible, serious soldiers.   In spite of the fact that saddle-fire is officially enjoined at this moment for " picked men " of the Mounted Infantry, I have heard it spoken of as though it were on a par with the beating of tom-toms, the throwing of stones or poisoned arrows and such unsoldierly pranks.   For ignorance of this sort no condemnation can be too strong.   Even fanatics may teach us lessons.   But the Boers were no more fanatics than the American troopers of Forrest and Morgan.   They were shrewd, sober, white men, valuing their lives, parsimonious of their ammunition, for fresh supplies of which during the guerilla war they had no domestic resources, and by no means inclined to extravagance or foolhardiness.   Their charges demanded not only dash, but high tactical discipline, a sure instinct for ground and skilled preparatory scouting.   Fire from the saddle requires good horsemanship and great manual skill.   If these be symptoms of fanaticism, the more fanatics we have in our army, the better.

And what were the results of these charges upon the progress of the war ?   Whether for their tactical lessons we dismiss them in footnotes or study them seriously, let us remember that they, like other aggressive Boer exploits, cost us many lives, many guns, many prisoners, and an amount of treasure at which we can only dimly conjecture—probably scores of millions of pounds.* Sannah's Post in March, 1900, changed the whole outlook of the Free Staters. To Vlakfontein, coupled with the night attack at Wilmansrust, can be definitely traced the decision of the joint Council of War (held on June 20, 1901), to continue hostilities throughout the winter of that year. But for Bakenlaagte, the Transvaalers, always the most inclined to peace, might have forced their will on the sister state, while De la Rey's successes in the early months of 1902 imperilled gravely the hopes of peace. Had the Roodewal charge, made during the progress of negotiations, succeeded, there might well have been a delay of several more months.

We on our side never succeeded in carrying the charging principle to the point to which the Boer veterans carried it. Saddle-fire was not, I think, in any instance practised. But in aggressive tactical vigour all our mounted men made remarkable strides during the guerilla war, in spite of the somewhat deadening effect of the driving system. The rifle was the inspiration. There was only one instance of an *arme blanche* charge during that period of the guerilla war in which the Cavalry carried steel weapons. This was at Welgevonden (February 12, 1901), in the course of French's great drive in the Eastern Transvaal, when Colonel Rimington's Inniskilling Dragoons got home among a Boer rear-guard, and disposed of some twenty Boers by death, wounds, or capture.† With this exception, every success we obtained was due to the dashing use of horse and rifle in combination. I have already mentioned the cases of Victoria Nek and Bothaville.

* Between May, 1901, and April, 1902, nine principal charging actions cost us 2,500 casualties and prisoners and 18 guns. The war cost about 5½ millions a month.

† *Times* History, vol. v., p. 173.

Wildfontein (March 24, 1901) was an excellent example of an energetic galloping pursuit, leading to the capture of guns, waggons, and a good many Boers. Roodekraal (February 3, 1902) led to similar results, and was distinguished by several genuine mounted charges of the Boer type, in which New Zealanders and Queenslanders, under Colonel Garratt, took part.* The systematized night-raids described in the previous chapter generally ended in something of the nature of a charge, in widely extended order, upon the Boer laager. Other small raids, pursuits and encounters, in which our men learnt to ride more boldly into rifle-range, were innumerable.

As I have often pointed out, this bold riding into a fire-zone is the principle which lies at the back of the charge. It is a question of tactical mobility, pure and simple. How far the ride can be carried rests on local circumstances, on the degree of surprise, on the nature of the ground to be traversed, on the quality of the enemy's troops, on their tactical disposition, and on the character of their defences, if any. But the whole scheme of offensive tactics is one ; the object, however attained, is always the same—to use the horse as the means of closing with the enemy as effectively as possible and as quickly as possible. Infantry, without the horse, pursue the same object. They move more slowly, but present less vulnerable surface. The horseman's problem is to neutralize greater vulnerability by greater speed and a larger measure of surprise. If we review the war as a whole, we cannot escape the conclusion that until the last year of hostilities the vulnerability of horses in rapid movement was exaggerated by both sides, and the effect produced upon the sighting, aim, fire-discipline, and equanimity of the defence underestimated. In our own case the error was aggravated by the fact that we came to the

* *Times* History, vol. v., p. 226, Wildfontein ; p. 475, Rocdekraal.

field possessing the tradition of a mounted charge, but in an obsolete form, inspired by the wrong weapon, and incapable of being associated with the right weapon —the rifle. This tradition was destroyed, and never adequately replaced. Outside the charmed circle of the Cavalry it was often too readily assumed that a principle had been discredited, not merely the false application of a right principle. Inside the Cavalry, whatever the various impressions of the time, the net official result now is to regard the tradition of shock as intact, and its failure in South Africa as a negligible incident of an " abnormal " war. The Boers started the war with no tradition, with a strong prejudice, indeed, against the exposure of the horse and an exaggerated reliance on the spade for passive defence and on stalking for offence. Their discipline, moreover, was not good enough for a form of tactics requiring exceptional discipline. Circumstances, moral and military, drove them to develop tactical discipline, and with it a charging tradition, and they attained it in a perfectly healthy, normal way. Our mounted men, Cavalry included, in so far as they approached the Boer standard, worked on the same lines of natural evolution.

Perhaps I ought to say one word more in regard to one of the strangest of the many paradoxical arguments which the defence of the *arme blanche* has evoked. I mean the complaint which I commented on *à propos* of Boschman's Kop—that the Cavalry were deprived of steel weapons just when the Boers were developing the charge, the assumption being, presumably, that but for this modification of armament the Cavalry would then for the first time have developed equally effective, if not more effective, *arme blanche* charging tactics of their own. I have never seen this view put forward in general terms by any high Cavalry authority, or, indeed, by any Cavalryman ; but it figures among the nebulous popular argu-

ments upon which the *arme blanche* thrives, and it sometimes finds accidental public expression. In July, 1909,
an anonymous correspondent of the *Times* propounded
it as a final and crushing answer to those who ventured to
see something instructive and important in the Boer
charges. Now, in the first place, the view is in conflict
with the facts. The Boers began to charge long before
the steel weapons were discarded. They charged at
Sannah's Post as early as March, 1900, and within view
of the Cavalry engaged in that action. They charged
mounted riflemen and attacked Cavalry with great perti-
nacity in the Eastern Transvaal during October, 1900;
and although no body of Cavalry was, so far as I know,
itself charged on horseback by Boers during the year 1901,
the steel weapon outlived the period of Vlakfontein, and
had not, I think, been more than partly abolished at the
period of Bakenlaagte. But dates are not material. The
discouraging feature of the argument is its total failure
to grasp the real nature and origin of the rifle charge, the
elementary physical and moral principles which distinguish it in tactical form, and, above all, in tactical
spirit, from the shock charge. And behind it, I am afraid,
we recognize an echo of Mr. Goldman's complaint that
the Boers, owing to fear of the steel, declined to " give
battle " with Cavalry on " open ground." I cannot
pause now to discuss that.*

We need not exaggerate, as assuredly we must not
minimize, the importance of the mounted charges in
South Africa. We must allow for the fact that the Boers
for the most part were veterans in the mounted rifleman's
art, and that the men against whom they were matched
never reached the same degree of excellence. What we
should do is to grasp the principle, and apply it to the
training of our mounted troops, especially to our professional troops, who are competent to learn anything to

* " With French in South Africa," p. 423. *Vide infra*, p. 285.

17—2

which they apply their minds and wills. Shock, at any rate, is gone. South Africa gave it its death-blow, and Manchuria, as I shall show later, buried it for ever. The rifle charge, whether on foot, mounted, or in any intermediate stage up to direct riding into contact, remains as a proved, tangible fact. Since 1870 and up to the present day (1910) shock has been pure theory.

CHAPTER XII

A PECULIAR WAR?

Such are the facts of the South African War, our only great war since the Crimea, and the first serious test for the whole world of the smokeless magazine rifle. What results can we place to the credit of the *arme blanche*?

1. The pursuit at *Elandslaagte* (October 21, 1899), on the second day of hostilities : Boers killed, wounded, and prisoners, say fifty. (No figures are forthcoming, but I think fifty is on the safe side.)

2. *Klip Drift* (February 15, 1900) : A " penetrating," semi-aggressive charge, in widely extended order, by a very large force, with a big backing of Infantry and Artillery, through a gap in a small hostile skirmishing screen. Boer casualties about fifteen.

3. *Diamond Hill* (June 11, 1900) : Two brave but insignificant little charges, which received as much punishment as they gave. Boer casualties about seventeen.

4. *Welgevonden* (February 12, 1901) : A small charge in the open. Boer casualties and prisoners about twenty.

Not a single example of true shock.

This gives a record of about a hundred casualties and prisoners due directly to the *arme blanche*. There may, no doubt, have been a few others in unrecorded episodes. To be well on the safe side, let us put the total at 200. All the other damage inflicted by the Cavalry, whether in offence or defence, was inflicted through the agency of the carbine or rifle. The opportunities lost through over-training in the steel and inexperience in the firearm are beyond computation.

With the exception of an unknown, but certainly small, proportion of casualties caused by Artillery, all the other losses in action, British and Boer, during the war were caused by the rifle, and all of our own casualties, close upon 30,000 in number, were (with the same exception) inflicted by mounted riflemen.

From the first to the last day of the war the rifle dominated every encounter, small or great, Elandslaagte and the rest included. Awaking finally to this fact, but at least a year too late, we converted our Cavalry into mounted riflemen. Every possible function and every possible species of encounter which mounted men can conceivably undertake in any war was illustrated again and again. In reconnaissance, in raids, in protective work and independent work, in pursuit and retreat, in battle and out of battle, acting as divisions, brigades, regiments, squadrons, troops, patrols, or as single scouts, the Cavalry were submitted to every sort of test during more than two and a half years. All our other mounted troops and all the Boer troops were submitted to similar tests. Out of it all emerges the single type of mounted rifleman, competent to do all duties alike, and incapable of doing any of them well unless he is as skilled in the rifle as he is on the horse—competent, too, if required, to perform functions never before dreamt of by any European Cavalry— to make, hold, and storm entrenchments, and to take his place in the main line of battle.

Here is a mass of evidence, vast, various, cogent. For the last time, I ask, was the war " peculiar "? Of course it was peculiar. Every war is peculiar. Terrain differs, races differ, degrees of civilization and stamps of military organization differ, quarrels and aims differ, aptitudes and temperaments differ, and, lastly, with the progress of science, weapons differ. That brings us to the point—

the only point relevant to our inquiry : Were the peculiarities of the Boer War such as to invalidate the conclusions developed in its course as to the armament and
tactics of mounted troops ?

Even that way of putting the question is a little too
wide. In Great Britain, at any rate, one big conclusion
is admittedly valid for all future wars—namely, that the
Cavalry must carry a good rifle, not a bad carbine, and
must be able to use it with far more freedom and skill
than they ever dreamed of before the war. We have got
that far, and stopped. Shrinking from anything radical,
taking refuge in compromise, we have fashioned in theory,
and only in theory, an ideal hybrid, perfect both in
shock and the rifle, and given him the formula for a
hybrid " Cavalry spirit," which is quoted at the beginning
of this volume. But—and this reservation is vital—
we have taught him in " Cavalry Training " to rely
mainly on shock and the " terror of cold steel," which
" nothing can replace."

That settles the final form of our question : Were the
peculiarities of the war such as to justify the re-establish-
ment of the lance and sword in their old position as the
dominant weapons of Cavalry ? Remember the proved
penalties of error, if error there be—the extra weight
and extra visibility of equipment, when every additional
ounce of weight and every additional inch of vulnerable
and visible surface tells, to say nothing of the complications, moral and physical, caused by allegiance to two
diametrically opposite tactical ideals and tactical systems.

The answer we shall give to the question carries with it
answers to many more. Are we justified in reverting to
exactly the same old view of " Mounted Infantry " as
existed before the war, and which the war, regarded as
an episode by itself, reduced to ridicule ? Was the war
so abnormal that we are still in our handbook of " Mounted
Infantry Training " to lay down, foremost among the

purposes for which that arm is to be employed, the purpose of " forming a pivot of manœuvre for Cavalry, of supporting them generally with their fire, and . . . of giving to the Cavalry such Infantry support, when they are acting at a distance from other troops, as will prevent the necessity of the Cavalry regiments being employed in any other capacity than that of their purely Cavalry rôle."* Prodigious indeed must be the abnormalities which would warrant the fresh enunciation of such a " general principle " ! Note the words " Infantry support," both in their context and in connection with the opening paragraph of the handbook, to the effect that " Mounted Infantry are Infantry soldiers governed in their tactical employment by the principles of Infantry training." Substitute the synonymous word " riflemen " for " Infantry " in the three cases where the latter word is used, and there is, indeed, a substratum of very sound truth in the proposition. But it is truth which would be heresy to the authorities. For them, apparently, it was Infantry who, under British leading, relieved Mafeking, charged at Bothaville and Roodekraal, pursued at the Biggarsberg and Wildfontein, saved the guns at Sannah's Post, and scouted, raided, and screened everywhere. It must have been Infantry, moreover, disguised as Cavalry, who held the Colesberg lines, intercepted Cronje on the Modder, and ran to earth Lotter ; Infantry, under Boer leading, who captured a third of the main army's transport at Waterval, intervened brilliantly at the climax of the battle of Paardeberg, ambuscaded and pursued at Sannah's Post, raided Cape Colony, Natal, and

* I am quite aware that under present arrangements our Mounted Infantry are allotted the duties of Divisional Cavalry, but this circumstance does not affect the general principles laid down for their action, which remain the same, and postulate the inferiority of mounted troops without steel weapons. The contradiction in terms exhibited by the nomenclature only serves to emphasize the confusion of thought involved.

the railway communications, and charged at Bakenlaagte and Roodewal. Was the war really so peculiar as to warrant such grotesque inferences as these ? Was a war which produced not a single example of true shock so peculiar as to justify the vague and unintelligible instructions to Yeomanry—namely, that they are to be " so trained as to be capable of performing all the duties allotted to Cavalry except those connected with shock action "? And what of our mounted forces overseas ? Suppose a war on Colonial soil against a European army —to my mind a far more likely contingency than a war on European soil—suppose (merely for the sake of argument) such a war in South Africa, where we should be aided both by Dutch and British mounted troops. Was the great war of 1899-1902 so peculiar as to warrant our telling the Boer troops or the Imperial Light Horse that they are not fit " to discharge Cavalry duties " ?

There is a big case, an authoritative case, an overwhelmingly convincing case, founded on a reasoned analysis of the campaign, to be made out here by the advocates of the *arme blanche* if they are to justify existing practice. When, where, and by whom has this authoritative case been presented ? I am at a loss to say. Directly we begin to grapple with this allegation of abnormality we find we are fighting with phantoms, with nebulous, elusive, and often mutually contradictory arguments held, some by one person, some by another. I scarcely know how far I need engage in this ghostly conflict. I have exhorted the reader from the first, in following my review of the war, to picture for himself parallel situations in a European war, distinguishing relevant from irrelevant peculiarities, and, without being led astray by mere names and labels, to test weapons and the tactical theories based on them by facts. I have endeavoured to assist him by analysis and comment, and I believe at one time or another I have dealt with every abnormality which is alleged to quash the verdict against the *arme blanche*. But I am not sanguine enough to hope that I have carried conviction, and I venture now to deal once more in a separate chapter with the allegation as a whole. In order to narrow the controversy within incontestably sound and fair limits, I will take the three powerful advocates of the *arme blanche* to whom I alluded in my first chapter, and from whom I have since frequently quoted—General Sir John French, Mr. Goldman, and General von Bernhardi. The last we may regard as the most powerful of all, since his book, " Cavalry in Future Wars," translated by Mr. Goldman, and furnished with an introduction by General French, is not only described by the latter officer as being the last word of logic and wisdom on all Cavalry matters without exception, but has been largely drawn upon in practice by the compilers of our own " Cavalry Training."

In General French's long and warmly written introduction, levelled avowedly against the " misleading conclusions " of those who criticize shock, only one short passage is to be found in which the South African War—our own great war—is so much as alluded to, and then only to be dismissed with a shrug of the shoulders as almost irrelevant to the controversy. Both the allusion and its context are, I am afraid, rather obscure, so I give the paragraph in full :

" In dwelling so persistently upon the necessity for Cavalry being trained to the highest possible pitch to meet the enemy's Cavalry, I do not wish to be misunderstood. I agree absolutely with the author in the principle he lays down that the Cavalry fight is only a means to an end, but it is the most important means, and I have thought it right to comment upon this because it is a principle which in this country, since the South African War, we have been very much inclined to overlook. *To place a force of Cavalry in the field in support of a great army which is deficient in the power to overcome the opposing Cavalry,* is to act like one who would despatch a squadron of war-vessels badly armed, badly trained, and ill-found, to blockade a distant coast-line defended by a powerful fleet.   What is the naval fight in the open sea but a means to an end ?   It would be as sensible to dwell on the inutility and waste of a duel between hostile fleets as to lay down the principle that the ' Cavalry battle ' in no way affects the mutual situation of hostile armies " (p. 26).

Sincerely desirous of understanding the General's meaning, I confess that this passage baffles me, and I scarcely know what it would convey to a reader fresh from the study of our war.   Do the words which I have italicized imply that the non-Cavalry portion of our " great army," the Infantry and Artillery, were not worthy of the " support " of our Cavalry, and denied that arm a chance of distinguishing itself in the " Cavalry fight "—that is, presumably the shock fight ?   That cannot be the sense intended, for the imputation not only would never be made by General French, but is in itself indefensible.   I need not argue that proposition again.   If any narrative of the war does not disprove it to the most cursory reader, my previous narrative and comments would add no further conviction.

We must arrive at some other interpretation ; and yet there seems to be no other that does not involve the writer in self-refutation.   Read literally, the sentence compares " a force of Cavalry " (sent out under the circumstances described) to a squadron of war-vessels badly armed, badly trained, and ill-found, while the unequal naval fight with the " great fleet," which results, is intended surely to be analogous to the " Cavalry fight." Both are " means to an end "—in the one case to landing and invasion, in the other to the destruction of a hostile army.   In the last sentence the simile becomes more precise, the " duel " between hostile fleets being expressly likened to the " Cavalry battle," and very aptly likened, if we do not assume with General French that the Cavalry battle must inevitably be a shock battle. It is true that in the case of the South African War the simile is impaired by the fact that the " opposing Cavalry," constituting as they did the entire hostile force, cannot be regarded as the counterpart of our Cavalry. But, disregarding that material point, where does the simile lead us ? To the conclusion that our Cavalry were badly armed, badly trained, and ill-found. That is admittedly true of armament and training ; for the rifle has been permanently substituted for the carbine, and " thorough efficiency " in its use officially enjoined ever since, while the steel weapon, during the war, failed. " Ill-found " might refer to horses. But the General, as the context shows, does not mean to take this dangerous line of argument. Who, then, were the troops referred to ? No part of the army was " ill-found " by comparison with the Boers, who in most of the resources possessed by great and wealthy nations were miserably ill-found, and were reduced for the last year to destitution. " Badly armed," except in the case of the Cavalry, is another misnomer. The Infantry were armed with the best modern rifle, and although the Artillery at first found their guns outranged, they soon received the aid of naval and other heavy guns, and always had an overwhelming numerical superiority over the Boers. " Badly trained " does, indeed, apply in a certain sense to the whole army, particularly to its practical organization for war. But it applies, too, to the Boers, and in the latter respect far more pertinently.

I have no desire idly to split straws. If the passage I have quoted formed part of a reasoned argument for the abnormality of our great war, I agree that it would be unfair to make too much of a case of obscure exposition. But it stands alone, and I am justified in criticizing the attitude of mind which permits so high a Cavalry authority

as General French, in an essay part of which is explicitly
directed against the advocates of mounted riflemen, to
treat so vaguely and superficially the great national
struggle which, for the time being, at any rate, did confirm their views. My justification is the greater in that
such an attitude of mind is strictly typical of a great
number of the adherents of the shock system. Pressed,
they are altogether unable to put into precise language
their reasons for disregarding the Boer War. In a later
chapter, when dealing with the Manchurian War, I shall
have to refer to General French's equally inadequate
treatment of the theme of another case of abnormality.

In the meantime I can do no better than take two
propositions from the paragraph quoted above, about
which there can be no doubt. (1) A " Cavalry battle "
without shock is inconceivable to General French. There
must be either shock or no battle, for surely no opponent
of shock would go so far as to argue that, shock being a
thing of the past, it was " inutility and waste " for
opposing sets of mounted troops to fight with one another
at all, in any way ? We have here, in an unusually
extreme form, that theory of the inevitable shock duel
between opposing Cavalries to which I alluded in my
second chapter. It occurs again on page xxii of the
same Introduction.

" How, I ask, can the Cavalry perform its rôle in war until
the enemy's Cavalry is defeated and paralyzed ? I challenge
any Cavalry officer, British or foreign, to deny the principle
that Cavalry, *acting as such against its own arm*, can never
attain complete success unless it is proficient in shock
tactics."

Here is the case complete, but, alas ! strangely qualified
by the words I have italicized. Is there some *arrière-
pensée* here ? What if the hostile Cavalry, like the
Boers, do not believe in shock ? Surely, the case thus

stated begs the whole question at issue. Observe that the underlying axiom is that the steel can always impose tactics on the firearm. Contrast this axiom with the facts of the Boer War, where the Boers were the " opposing Cavalry," and were admittedly strong enough, though in what way we are not told, to throw into prominence the many defects of the great army sent to overcome them. And, by the way, we may remind the General that it *did* overcome them in the end, mainly through the improvisation of mounted riflemen (whom he ignores altogether), and through the assimilation of the Cavalry to that type.

(2) The other clear deduction from the paragraph is this, that the Boers were, on the whole, from whatever cause, a formidable enemy. They are compared to a powerful fleet, and we are represented, in whatever capacity, as suffering from certain weaknesses. That is the general colour of the argument, and I draw the reader's attention to it, because the gist of Mr. Goldman's argument is of a precisely opposite character ; and this contradiction, in one form or another, runs through all the hazy generalizations that one hears expressed in public or private on the topic of abnormality.

To the best of my belief, Mr. Goldman is the only writer who has had the courage to set forth categorically, in the form of a reasoned argument designed expressly to prove the superiority of Cavalry over mounted riflemen, the various grounds for regarding the South African War as abnormal. He does this in his Appendix A. to " With French in South Africa " (1903), and again in his preface to Von Bernhardi's " Cavalry in Future Wars."

Before examining these grounds it is essential to know what Mr. Goldman means by a " mounted rifleman." Here is his appreciation, on page 408 of the former book : " . . . the horseman armed only with a rifle. We may assume that he has received the special Cavalry training aforesaid, and that in every way he is qualified to perform the duties of Cavalry." (I do not know what to make of this curious admission.) "But he is equipped solely to fight on foot. Hence, no sooner does it become necessary for him to assume the offensive than he is forced to dismount, and from that moment his rate of progress depends solely upon the pace he can walk."

Truly, a poor creature ! But we think of South Africa and rub our eyes. Was this the figure cut by mounted riflemen, Boer and British, in South Africa ? It may be said without exaggeration that all the " offensive " mounted work was done by mounted riflemen or by Cavalry acting as such. And think of the charges— Bakenlaagte, for example. At what moment did Botha's men begin to " assume the offensive " ? According to Mr. Goldman, when they " dismounted." And when was that ? Within point-blank range of our guns, after a charge of a mile and a half.

To proceed with the quotation : " Moreover, he has given hostages to fortune. His led horses being an easy prey to a handful of mounted horsemen, he cannot leave them far behind, for, should he lose them, his usefulness for reconnoitring purposes is gone ; the opposing Cavalry will merely push on and through the gap he has left in his screen." We rub our eyes again. When did Boer led horses fall a prey to Cavalry, acting as " Cavalry "? Not in a single instance. As for the idea that the mounted rifleman is handicapped for " reconnoitring purposes "— after all the bitter losses and humiliations from which we suffered in South Africa through imperfect recon- naissance, one can only regard the suggestion with re- spectful amazement. Similarly with the suggestion about " pushing through gaps in screens." This, as I have repeatedly pointed out, is what the Cavalry could *not* do. Their inability to do it was the predominant charac- teristic of all the fighting in which they were engaged—

with one only apparent exception—the Klip Drift
charge, where the screen was not a screen, but an
isolated skirmishing line of 900 men and 2 guns, which
was pierced without shock, and almost without blood-
shed, by 5,000 horsemen, covered by the fire of 56
guns, and supported by a division of Infantry.

To proceed : " It must be remembered that the mounted
rifleman cannot fight on horseback.   He has no weapon
for that purpose, so that his only means of taking the
offensive is to act on foot. . . .   If in open country, the
mounted rifleman cannot hope to meet the Cavalryman
mounted.   In these circumstances he is practically unarmed ; for the firmest believer in the rifle will scarcely
maintain that the rifle-fire of mounted men is a serious
quantity ; anyone who has experienced it knows how
perfectly ineffective it is."   Well, I leave the reader to
judge of the soundness of all this, in view of our experiences in South Africa.   It reads like a dream.   Is it,
to say the least, an adequate treatment of the theme ?
Surely it would be wiser to make some overt reference
to the fine examples of aggressive mobility shown by
our Colonial irregulars, or to the Boer charges, if only for
the sake of proving their negligibility.   This particular
passage may have been written before Mr. Goldman
(whose narrative of the war ends at Komati Poort) had
had full opportunity to study final developments, but his
book was published in 1903 ; he was cognizant when he
wrote, at any rate, of Sannah's Post, and in his preface to,
and notes upon Bernhardi (1906 and 1909), he maintains
an equally icy silence upon the achievements of mounted
riflemen in South Africa, until a passage of warm praise
from Bernhardi himself extorts from him the footnote,
inaccurate as to facts and mistaken in criticism, which
I quoted in the last chapter (p. 254).

I need not pursue this quotation further.   The writer
eventually admits that in an " enclosed country " (what

of the South African terrain ?) the mounted rifleman has a certain value, but the most he will yield is that here the " mounted rifleman and the Cavalryman are on an equality." Truly, an astonishing conclusion ! Surely part of this Appendix must have been written before the war and left unrevised ? Even then the writer was old-fashioned, for the Mounted Infantry Regulations of 1899, while warning that arm in a general way that they " needed the assistance of Cavalry," told them that when they cannot get this assistance, their " best security was to be keeping in broken, intersected, woody, or marshy ground, where they would have a *great advantage over Cavalry.*" It is indisputable that men who spend their whole time in practising rifle-tactics, must be more efficient than men who spend half or more than half their time on shock-tactics. The strange thing is, that Mr. Goldman, in another connection, himself quotes the official warning with approval, as putting the mounted riflemen in their right place. Yet, we may well ask, when in South Africa did mounted riflemen ask for the assistance of Cavalry— that is to say, of Cavalry " as such," to use General French's expression ? How often, on the other hand, did Cavalry, as such, ask for the support of mounted riflemen, as such ?

And these mounted riflemen of ours, who came in so many thousands from so many lands, to do such splendid and such absolutely indispensable work for the Empire ? Not a single allusion to them either in this essay or in the Preface to Bernhardi. Boers alone are used for illustration. Anyone without knowledge of the war would infer that the whole of the mounted work on our side had been done by Cavalry. Nor is the conversion of the Cavalry themselves into mounted riflemen mentioned.

One further question of definition before I proceed to the " peculiarities " of the war. What does Mr. Gold-man mean by " shock "? He does not define it, nor does

" Cavalry Training," wisely enough, attempt a definition ; but under the heading "Shock Action " (p. 410), he adduces as an example of shock the Klip Drift charge, where the Cavalry files were eight yards apart, and the immediate objective of the charge was a sprinkling of extended skirmishers. I should weary the reader if I again exposed this fallacy at length. Shock means impact. This charge was not shock, by any interpretation of that word, nor in the sense in which Bernhardi or any European Cavalry understands it. It was the right pattern of charge, but, as after experience proved, it was essentially the pattern of charge appropriate to mounted riflemen, and it was through blindness to this fundamental difference that the Cavalry never made another like it.

Now for Mr. Goldman's " abnormalities."

1. *Terrain.*— To take this point first, as the least important. Indeed, I scarcely know whether to take it seriously or not. It is rarely expressed elsewhere, and I think Mr. Goldman himself regards it as a desperate resource. After saying, broadly, that " certain physical and local conditions go far to explain why the Cavalry were not more effective with the lance and sabre,"* he complains that the " boundless plains " were " seamed with ridges and watercourses," while " the shock-tactics of Cavalry require open ground free from large obstructions like rocky kopjes, thick bush, and strong fences " (*i.e.*, wire fences, which, as he admits, were easily cut, and in time became no hindrance). But, while condemning, apparently, the whole of the Transvaal, he cautiously admits that in the Free State " the conditions were favourable." Was there ever a more remarkable example of under-statement ? What does he expect ? Where is his ideal battle-ground of the future ? Taken as a whole, South Africa, though its rolling plains were not quite so flat or so free from fences and dongas as the

* " With French in South Africa," p. 422.

plains of Northern Manchuria, may be regarded as one of the most perfect manœuvring grounds for Cavalry which the civilized world contains. Of course, there were " obstructions " even in the most favourable areas, and, of course, these obstructions had a way of coming into prominence when fighting was afoot. Battles are not fought on billiard-tables. One side or the other usually seeks defensible positions. And why should Cavalry complain of irregularities ? How effect surprise on a dead-level plain ? It was by *using* irregularities that mounted riflemen won their most brilliant successes in South Africa. Shock is extinct, precisely because the ground which it imperatively demands makes Cavalry most vulnerable to fire and least capable of surprise.

2. *Bad Condition of Horses and Poor Remounts.*—I dealt with this point in Chapters VI. and VII. The difficulties of the long voyage and acclimatization, and the imperfections of the remount system, are well known. A preventable cause of wastage, careless management and riding, is also scarcely disputed. On the debatable point of over-weight Mr. Goldman, in a separate Appendix, contends that the horses were needlessly over-loaded. All causes together do not explain away tactical facts covering two years. The more closely these facts are scrutinized—even those of actions like Poplar Grove, where the excuse has been most loudly raised—the less adequate the explanation. On inspection it always turns out that the enemy's skill with the firearm, and our own deficiencies in that respect, are the principal cause of imperfect achievement. Where the Cavalry showed skill with the firearm there they obtained their tactical successes, irrespective of the condition of their horses. In the excellent Colesberg operations no complaint was raised about the horses. When were sabres drawn ? Once, but without result, owing to delaying rifle-fire. In the arduous operations for the relief of Kimberley,

when the horses were at their worst, the Cavalry achieved their most important success, by intercepting and containing Cronje.   On the strategical aspect of these operations, the use of lance and sabre, as combatant weapons, had no bearing whatever.   Men do not ride better or quicker for carrying steel weapons ; on the contrary, the extra weight and the habits instilled by the shock theory are a hindrance to mobility.   Tactically, the Cavalry succeeded or failed in proportion to their skilful or unskilful use of carbine and horse combined ; succeeded signally at the Drifts, where they held up Cronje ; failed signally in the pursuit north from Kimberley.   On the Natal side, the Cavalry horses were as fresh at Talana, a case of failure, as at Elandslaagte, the solitary case of a successful charge.   As for Poplar Grove, which Mr. Goldman singles out for illustration, let me give his own words : " How could horses pursue a fleet and mobile enemy after a long day's engagement, in which they had covered forty miles, and had turned the Boers out of position after position ?"   How indeed ?   Does Mr. Goldman seriously expect or demand that in our next war, after four months of hostilities, we shall be provided with super-horses capable of the kind of feat suggested— that is, of beginning a galloping pursuit *after* fighting over forty miles of country ?   But this is a case where the reading of facts makes such a difference.   In point of fact the *conditions of pursuit* began to be present after twelve miles.   The full forty miles can only be arrived at (as I pointed out in my narrative) by counting the unnecessary détours and countermarches caused by failure to break down or ride past trivial flank and rear-guards. In these and many other later operations I have pointed out the intimate connection between horse-wastage and deficiency in direct aggressive power.

From the capture of Bloemfontein to the end of the war the complaint about horses has less and less force.

The remount system, of course, was greatly improved. Although the difficulty of acclimatizing foreign animals was never properly overcome, owing to the ceaselessly voracious demands of the field-columns, horses poured into South Africa from all quarters of the globe at an enormous rate, while no less than 158,000 native South African ponies (exclusive of large numbers captured on the veld) were supplied by the Remount Department. Whatever the condition of the horses from time to time, the tactical incidents are of the same general character. Nor, it need scarcely be added, was the disability confined to the Cavalry. All our mounted troops were similarly affected, and the Boers, in spite of their possession of the hardy native pony, must be regarded as being on the whole in a worse position. From first to last they were confined to their domestic supply, and, as I have pointed out, from Paardeberg onwards they suffered considerably from shortage of horses.* Their advantages were a light load and good horsemanship.

Lastly, let me remind the reader of what I believe to be the real gist and essence of this complaint about horses. The theory of shock among several other rigorous conditions presupposes the presence at any and every moment of fresh horses capable of bearing down upon their objective at a gallop, and during the last fifty yards at the " charge," and in perfect formation. This condition alone is enough to make shock a negligible factor in future wars—*if*, that is, Cavalry are going to play the great part in war which they should play, but which they have not played for the last forty years. Mounted rifle-

* On the subject of horses see *Times* History, vol. vi., part ii., chapter vi. The total number provided for the British army was 518,794 (mules 150,781). The net wastage accounted for was in horses 347,007 (mules 53,339). The Boers took the field with 50,000 to 60,000 horses, which were renewed several times. Their net wastage is estimated conjecturally at 100,000.

men are subject to no such conditions, and would lose half their value if they were.   Picture a Boer charge— the little grass-fed ponies breaking from their " trippling" trot to what would correspond in European Cavalry to a moderate canter.

3. *Lack of Opportunity.*—From ground and horses we pass to the more important part of Mr. Goldman's case for " abnormality." *   Though he never admits that Cavalry work fell short in any respect in South Africa, he is evidently conscious that this perfection needs much special proof, and he falls back on the proposition that they did not have a proper chance of distinguishing them-selves in their own special line.   Two absolutely distinct causes—the one domestic, the other external—are repre-sented as having produced this lack of opportunity :

(*a*) They were not employed properly—*i.e.*, as the con-text shows, by Lord Roberts in particular, though he is not named.

(*b*) That the Boers, owing to their habit of retiring without " fighting to a finish," did not permit the Cavalry to " discharge Cavalry duties."

I have alluded in previous chapters to both those points. Let me add a word more.

As to (*a*), Mr. Goldman's argument is vitiated from beginning to end by that old confusion between strategy and tactics, between mobility and combat, which lies at the root of *arme blanche* doctrine.   The express point he is arguing, remember, is the relative value of Cavalry and mounted riflemen, of the steel weapon and the fire-arm, or, to be more accurate, the steel weapon plus the firearm, and the firearm alone.   Now, the horse, whether

---

* I ought, perhaps, to allude to another argument which appears in Mr. Goldman's Preface to Bernhardi, though it is expressed in very vague terms, and the meaning is beyond me : " The Cavalry, after the first few weeks of 1900, as an effective force had practically ceased to exist." Figures of strength and disposition will be found in my previous chapters.

used strategically or tactically, is common to both types. Weapons are used only in combat. We are concerned, then, purely, with a question of weapons and of combat. Strategy only concerns us in that the ultimate end of all strategy is combat. If there were to be no combat, equipment for a strategical errand would be vastly simplified. We should discard all weapons and all ammunition, and use the lightest men we could possibly find. In defending the steel weapon, therefore, and in showing that it had not its proper opportunities, we should expect to find Mr. Goldman dwelling on tactical opportunities. Quite the reverse. His complaint—both in the Appendix to his own book and in his Preface to Bernhardi—is that the Cavalry were denied strategical opportunities. If he proved this up to the hilt, he would not have furthered the *arme blanche* theory one whit. But does he prove it ? " Strategical " is, of course, ambiguous, but let us follow his loose employment of the word in calling the Kimberley raid " strategical." He would not —and, indeed, does not—contend that at that period Roberts denied the Cavalry independent opportunities. He begins with the general advance of May, 1900.

But, again, we must pause to define the terms we are using. Mr. Goldman's definition of the " strategical use of Cavalry " is on page 412 of " With French in South Africa " : " The use of that arm in such a fashion that, *without of necessity engaging in any tactical action*, certain well-defined effects are produced." Note the words I have italicized, for they prepare the way in advance for Mr. Goldman's appreciation of the action of Zand River, which he gives as a " concrete case to explain his argument." " At that action French's Cavalry division was employed on the extreme left flank of the army to produce a *purely tactical effect*. . . . His operations *could only, and did only*, have the effect of causing the enemy gradually and in perfect order to withdraw from the position commanding the river. . . . The effect was *purely tactical*, for the early withdrawal of the enemy, un- beaten, undemoralized, gave no chance to Cavalry shock action." What is the inner meaning of this contempt for " purely tactical effects "? Simply this, that our Cavalry, owing to their armament and methods, were outmatched in combat by the Boers. Let the reader examine once more the facts and maps of this action in the " Official History," the *Times* History, Mr. Gold- man's own narrative, or any other. He will see that " could only " and " did only " are synonymous terms to Mr. Goldman. Eight thousand Boers held a twenty- five mile front, with their main strength in the centre and left, against nearly 40,000 British troops, of whom 13,000 were mounted. Aiming at envelopment and destruction, Roberts gave the Cavalry a supremely important tactical object. Of the two turning forces employed, two brigades of Cavalry, supported by 2,200 mounted riflemen, were to make an extensive sweep round the Boer right flank, and gain an intercepting position at Ventersburg Road Station. The Cavalry got well round to the rear in very good time (for the move ment was a complete surprise to Botha), but were sub- sequently checked by small flank-guards. One brigade was badly mauled, and the whole division was delayed long enough to enable Botha to withdraw his whole force in safety. The Lancer brigade, near the railway, and next in line to French's division, though lightly opposed, showed no greater aggressive capacity (see " Official His- tory," vol. iii., p. 56, and map), and the same applies to the remaining Cavalry brigade on our extreme right. Mr. Goldman is content : there could not have been any " tactical effect." The logical inference is that Cavalry can have no tactical value at all.* For he does not

---

* This, as I shall show in the next chapter, is precisely the conclusion reached unconsciously by Bernhardi, and consciously by Wrangel.

suggest *any tactical* alternative for them. One tactical retort to these immense Boer extensions was, as I indicated, a piercing movement ; but Mr. Goldman makes no such suggestion, although in the same Appendix (under " Security and Information ") he expressly gives as one of many normal Cavalry functions that of " piercing the opposing Cavalry screen with a division or divisions cut loose from the main army." As I have pointed out, for purposes of analogy, the Boer army on this, as on so many other occasions, did represent a Cavalry screen.

And what is his suggested strategical alternative ? This, that the Cavalry division should have been, say, " 100 miles to the north of the main army, moving south, while our main army moved north." The effect on the " ill-disciplined Boer troops " would have been " incalculable," and then, in some unexplained way, would have come the " opportunity for the shock tactics of Cavalry." How wonderfully simple war seems to Mr. Goldman, and how carelessly he must have read his master, Bernhardi, who makes short work of this conception of miraculously easy and effective raids in modern war ! But let us look a little closer. The Cavalry had arrived from Bloemfontein at Smalldeel, freshly remounted, on the 8th. On the 9th French's two brigades covered twenty miles of their turning movement. On the 10th, the day of the battle, they covered upwards of thirty miles, and their horses were too tired for them to be able to act on the suggestion of Roberts for an enveloping march that same night round the Boer army and to the north of Kroonstad. Starting at 6.30 a.m. next day, they were too late to produce any important results.

The tasks set the Cavalry, whether we call them strategical or tactical, were as heavy and responsible as

---

Their only tactical rôle *with the steel* is in the " collision of Cavalry masses "—*i.e.*, between masses of Cavalry who both believe in the steel and engage on that understanding.

the most ardent leader could desire. This craving for grandiose strategical " effects " without combat is thoroughly unhealthy and distorted. I venture to lay down the proposition that no Cavalry has a right to complain of strategical mishandling until it has proved beyond question high combative capacity. With carbines and inadequate fire-training this high standard was beyond the reach of the Cavalry. It has been said that Roberts misused them in the Middelburg operations of July 23-25, 1900. Study the facts. French had planned a very extensive circuit. Roberts, who had no spare mounted troops for his main columns, prescribed a shorter curve. On the 24th both Cavalry Brigades, even with the help of Hutton's mixed force of 3,000 men, were held up for four hours by a small rear-guard. Casualties, two men wounded. It is impossible to assume that a wider circuit against so mobile an enemy would have produced important results.

Genuine strategical independence for a purely Cavalry force, on the lines of the great Civil War raids, was never in question during this period, and would have been useless if feasible.* The nearest approach to such an expedition was the futile divisional march of 173 miles across the Eastern Transvaal in October, 1900, where some Infantry and a few mounted riflemen, besides masses of ox transport, accompanied the column. There was no mobility worth the name ; the column became nothing more than an escort to its own transport. The Kimberley raid was not, of course, one of strategical independence. The division as a whole was never more than twenty miles from large portions of the main army, and was not rationed independently for a longer period than three days. Kimberley was a friendly town, and after the return of the main army, on which the force was dependent for all but temporary supplies, forage ran out

* See Bernhardi's warning, " Cavalry in Future Wars," pp. 169, 170.

owing to De Wet's stroke at Waterval. Mounted riflemen were associated with Cavalry, and the Cavalry themselves won success by acting well as mounted riflemen.

Mr. Goldman's idea that hundred-mile circuits would end in " opportunities for shock " is utterly chimerical. It is against all evidence, from this war and others, European, American, or Asiatic, and Bernhardi scouts it.* The ride from Kimberley on February 15, selected by Mr. Goldman as a case where for once " Cavalry " were used in a proper " strategical " manner, did not end in shock ; on the contrary, it ended in tactical fire-action pure and simple. The chance for interception was of the same tactical character at Zand River. In point of fact, at one moment during the latter action an attempt was actually made at an open-order Cavalry charge, by a brigade against about 200 Boers.† It came to nothing. And the reason, as given by Mr. Goldman and the Official Historian ? Horses too much blown. And yet Mr. Goldman cries out for hundred-mile expeditions which are to culminate—with fresh horses—in shock.

No one, of course, would go so far as to assert positively either of Roberts or of any Commander-in-Chief in any war that he never once missed an opportunity for the strategical use for *mounted troops*. That is a different matter altogether. The issue lies between steel-armed troops and the mounted riflemen, whom Mr. Goldman ignores. Why not a bare allusion to Plumer's brilliant defence of Rhodesia, or to the relief of Mafeking—a strategical march of 250 miles in fourteen days, with fire-fights *en route*, by irregulars ?

With regard to General Buller's use of Cavalry I need add nothing to my criticisms in Chapters VIII. and IX.

---

* " Cavalry in Future Wars," p. 51. Non-frontal pursuits, especially " strategical " pursuits, are to be by fire-action.

† Mr. Goldman's estimate. The *Times* Historian speaks of a " party," the Official History a " commando." The total force detached by Botha against the division was certainly very small.

His fault was to carry disbelief in the steel for the Boer War to the extent of disbelieving in Cavalry altogether for that war, a wholly unwarrantable point of view, derived from an equally distorted conception of the utility of Cavalry.

(b) *Refusal of the Boers to Stand.*—The facts speak for themselves. Only by avoiding the whole topic of Boer aggression, and by treating Boer rear-guard skill as a non-Cavalry quality which "made pursuit practically impossible," is the point even arguable. Indeed, I approach it again with the utmost reluctance; for Mr. Goldman's *idée fixe* that the Boers were from first to last mortally afraid of the lance and sword carries him to lengths where no upholder of mounted riflemen who respects and admires the Cavalry and attacks only their weapons and methods can consent to follow him. I shall refrain from making controversial use of these passages, and shall confine myself, briefly, to less difficult ground.

Mr. Goldman is probably thinking mainly of the operations of Lord Roberts, though his proposition is general (p. 420). He would scarcely contend that the Boers did not " stand " from November, 1899, to March, 1000, on the Tugela heights, or that they did not show positively aggressive qualities and outmatch our Cavalry at Talana and the battle of Ladysmith. With all his belief in the steel, he would scarcely in set terms allege that regular Cavalry would have defended or attacked Spion Kop or Pieter's Hill better than they were in fact defended and attacked. But these were tactical occasions, presumably with no " tactical effects " to be produced. What, then, of Elandslaagte ?

As for the main operations under Lord Roberts, has Mr. Goldman ever seriously reflected upon the relative numbers engaged ? Of course, the Boers frequently showed moral weakness—we ourselves were not exempt —but they did not fear the *sword.* Assuredly they

" stood " at Paardeberg to their ruin ; but was there shock at Paardeberg ? Assuredly they may be said to have stood at Dornkop and at the two days' battle of Diamond Hill, where Cavalry were hotly engaged, and at Bergendal, where seventy-four Boer Cavalry (though Mr. Goldman would never admit they were " Cavalry ") delayed an army and were ejected by Infantry. In the other actions of this period, as I have pointed out, their retreats were conducted in an orderly manner and with small loss.

Let me lay down another proposition, which I believe all Cavalrymen will agree to. No one on behalf of Cavalry has a right to make a general complaint of pusillanimity or insufficient resistance on the part of the enemy, unless (*a*) that enemy has had something approaching numerical equality ; or (*b*) has been forced into disastrous retreats, with loss of guns, transport, etc. ; or unless (*c*) the Infantry and mounted riflemen associated with the Cavalry have not been seriously engaged. On this latter point the facts of the war and statistics of losses are decisive. There is something that makes the brain a little dizzy about the first two conditions, but the whole case for the *arme blanche* teems with paradoxes which can only be met by the method of *reductio ad absurdum.*

Finally, I ask again, as I asked above, what is the real meaning of this complaint about lack of resistance ? Simply this, that the Boers would not engage in shock and imposed fire-tactics on the Cavalry. In his remarks on terrain (p. 423) Mr. Goldman reveals the truth. " Favourable on the whole as the ground was in the Free State, in the presence of Cavalry operating on favourable ground the Boers refused to give battle." Well, I can only ask the reader to study as one example among scores Mr. Goldman's own example, Zand River, noting (1) that we were nearly five times superior in total strength, and in guns, and that the regular Cavalry, reckoned apart from mounted riflemen and Infantry, amounted to five-eighths of the whole Boer army ; (2) that the terrain was as suitable for shock manœuvre as any Cavalry could expect to obtain, and such as they very rarely would obtain in any probable European battle-field ; (3) the tactical incidents of the Cavalry turning movement, the offensive strokes by the Boers, and the failure of our charge. How could the Cavalry lose 224 horses and 161 men in casualties and prisoners and fail in their tactical task, unless someone " gave battle "? In other words, " battle " is synonymous with " shock." Nothing but shock counts.

Time has convinced Mr. Goldman more and more strongly of this truth. In his Preface to Bernhardi he lectures the Boers in a vein of compassionate condescension on their ignorance of the " Art of War." It is true enough that there was much in the art of war which the Boers did not understand, or understood fatally late. But what does their mentor, for the purposes of his argument in this Preface, mean by the " Art of War "? He means shock, though he gives it the customary name of " mounted action."

" Had the Boers understood the Art of War and taken advantage of the openings which their superior mobility gave them, or had they been possessed of a body of Cavalry capable of mounted action, say at Magersfontein, they might repeatedly have wrought confusion in our ranks."

This passage sets the crown upon the case for " peculiarity." I leave it as it stands without further comment.

Such are Mr. Goldman's reasons for regarding his South African War as a vindication of the *arme blanche.* I have not discussed them at excessive length. They are extreme views, but such views, if honestly expounded, as Mr. Goldman expounds them, must be extreme. Many people vaguely entertain similar ideas, but if they take the pains to work them out with facts and maps, they will either be forced to similar extremities or will abandon them altogether. In my next two chapters I shall give further proof of the astounding contradictions in which *arme blanche* doctrine abounds.

I come to the last of the triumvirate, General von Bernhardi himself. It is a relief. We begin to breathe fresh air after an atmosphere which, I believe the reader will agree with me, becomes sometimes almost unbearably close and enervating. When censure of the Commander-in-Chief, depreciation of a brave enemy, implied depreciation of our own mounted riflemen, complaints about ground, complaints about horses, complaints about anything and everything but the one thing which really merited complaint, when apology and insinuation are carried so far, we begin to long for something stimulating and straightforward, and in Bernhardi we get it. On his work I shall have to write more fully in the next chapter. At this moment I wish only to call attention to his view of the " peculiarity " of the Boer War. It is contained in half a dozen lines on page 56 of " Cavalry in Future Wars." He has just been praising the Boer charges as having achieved " brilliant results," in spite of " any kind of tactical training for this particular purpose." (What a curious sidelight that latter remark throws on official views of " training " !) He adds :

" Certainly weapons and numbers have altered materially since the days of the American Civil War, and the experiences of South Africa, largely conditioned by the peculiar topographical conditions and the out-of-door habits and sporting instincts of the Boers, cannot be transferred to European circumstances without important modifications."

That is all he explicitly says about the Boer War. But the reader will see at once that here is a totally different point of view from that of Mr. Goldman, whose thesis is that the Boers were not formidable enough to be fit adversaries for our Cavalry, that they would not "stand," and that their great deficiency was lack of a steel weapon and shock power. The idea underlying Bernhardi's vague words is much more akin to that contained in the passage quoted from Sir John French, and, of course, it is essentially the right idea. I pass by the "peculiar topographical conditions." Without further elaboration, we need not take the words to mean in set terms that South Africa was less favourable for shock manœuvre than Europe. The kernel lies in the "outdoor habits and sporting instincts," creating conditions which ":cannot be transferred to European circumstances without important modification." These words, read in connection with the "brilliant results" of the Boer charges, can only signify that town-bred Europeans cannot hope to imitate methods, excellent in themselves, but demanding outdoor habits and sporting instincts.

This idea, expressed in one shadowy form or another, of an element of superiority in the Boers, is very common ; commoner, I think, on the whole than its antitype, the idea of inferiority, though I have more than once heard both propounded, unconsciously, in the same breath by the same person. But it is never in this country voiced authoritatively ; and with good reason, for it shakes to its foundations the whole fabric of the shock system and opens up a line of thought which can end only in one way. Mr. Goldman does not even hint at it, except in connection with that strange faculty for fighting *defensive* rear-guard actions which he regards as quite outside the topic of Cavalry. General French, while implying that the Boers were formidable, is silent about the reason.

Let us face this shadowy argument for what it is worth. What does it mean ? That we cannot train our Cavalry to become genuinely mobile mounted riflemen, with the rifle charge as their tactical climax instead of the shock charge, which is not a climax at all, but an isolated species of encounter in glaring conflict with real battle conditions ? The contention, if it is really made, is absurd. If we cannot artificially create inbred instincts and habits so strong as those of the Boers, we have the advantage of moral and tactical discipline, acquired only too late by the Boers. We can work in the right direction on the magnificent material we have, and instead of imbuing the wrong spirit deliberately imbue the right spirit. We can teach our men to " fight up " to the charge and rely on one and the same weapon both for the process of " fighting up " and for the charge itself, when and where the actual mounted charge is necessary. The tactical form of the Boer and British rifle charge—that is, in successive lines and with wide intervals—was precisely the same as our own open-order steel charge as practised at Klip Drift and at the present moment. The crucial difference lay in spirit and object ; the spirit leading up to the charge was that of the rifle, and the object was that of overcoming the enemy with the rifle, not necessarily in a mêlée unless by way of pursuit, but at decisive range.

Is saddle-fire an accomplishment our Cavalry cannot acquire—an accomplishment which at this very moment we inculcate for " picked men and scouts " of the Mounted Infantry, a force with not a quarter of the mounted training that the Cavalry receive ? For professional troops it cannot be more difficult to acquire than skill with the steel weapon on horseback. That is an art which, as everybody knows, demands long and continuous drill and practice. Indeed, it must demand longer drill and practice, because true shock—that is, heavy impact—involves close, knee-to-knee formations, rigid, mechanical, symmetrical, not only difficult to attain in themselves, but exceedingly difficult to combine with the free and effective use of steel weapons. Obviously, neither saddle-fire nor

the use of steel weapons can safely be enjoined in times of
peace for volunteer troops like our Yeomanry, for example, who obtain at the most a fortnight's continuous
field training in the year.

I ask the reader seriously to follow out the train of
thought suggested by those pregnant words " outdoor
habits and sporting instincts." Is it not common sense
that these habits and instincts, fortified by drill and discipline, must be the very foundation of mounted success
in war, and is not a system of tactics founded upon them
likely to be a good system ?   Should it not be the aim of
a highly-civilized industrial people to aim at approxi-
mating as far as possible to such a system ?   Or, taking
as their starting-point indoor habits and urban instincts,
are they to persist in working in the opposite direction ?
Was it not the possession of these habits and instincts
by such a large number of Americans at the time of the
Civil War that led to the brilliant achievements of
Cavalry in that war, mainly through trained reliance on the
firearm, imperfect weapon as it was ?   Was not our own
possession of sporting and hunting aptitudes, embodied
in Englishmen and Colonials alike, our very salvation in
South Africa ?   Of course it was.   Wherever these
natural instincts were strong enough to burst the bonds
of ancient tradition, there we obtained enterprising
Cavalry leaders.   The same instincts called into being
many good leaders among Infantrymen, gunners, and
sappers, and among ordinary civilians from every quarter
of the Empire.

Do we not pride ourselves on this fact ?   Is it not a
commonplace in every Englishman's mouth that, hard
and bitter as the struggle was, " no other nation "—and
among other nations Germany is often instanced—could
have engaged in it so successfully as ourselves ?   There
is sound truth in the boast.   But it is the emptiest and
silliest of boasts if we do not recognize the meaning behind

it, which is nothing but this—that we have a greater proportion of men in our Empire who possess those outdoor habits and sporting instincts which take shape in skilled mounted riflemen. And when we envisage a European war, are we to forget this boast and, ignoring not only our own priceless experience but our own innate capacities, revert to the antiquated European system ?

If there are other arguments for " peculiarity," I do not know them. But if I have carried my readers with me, they will agree that in this chapter and every other, in investigating and combating alleged peculiarities I have, in fact, been pursuing phantom arguments round the circumference of a vicious circle. Disguise it as we may, the real peculiarity of the Boer War was that the Boer horsemen did not carry steel weapons. European Cavalries do. Let us turn to Europe.

CHAPTER XIII

BERNHARDI AND "CAVALRY TRAINING"

THERE, indeed, is the grand paradox. Quite convinced as patriotic Englishmen that we did better in South Africa than the Germans could have done, we nevertheless turn to Germany for light and leading on the mounted problems of to-day. Though I name Germany in particular, and would be justified, for the purposes of my argument, in confining myself to Germany, it need scarcely be added that Continental practice in general has a fatally strong influence on British practice. One may argue interminably, and perhaps not without some success, against the alleged peculiarities of the Boer War, but in the last resort one meets that most exasperating, because most intangible and inconclusive, of all arguments—" other nations believe in the *arme blanche*. Germany, for example, believes in it. Germany has a large and magnificent army ; therefore, Germany and the other nations must be right." As a moderate and sober expression of this view, I quote the following from a leading article which appeared in the *Times* of September 16, 1909—an article itself founded on the views of the able Military Correspondent of that journal, given after the manœuvres of 1909 :

" Prominent among these "—*i.e.*, erroneous schools of thought arising from South African experience—" is that which, in the campaigns of the future, *assigns to Cavalry the rôle of Mounted Infantry*. As our Military Correspondent points out, Continental nations, to whom our own records, as well as those of the Russo-Japanese War, are equally open, and who are among the most intelligent and *experienced* in military affairs, maintain large forces of Cavalry, and train them in a certain manner for a certain purpose. As our army is officially designed to fight a *civilized* enemy, it follows that we *must not be deficient in a weapon possessed by potential foes.* It is therefore necessary that the one Cavalry division we possess should compare favourably in quality with the squadrons that it may have to meet, whose *numerical superiority* is not a matter of doubt."

Although almost every word in this paragraph invites criticism, I need call attention only to those I have italicized :

1. " The rôle of Mounted Infantry," in effect, begs the whole question. It instantly calls up the starved and stunted functions of that arm, as it is now organized and trained, and by innuendo suggests something utterly devoid of dash and mobility.

2. " Experienced." Russia I shall come to later. When have Germany, Austria, or France had national experience, in civilized war, of the smokeless magazine rifle ?

3. " Civilized." Were the Boers not a civilized enemy ?

4. " Numerical superiority." The suggestion is that, having a small force of Cavalry, we should be all the more careful to obtain excellence in the *arme blanche*. This is, indeed, an amazing argument. Is our solitary division to court brute physical collisions with the Continental masses ? Even " Cavalry Training " admits that the smaller the force, the greater the necessity of relying on the rifle. Think of South Africa—of Bergendal, for example, and scores of other actions ! The admission, of course, gravely imperils the *arme blanche*, because it implies, what is the literal truth, that the rifle can impose tactics on the steel. But how escape the admission ?

5. " It follows that we must not be deficient in a weapon possessed by potential foes."

That will serve as a text for this chapter. Observe that the doctrine of mere imitation is put in its frankest form. Our Lancers already carry three different weapons. If Germany were to add a fourth or a fifth, in that case, too, it would "follow," no doubt, that we must "not be deficient." If we act on this principle at all, it was surely a pity that we did not act upon it when the Boer War was imminent. Our "potential foes" then possessed a weapon in which our Cavalry were lamentably deficient, and lacked a weapon which proved to be nothing but an encumbrance to our Cavalry. Did those circumstances prevent us from sending our Cavalry to the war equipped and trained on Crimean lines, more than forty years out of date? Do they prevent Mr. Goldman, even now, from denying that, even for South Africa, that equipment and training were wrong? What I want to lay stress on is the absence of any recognition that there are some general principles at stake. Votes are counted, selected foreign votes, given by "potential foes" to whom our "records are open," being regarded as equal in value to our own. America, not being a "potential foe," has no vote. Colonel Repington himself, in the *Times* of September 14, briefly disposed of the question in just this way. Yet he is too able a man not to know that imitation is not a principle, that counting votes is not decisive, and that the *arme blanche* must be justified by arguments based on the facts of modern war. Is he prepared so to justify it? I have never seen his full profession of faith. I always seem to detect in his writing the attitude of one who on this matter passively accepts the official doctrine as it stands, and who works with enthusiasm and vigour to make a success of an existing system. After all, I seem to hear him saying, we cannot go far wrong, because our potential foes believe in the same system. I may be in error, but I venture to issue the challenge to him to expound, illustrate, and justify the *arme blanche* theory;

to declare for the " terror of cold steel," for the dash which can only be inspired by the steel weapon, for the power of the steel to impose tactics on the rifle, for the inevitable shock duel ; and to state whether he agrees with General French, or Mr. Goldman, or General von Bernhardi, as to the nature of the abnormalities which make the lesson of the Boer War negligible. If he will help with his keen logic to illuminate the maze of contradictions through which I shall thread my way in this and the next chapter, he will do a still greater service to the true interests of the Cavalry. He will admit that he has undergone conversion since 1904. At a time when he and all the world were under the hallucination that the Cossacks were good mounted riflemen, he wrote that the tactics necessary to destroy them would be the Boer tactics, and that they were " not to be beaten by serried ranks, classic charges," and " prehistoric methods " of that sort (*Times*, April 2, 1904).

General von Bernhardi's work, " Cavalry in Future Wars," admittedly inspires British Cavalry practice. Is he, *in the matter of the steel weapon*, a trustworthy guide ?

Let me first recall the attitude of the German General Staff towards the mounted problems raised by our war. The whole of the issue we are discussing is " taboo " to them. Indeed, the whole mounted question is " taboo " to them. In the rare comments on mounted action— comments confined mainly to the Kimberley operations, and referred to in my own Chapters VI. and VII.—the German Official Historian never so much as by a line even indirectly contrasts the relative powers of mounted riflemen and Cavalry. During the period covered by the History, he speaks of the Boers nearly always as though they were Infantry, and alludes in general terms to their " purely defensive powers," in spite of incidents—rare, no doubt, in the early stages, but strongly suggestive of the future—like Talana Hill, Nicholson's Nek, Wagon

Hill, Spion Kop, Waterval, Kitchener's Kopje, Sannah's Post, all of which occurred within the period described. And just at the time of Sannah's Post and De Wet's raids, when the Boers were beginning a consistent development of aggressive mobility, not in the " regular " battles, where in numbers they were hopelessly outmatched, but in independent adventure ; just, moreover, when aggressive mounted effort on our side was beginning to be more urgently necessary than ever before, the detailed narrative ends. After March, 1900, " the battles furnish in their details little instruction of tactical value,"* and the whole campaign from Bloemfontein to Komati Poort receives only a brief summary. The guerilla war—a wholly mounted war—obtains half a page.

Then comes a " tactical retrospect," in which it becomes perfectly clear that for the writer the whole interest of the war centres in the development of fire-tactics for riflemen. Whether they have horses in the background or not seems to be immaterial, and for practical purposes he assumes that they have not. This assumption destroys the value of more than half his criticism. The whole point was that the Boer riflemen were mounted riflemen, able, by the rifle, to defend a position in small force against superior force, and, by the horse, to leave that position when it became too hot. Obviously these men, though they could be, and were, attacked vehemently by Infantry, could never, unless they courted suicide, be defeated and destroyed by Infantry, who walk and do not ride. Obviously, too, you cannot expect even the best Infantry under the best leaders eternally to sustain at the highest level the ardour of the fire-fight on foot unless they know that riflemen equal in mobility to the enemy—that is, mounted riflemen—are co-operating with equal ardour and efficiency for that defeat and destruc-

* " The War in South Africa " (March to September, 1900), (translated by Colonel Du Cane), p. 288.

tion of the mounted enemy which mounted men can alone ensure. This sense of skilled and effective co-operation is exactly what our Infantry did not have, from causes I need not enter into again. The German critic is blind to the defect, because he is blind to the whole mounted problem. Regarding the Boers as Infantry, he regards our Infantry and the Generals who controlled them as solely responsible for the incompleteness of our victories, and goes to the monstrous length of attributing this incomplete achievement partly to the " inferior quality of a mercenary army."

The writer of the retrospect knew that the Boers had horses, for in one passage he alludes to their " mobility," and he knew that we had a large body of Cavalry and mounted riflemen, for in another solitary passage he casually alludes to their ineffective turning movements. But the " Infantry fight," which in all war " decides the battle," is the main theme throughout, and remarkably interesting the critic's observations are. So far as they go, they apply just as closely to mounted riflemen as to Infantry, though the critic himself is wholly unconscious of the analogy and of the implied condemnation he over and over again makes on the theory underlying the steel armament of Cavalry.

If he had proceeded with a study of the war, and had thoroughly digested the fact that the Boers not only had horses, but could attack, what would have been his conclusions ? If only he had thoroughly realized that our Infantry had not horses, he would, I am sure, have modified some of his strictures on the use of that arm, on the excessive " dread of losses," and so on. Some inkling of the truth that mobility often transcends vulnerability, and that mounted riflemen can in the long run be thoroughly defeated only by mounted riflemen, would have dawned upon him. But who knows ? So strange and persistent is his reticence about the *arme blanche*, so outspoken his surprise and delight when—for example, at Paardeberg—he finds Cavalry using the carbine with success, that one would almost imagine he had received the *mot d'ordre* for silence on the whole topic. However, let this be clear, at any rate : (1) That there is no explicit comfort for the *arme blanche* in any page of these two volumes ; (2) that there is no suggestion of any peculiarity or abnormality in the Boer War which renders its lessons inapplicable to future wars. Mr. Goldman's case for peculiarity crumbles in the light of this searching analysis of fire-tactics. Substitute " mounted riflemen " for " riflemen " in cases where the facts obviously demand the change, and the whole structure of " strategical mishandling " and slack Boer resistance falls to pieces. The idea that the Boers needed only the *arme blanche* to make them formidable is refuted a hundred times by implication.

And now let us turn to Bernhardi. Here, by a welcome contrast, we have an enthusiast for the mounted arm. Not a disproportionately ardent enthusiast by any means. Armament apart, not a word he says in support of the profound importance of Cavalry in future wars is exaggerated. On the contrary, he underrates their rôle, as I shall show. The Boers, in the one allusion to them, are not " Infantry " for him, but " Cavalry," and he has evidently been deeply impressed by the bearing of our war upon Cavalry problems—how deeply impressed it is impossible to say. His first edition was published in 1899, just before the war began ; the second, which Mr. Goldman has translated, in 1902, when it was barely over. His strong views on the great importance of fire-action were evidently inspired by the American Civil War and by the poor performances of the shock-trained European Cavalries, including those of the Prussian Cavalry, in the wars of 1866, 1870, and 1877. In his second edition he never illustrates specifically from our war, probably from lack of sufficiently full information. But his allusion to the remarkable character of the Boer charges is in harmony with the whole spirit which pervades his chapters on fire-action.

Any Englishman who is aware of the fact that our own "Cavalry Training" is based, sometimes to the extent of textual quotation, on Bernhardi's work, and, on the recommendation of General French, resorting to that work not merely as the most complete and brilliant exposition of modern Cavalry theory, but as a refutation of the opponents of shock, must be struck at the very outset by two singular circumstances :

1. The dominant feature of the book is insistence on fire.

2. So far from representing German practice, Bernhardi writes avowedly as the revolutionary reformer of a dangerously antiquated system, upheld by authorities whom long years of peace and the memories of a war far too easily won have drugged into unintelligent lethargy. In 1899, when, without a suspicion of our own defects, we were complacently beginning a war which threw Cavalry defects into the strongest possible light, Bernhardi was fiercely combating these very defects in the face of a strongly hostile professional and public opinion. In the preface to his edition of 1902, when our war was ending, he complains that " of the demands which I put forward concerning the organization and equipment of the [German] Cavalry, none have as yet been put into execution," though he concedes that the " necessity of reforms " has " made progress." Organization is of no immediate concern to us. By equipment we find later that he refers (among other less important points) to the rearmament of the Cavalry with a firearm " ballistically equal in all respects to the rifle of the Infantry "—that is, to a reform adopted by us during the war, and retained ever since. Some of his recommendations for the educa-

tion of Cavalry officers in the rudiments of fire-tactics would make our youngest Yeomanry subaltern blush. On the importance of fire for Cavalry there is nothing in the book which has not been commonplace to all intelligent critics of the American Civil War of 1862-65.

Now I want to give the reader a warning and a suggestion. The warning is not to assume that Bernhardi is representative of " other nations." The German Cavalry is now only just about to be equipped with a good firearm. Count Wrangel is preaching to the Austrian Cavalry a doctrine in flat contradiction to Bernhardi's. The French Cavalry, General de Negrier tells us, *s'obstinent dans leur rêve* of classic charges and contempt for fire-tactics.* My suggestion is this—that we should measure Bernhardi's views by the reactionary views which he set out to fight. He is a German, writing exclusively to Germans, ruthlessly exposing German defects, and making his remedies conform to these defects. His only allusion to British Cavalry is when he speaks, on page 185, of "Anglo-maniacs and faddists " in connection with a question of breaking horses. After all, the most passionate reformer must limit himself to more or less feasible aims. I do not mean for a moment that the General consciously refrained from giving overstrong meat to babes ; but when we remember the *milieu* in which he lived, the influence to which, during his whole life, he was subjected, and the mountains of prejudice which he had to surmount, it seems marvellous, not that he should go no farther than he does go on the path of intelligent reform, but that he should have gone as far. As a matter of worldly wisdom, de Negrier is probably wrong in telling to a yet more backward Cavalry the full, logical, scathing truth about the archaic absurdities of shock.

Read Bernhardi in the light of these circumstances. The early chapters must, I think, have fairly horrified our

* *Revue des deux Mondes*, August, 1908.

arme blanche school. He runs amok among all the cherished traditions which held good from the Crimea to Talana Hill.

" The Art of War has been revolutionized (*inter alia*) by ' arms of precision ' " (p. 1).

Compare Mr. Goldman's definition of the Art of War, in so far as that art was misunderstood by the Boers.* On page 9 Bernhardi says :

" As far as the Infantry are concerned, it will be quite the exception to encounter them in closed bodies ; generally we shall have to ride against extended lines, which offer a most unfavourable target for our purpose."

Absolutely correct, if we remember that by " our purpose " he refers to the steel weapon, showing at the outset that he does not realize the nature, as he certainly does not contemplate the adoption of the mounted rifleman's charge.

" Thus, essentially the Cavalry has been driven out of its former place of honour on the battle-fields of the plains, and has been compelled to seek the *assistance of the cover the ground affords* in order to carry its own power of destruction into immediate contact with its enemy, and only under most exceptionally favourable conditions will it still be possible to deliver a charge " (he means an *arme blanche* charge) " direct across the open " (pp. 9, 10).

He should add, of course, what South Africa proved, and the Japanese Cavalry confirmed on the plains of Mukden—that mounted riflemen have taken the " place of honour " vacated by Cavalry. But his instinct about terrain is sound at bottom. Contrast the demoralizing doctrine of " Cavalry ground," and Mr. Goldman's complaint that even South Africa was not " open " enough for Cavalry. Contrast his view of " obstructions," and his failure to perceive what Bernhardi clearly perceives— that inequalities and obstructions, so far from being a

* *Vide supra*, p. 286.

hindrance to mounted troops, are in modern war increasingly necessary for effective action in surprise, and ought to be a matter of rejoicing, not lamentation.

" The possible participation of the civilian inhabitants of the invaded Nation in the War will hamper most severely all forms of Cavalry action other than on the battle-field " (p. 10).

This, of course, is an allusion to the *francs-tireurs* of 1870, who made it unsafe for the Prussian Cavalry to go about alone. I commend it to those who regard our guerilla war in particular as of no concern to Cavalry. The implication, of course, is that the steel is useless in these conditions. And the same is implied elsewhere of all the duties of scouting and reconnaissance, save alone for the gigantic preliminary shock duel which is to clear the road for reconnaissance, and to which I shall have to recur later.

On the steel in pursuit, Bernhardi is almost ironical. Only when

" troops of low quality, beaten, without officers, weary and hungry, lose all cohesion, when with baggage, wounded and stragglers, they are driven back over crowded roads, and then, no matter how well they are armed, they are an easy prey to a pursuing Cavalry. The man who throws his rifle away, or shoots in the air, will not find salvation either in clip-loading or smokeless powder against the lance in the hands of a relentless pursuing Cavalry " (p. 15).

We may add—and I am sure he would admit—that men who throw their rifles away are an easy prey to any form of physical compulsion. They will surrender to a riding-whip. For sheer rapid killing just conceive of the frightful efficacy of the rifle, as proved by our war ! If the horsemen insist on remaining on their horses among these terrified sheep, and if they do not use rifle-fire from the saddle, would not a revolver be at least as effective as a sword or lance ? Of course the whole conception of

such a pursuit with the steel on any considerable scale is
the old Cavalry chimera so rarely seen in practice, never
seen in the European wars from 1866 onwards, never
seen in the Boer War, never seen in Manchuria.   In other
passages Bernhardi himself practically admits that it is a
chimera.

"The same holds good for the fight itself. We cannot
attack even inferior Infantry as long as it only keeps the
muzzle of its rifles down and shoots straight ; but once it is
morally broken and surprised, then the greatest results are
still to be achieved even on an open battle-field " (p. 15).

The amazing thing is that in passages like this, where
he is thinking mainly of the deficiencies of the steel,
Bernhardi seems for the moment to forget that pure
mounted riflemen, and even the hybrids, perfect in both
weapons, who represent his own ideal, have the same
defensive power as Infantry, to say nothing of the additional offensive (and defensive) power conferred by the
horse.   When, in other passages, he is thinking mainly
of the excellence of the firearm, he is fully alive to the
close analogy with Infantry, and goes to the extreme
length of insisting that Cavalry shall actually be as good
as Infantry at their own game of *fire*.   They *can* be as
good, he says, and if they are not as good, for Heaven's
sake, don't tell them so, or you will destroy their *dash !*
(p. 249).   And they should have a firearm superior even
to the Infantry rifle (p. 176).   These three passages, on
pages 15, 176, and 249, read together, give us in one more
form the *reductio ad absurdum* of the steel weapon.
Postulating equal fire-efficiency for Cavalry and Infantry,
read the first passage over again, substituting " Cavalry "
for " Infantry."   " We cannot attack [*i.e.*, with the steel]
even inferior Cavalry [much less inferior mounted riflemen of the pure type] as long as it only keeps the muzzles
of its rifles down and shoots straight."   The rest is a
truism : morally broken troops of course get beaten.   And

now postulate superior Cavalry, or, better still, superior mounted riflemen of the pure type, with their full aggressive powers. What becomes of the steel ? In Bernhardi part of the confusion is due to the fact that he does not recognize the pure type of mounted rifleman at all, not even in the half-developed form of our Mounted Infantry. Having started from the *a priori* unreasoned dogma that however reduced the opportunities for the steel, it must be retained, he is continually endeavouring to obtain the benefit of both worlds, and involving himself thereby in palpable contradictions and inconsistencies. Our own authorities are more careful in avoiding the direct *reductio ad absurdum*. In borrowing from Bernhardi for the purposes of " Cavalry Training," they eschew passages like those I have quoted hitherto, which to English ears would mean the downfall of the steel, and rely on less compromising matter.

In Chapter IV., " Increased Importance of Dismounted Action " (note in " dismounted action " the old, ineradicable assumption that " mounted action " is only associated with the steel), he is in the height of what I may call his " fire-mood," and is very reticent about the *arme blanche*. The firearm, which, remember, should be a *better* weapon, if anything, than the Infantry rifle, is given many offensive as well as defensive rôles. Pursuits, for example, must not be " frontal," because " Cavalry can easily be held up by any rear-guard position in which a few intact troops remain." But who, we wonder, are these " intact troops " ? Why not Cavalry, or mounted riflemen, as in South Africa ? Is not rear-guard work a conventional and normal function of Cavalry itself ? And if it is a case of Cavalry versus Cavalry, why not shock, at the compulsion of one side or the other ? On the next page the General himself is demonstrating the value of Cavalry in rear-guard work, and insisting on the paramount importance of the firearm in it.

His further views on pursuit have been incorporated in
"Cavalry Training." Pursuits are to be on "parallel
lines" and on the enemy's flanks, or by way of anticipa-
tion, on his extreme rear—circumstances where the
"principal rôle falls to the firearm, for only in the fire-
fight is it possible to break off an attack without loss in
order to appear again at some other point." This passage,
of course, is another implicit abandonment of the whole
case for the steel. Think it out, and you will see that I
am not exaggerating. It is transferred textually to
"Cavalry Training" (p. 229), but, wisely enough, it
appears at the respectful distance of forty-two pages
from the general remarks on the "Employment of
Cavalry," where, among opportunities for the use of the
firearm (pp. 186, 187), pursuit is not mentioned, and
where the whole tenor of the instruction is that fire-action
is only to be used when "*the situation imperatively demands it.*" Think this matter out in the light of "fire-
fights" in South Africa (Roodewal, for example) or anywhere else, including, of course, fire-fights between or
against Cavalry or mounted riflemen. What is the use
of a weapon which admits of no tactical elasticity, for
that is what it comes to, which can be used only when you
are so certain of complete and *final* success that you need
not even contemplate another attack at another point ?
This, of course, is the real reason for that idleness on the
battle-field, that strange lack of dash which, by the
admission of their own military authorities from Von
Moltke downwards, characterized the Cavalries engaged
in the wars of 1866 and 1870. And then there were no
magazine rifles. Cavalry dash in South Africa was sapped
by faith in the steel, and only partially restored by faith
in the rifle. It is the old story : the charge must be the
climax of a fire-fight, and therefore it must be inspired by
fire. Under modern conditions you cannot mix the two
sets of tactics ; they are antagonistic and incompatible.

The passage goes on : "The charge, then, will only secure a greater result than dismounted action when the tactical cohesion of the enemy has been dissolved and his fire-power broken—that is to say, generally it will be of greater service in tactical than in strategical pursuits " (pp. 51, 52). We know from the passage quoted on page 302 what Bernhardi means by "dissolved tactical cohesion." He means circumstances in which any weapon and any charge will secure surrender. In the next words he falls accidentally into the old error of confusing combat with mobility. What difference does it make to the efficacy of a weapon whether combat has been brought about tactically or strategically ?

But, taking the words as they stand, what a light they throw on South Africa and the complaints of strategical mishandling and lack of opportunity ! How in the world does Mr. Goldman reconcile them with his contempt for " tactical effects " and his conception of vast *strategical* circuits ending in *shock*-tactics ? I need scarcely remind the reader that in all the actions on the main line of advance from Paardeberg and Poplar Grove to Bergendal, from February to September, 1900, the conditions of pursuit may be truly said to have been present from the very outset, owing to the great disparity of forces. Roberts was continually endeavouring to do exactly what Bernhardi recommends, to initiate for his mounted troops, not frontal but parallel pursuits, or anticipatory pursuits on the enemy's extreme rear. He failed because (1) the enemy were themselves skilled mounted riflemen, who were able to hold very extensive fronts with very few men ; (2) because our Cavalry were deficient in the very quality which Bernhardi says is essential—fire-power. And now let us read a little farther and see what Bernhardi says in contemplating this very contingency of wide fronts on pages 53, 54, under "Turning Movements Impracticable." Here he strongly censures the fallacious idea that Cavalry "possesses in its mobility the infallible means of circumventing points of resistance." "Width of the (enemy's) front" (and the reader will remember the prodigious extent of the thinly-held Boer fronts) is one of the first obstacles named. Others are summarized in the following paragraph, which I commend particularly to Mr. Goldman :

"The theory that Cavalry, thanks to its mobility, can always ride round and turn the positions it encounters, breaks down in practice before the tactical and strategical demands upon the arm, partly by reason of the *local conditions*, and partly because of the consideration which has to be given to *time*, to the *endurance of the horses*, and the position of the following columns" (p. 54).

Apply these remarks to battle-fields, such as Diamond Hill and Zand River, upon which I commented in Chapters IX. and XII. The logical alternative to circumventing tactics was, as I pointed out, piercing tactics, not the still wider circumventions which French favoured. But piercing tactics signified fire-tactics, and, since the enemy was mounted, swift, aggressive fire-tactics, either into decisive range or through the whole of a fire-zone, with a wheel back from the rear, should the enemy hold their ground. Bernhardi's alternative is of precisely the same nature. "The actual assault remains necessary now," and it is the assault by *fire*. Only, alas! it is always the wholly "dismounted" assault.

Two pages later, after censuring another error, which I have several times alluded to—namely, that of "overrating the power of Horse Artillery to clear the road for Cavalry" (pp. 54 and 178), we come to his allusion to the Boer charges on horseback (p. 56). Surely these must have given him, after all he has said, *furieusement à penser*. But no. What have "habits and instincts" to do with immemorial official creeds ? A page later he is qualifying his remarks about Horse Artillery for the express purpose of admitting that guns are very necessary indeed for covering Cavalry *fire-tactics*, which, by his hypothesis, must be "dismounted." I would give much to know exactly what effect upon his mind was made by Mr. Goldman's deprecatory footnote to the effect that the Boer charges were not "Cavalry" charges, but Mounted Infantry charges ; for, remember, he does not recognize Mounted Infantry at all. The real truth is, of course, that when Bernhardi wrote his second edition he knew very little about the last half of our war. No foreign observers were there, and the German official witnesses had decided that there was to be no "tactical interest" after March, 1900. It is doubtful whether the greater number of the charges had even taken place when Bernhardi went to press. Mr. Goldman takes pains to assure him that there were only "one or two" after all. And the whole of our Cavalry school has been assuring him ever since that the war, and especially the guerilla war, was so abnormal as to be quite uninteresting to Cavalry. So error propagates error.

We are prepared, then, for the inevitable. Since for Bernhardi Cavalry must have some "mounted" tactics, clearly those mounted tactics must be derived from the steel. Yet, by the end of Chapter iv., what a chasm seems to have intervened between the firearm and the steel! For the latter weapon he has, explicitly or implicitly, eliminated every combative opportunity save those of complete demoralization in the enemy. The General leaps the chasm with splendid intrepidity. Hitherto the natural inference from his writing is that the firearm has far surpassed the steel in importance, and in several later passages, after leaping the chasm, he speaks of its importance as "equal." But in the first lines of Chapter v., "Tactical Leading in Mounted Combats," when his revolutionary instincts must be curbed, all he admits is that dismounted action has "increased considerably in importance." Then follows the explicit recantation, the confession of the true faith :

" It nevertheless remains the fact that the combat with cold steel remains the chief *raison d'être* of the Cavalry, and when the principles have to be considered according to which troops have to be employed upon the battle-field, the actual collision of Cavalry ' masses ' remains the predominant factor."

The logical hiatus, so familiar in all writers on shock, is complete. There is no attempt made to bridge it. One can almost hear the ghost of Frederick the Great whispering in the impious General's ear : " What is all this despicable talk about dismounting ? Betray the steel ? Never !"

Remark that in making this sudden transition the General passes instantly from a general consideration of the uses of Cavalry in war, mainly fire-uses (where any weapon is mentioned at all), to the specific consideration of the " collision of Cavalry masses," which I will assume for the moment to mean the inter-Cavalry shock fight, the absence of which, from modern battle-fields, he, like General French, seems to regard as unthinkable. " Battle-field," in its context, evidently means " general battle-field of all arms." Previously, in Chapter ii., he has referred to that other opportunity for the " Cavalry duel "—namely, in strategical reconnaissance by the independent Cavalry, where, also, I take him to assume that the duel is a *shock* duel. This battle-field " collision " is the " predominant factor," and it is here, if I read his real inner meaning aright, and, for practical purposes, here only, that the steel weapon will find its opportunity.

' If I read his real inner meaning aright ;' I am bound to make that reservation. One has to make such reservations in criticizing all " shock " literature at the present day, because the irruption of the unruly firearm into the sacred precincts of shock results in obscurities the task of unravelling which can only be compared to the elucidation of a difficult Greek text. Two incompatible things have to be reconciled, and it is beyond the wit of man to depict their reconciliation in clear and logical language. How easy it would have been for Bernhardi (if he really meant it) to say early in his book, " For Cavalry the predominant factor is the collision (*i.e.*, the *mutual* collision) of Cavalry masses. In this inevitable class of encounter the steel is, and must be, supreme ; therefore the steel must be the dominant weapon for Cavalry. Otherwise, and for all other purposes (except, for example, the pursuit of utterly demoralized Infantry and one or two other very rare opportunities) the firearm has usurped its place," and then arrange his treatment of the subject frankly and clearly from this point of view. Then—if one only could extort from him his definition of a " mass "—one would have something concrete and definite to deal with. But such a course would have compelled him to rewrite his entire work, and to open his eyes to the inconsistencies with which it teems, just as the same course would compel the compilers of " Cavalry Training " to court self-stultification. It is ludicrous first to vest Cavalry with the full fire-power of Infantry, who are to have no fear of Cavalry, and then to say that the steel weapon must decide the mutual combats of Cavalry, who are riflemen plus horses. Even as it is, the jar of the ill-locked points (if I may change my metaphor) is audible as Bernhardi passes from one set of rails to the other. By the time he has reached this Chapter v. he has already, thanks to fire, almost banished the " battle-field " from consideration. " Cavalry has been driven out of its former place of honour on the battle-fields of the plains " (*i.e.*, from the only terrain fit for shock). But surely the collision of Cavalry masses on the battle-field, this " pre-

dominant factor," must involve a "place of honour."
What can there be more honourable than the defeat of
the enemy's mounted troops ? In South Africa such a
defeat would have signified the defeat of the whole Boer
army on any given occasion. But I do not want to cavil
over words. Take the General's summary at the end of
Chapter ii., " Duties during the War."

" If, after this short survey of the many fields of action open
to horsemen in the future, we ask the decisive question, ' Which
tasks in the future will need to be most carefully kept in mind
in the organization and training of this arm in peace-time ?'
we shall not be able to conceal from ourselves that it is in the
strategical handling of the Cavalry that by far the greatest possi-
bilities lie. Charges even of numerically considerable bodies
on the battle-field can only lead to success under very special
conditions, and even for the protection of a retreat our rôle
can only be a subordinate one. But for reconnaissance and
screening, for operations against the enemy's communications,
for the pursuit of a beaten enemy, and all similar operations of
warfare, the Cavalry is, and remains, the principal arm.
Here no other can take its place, for none possesses the
requisite mobility and independence."

The meaning of this is plain, if we remember that Bernhardi contemplates only one type of horsemen, Cavalry,
which are the only troops with the " requisite mobility
and independence " to reconnoitre, screen, and pursue.
It is a truism that horses facilitate these objects. Their
weapon is a distinct question, and all that precedes is an
implicit condemnation of the steel, at any rate for anything in the nature of mixed combat. The reader will
bear in mind the passages on pursuit.

Now, in the light of this passage and all that precedes it, read the chapter on " Leading in Mounted
Combats." Combats against whom ? Surely against
mounted Cavalry ? Surely " collision " must, in its
context, mean that ? Yet for twenty full pages we read
on, more and more bewildered, through passages more and

more suggestive of mixed general combat, until on page 83 we come with a shock to the isolated consideration of " Cavalry duels," which he declares to be " essential," though he admits that they led to " mutual paralysis " and " deadlock " during the war of 1870. A moment later, and for the rest of the chapter, he is deep once more in fire and all that appertains to fire on the modern " battle-field." And he ends with an eloquent purple patch on the " real work " of Cavalry being in *pursuit*.

Happily, in the case of Bernhardi, one is dealing with what *au fond* is not a complex mental structure. He does not arrange his subject with any ulterior purpose. He does not seriously attempt to reconcile faith with science, the *arme blanche* with the firearm. He passes from one to the other with complete *insouciance*, instinctively locking the thought-tight door which divides them, and bestowing on both the enthusiasm of an ardent nature. But the enthusiasm is of significantly different qualities. For the firearm it is predominantly technical and scientific ; for the *arme blanche* it is romantic. In this very chapter, having delivered himself of the *raison d'être*, he enlarges on the difficulties of man-œuvring and leading masses of Cavalry for shock, and shows himself acutely alive to the artificiality of the whole system, to its liability to fall to pieces under stress of a few rifle-shots, and to the absolute impossibility of effecting a sudden tactical transformation to fire-action under pressure of unforeseen conditions, after an advance has begun. The steel is treated poetically. For some reason it has always been regarded as a poetical element in war. In these days of scientific brutality, the less poetry unfounded on hard science and hard facts the better. It is better to be busy in battle with a prosaic weapon than to be idly weaving dreams which never come true. In Bernhardi, the poetry being on the surface, the profound physical and moral fallacies, underlying the *arme blanche* for Cavalry, become the more patent.

Take, for example, this conception of the indispensable inter-Cavalry *shock* fight, which, as I say, I think he really believes to be the only serious rôle of the steel, though, by the way, he never explicitly says in speaking specifically of the Cavalry duel, that it must be a *shock* duel (p. 83). I suspect that such a categorical axiom would revolt his common sense. Remember once more that he regards the ideal Cavalry *qua* riflemen, as the *equals* of Infantry, technically and morally. Read back, or forward, and see what he says about the steel versus Infantry, about Cavalry having been driven out of their place of honour on the battle-fields of the *plains*, about the revolution in conditions caused by arms of precision, etc. Then recollect that Cavalry, unlike Infantry, have horses, allow for country which is not a plain, and construct your own picture of the duel. Lastly, test your picture by South African experience, where the duel, without a trace of shock, lasted for two and a half years, and include, as the finishing touch, the fact, which Bernhardi only once dimly adumbrates and has not seriously envisaged, that mounted riflemen can charge.

One searches the whole of his volume in vain for light upon the profoundly difficult questions which arise from this intermixture of steel-tactics and fire-tactics in one Arm. Though in spirit the whole book is a recognition of the fact that the firearm is absolute arbiter of modern combats, directly he regards the steel in isolation he becomes completely absorbed in " mass " formations, and in every species of drill and manoeuvre which is antagonistic to, and abhorrent to, fire-tactics. In this steel mood there is no confusion in his mind about the meaning of " shock." There is no compromise toward " extensions." For Cavalry charging against Cavalry (pp. 221, 222), " it is a vital article of faith that only the closest knee-to-knee riding—jamming the files together by pressure from the flanks—will guarantee victory or their personal safety." Against "Infantry" (and why not against dismounted Cavalry ?) the utmost he concedes is that the "files must be loosened, and every horse go in his normal stride," but perfect cohesion and symmetry must be maintained. In other words, the essence of true shock—heavy impact—is retained without any qualification. The General, from his own point of view, is perfectly right. Unlike Mr. Goldman, he would have ridiculed the idea that there was shock at Klip Drift with the troopers many yards apart.

And now contrast the directions of our own "Cavalry Training," whose compilers, more sophisticated than the innocent Bernhardi, cannot proceed too far in defining shock and the purposes of shock for fear of falling into transparent solecisms. Section 103 (p. 125) is entitled "Instruction in the Attack against Cavalry." (Note the tacit assumption that Cavalry are always on horseback and always on plains, for on any other interpretation the section is meaningless.) The charge, it is laid down, must have "rapidity and vehemence . . . firm cohesion, highest speed, and determination to win, . . ." but "cohesion " is only further defined as "riding close." If this is a symptom of compromise, it is fatal compromise from the point of view of shock ; for I noticed that in criticizing inter-Cavalry charges at the Cavalry manœuvres of 1909, the Military Correspondent of the *Times* repeatedly censured the lack of cohesion and "boot-to-boot " riding as likely to cause failure against "the best foreign horsemen."* What a satire on our imitative policy ! But in Section 104 (p. 129), "Instruction in the Attack against Infantry and Guns," a reason appears for some anticipatory tinge of compromise. "The troop will usually attack in an *extended formation*." And here,

* *Times*, September 2, 16, etc., 1909.

too, according to Colonel Repington, the Cavalry in 1909 were not up to the mark, this time from excess of cohesion.* Again we see the fatal results of compromise.

All this would be anathema to Bernhardi, who by a singular irony is the model of our Cavalry School. He knew what shock was, and however flagrant the inconsistencies he was drawn into, clung honestly to that true conception. Our authorities know perfectly well that these extended formations are utterly incompatible with shock, and ought to know from South African experience that they are only strictly compatible with a fire-object and a fire-spirit. Then, indeed, they are formidable.

Had I space I could multiply examples of inconsistency in Bernhardi's book. How, after war experience of our own, the *arme blanche* school in this country had the courage to enlist under his banner was a mystery to me on first reading his book, until I came to that blessed formula on page 90, which I had better repeat once more.

" Moreover, in the power of holding the balance correctly between fire-power and shock, and in the training for the former never to allow the troops to lose confidence in the latter, lies the real essence of the Cavalry spirit."

This is his solitary attempt at verbal reconciliation. It is, of course, only verbal. The counsel of perfection is never fortified by practical instruction. There is scarcely an attempt to show that it is humanly possible to create the ideal hybrid, or to show, even if it be created, how to combine harmoniously the two sets of incompatible functions in one scheme of tactics. On the contrary, the deeper he gets into the topic of training the more patent becomes the impossibility of performing this miracle.

The Austrians are more logical. Count Wrangel says :

* *Times,* September 16, 1909.

" The ideal would perhaps be for them [*i.e.*, Cavalry] to do each equally willingly—*i.e.*, to be equally efficient with the carbine as with the *arme blanche ;* in this we include, besides sword and lance, horsemanship. *The attainment of this ideal is, in our opinion, practically impossible.* Not only on account of the short service, which scarcely is sufficient to make a man at one and the same time a clever rider, swordsman, and shooter, but also because the sword and the carbine are such *different masters* that the Cavalryman simply cannot serve both with the same love.

" It requires quite a different temperament to ride to the attack with drawn sword at the gallop than it does to wait for hours placidly aiming in a fire position." (Observe that Wrangel has never heard of rifle charges, and thinks that both sides in South Africa sat out the war " placidly aiming.")

" As long as we lay principal stress on good dashing horsemanship and the clever handling of the *arme blanche*, and relegate training with the rifle to the second place, so long shall we foster the *offensive* spirit of our Cavalry " (" Cavalry in the Russo-Japanese War," p. 55).

Wrangel is wrong, but he is frank. De Negrier is both frank and right in dismissing the steel save for occasions when ." *la panique saisit les troupes en désordre.*" Right, too, are the Americans.

Bernhardi's book is a crushing refutation of Wrangel, and a vindication of de Negrier. Indeed, in his heart of hearts I believe he suspects his formula of balance to be only a counsel of perfection, for in the lines which immediately precede it he implies that only a leader of very rare genius will be capable of combining both systems. As for the men—silence. The formula, moreover, must be read in its context. At the moment he is in his firemood, addressing remarks on the " tactical conduct of dismounted actions " to a Cavalry of whose abysmal ignorance and incapacity in that branch of war he cannot speak too strongly. He is sweetening the pill to the refractory patient.

Our own soldiers refuse to follow Lord Roberts and

de Negrier, and cannot officially say what Wrangel says, because there are still some memories of South Africa left, and Wrangel's opinion is simply pre-South African opinion as embodied in the pre-war Manual. So they have taken Bernhardi's formula ("Cavalry Training," p. 187), add on their own account that "thorough perfection" in both weapons is necessary (Wrangel's impossibility), and by an ambiguous mixture of contradictory counsels manage to save their face in the matter of fire while actually insinuating the full truth of Wrangel's view as to the paramount importance of the steel. The formula of balance is sandwiched between two passages on the same page which reduce the idea of "balance" to a nullity, and which I must now repeat again. The first is :

"Squadrons must be able to attack on foot *when the situation imperatively demands it.*"

The second is :

"It must be accepted as a principle that the rifle, effective as it is, cannot replace the effect produced by the speed of the horse, the magnetism of the charge, and the *terror of cold steel.* For when opportunities for mounted action occur, these characteristics combine to inspire such dash, enthusiasm, and moral ascendency that Cavalry is rendered irresistible."

And we may add that immediately before this latter passage comes another which suggests Wrangel's idea that fire-action is mainly defensive. "Experience in war and peace teaches us that the average leader is only too ready to resort to dismounted action, which often results in acting defensively." It is true that the compilers add that it is important to lay stress on offensive tactics for Cavalry, *even when fighting on foot,* but what chance has that little proviso when they are told in the next breath that dash comes from the steel ?

That assertion is far more sweeping and positive than anything to be found in Bernhardi, who would stultify himself if he spoke in such a general way of the " imperative demands of the situation," of the " defensive " function of the firearm, or of the " terror of cold steel." His whole work is a demonstration, not only of the pressing importance of dash in aggressive fire-action, but of the fact that " even inferior " riflemen, unless in a state of abject panic, do not and need not have the smallest fear of the sword and lance, and to say in so many words that the only persons terrified by those weapons are the Cavalry themselves (who are also riflemen) is more than he could do. I have pointed out that he does make a belated attempt to define, at any rate inferentially, the function of the steel. " Cavalry Training " makes none. Hence " terror " is permissible.

Of course, our official drill-book, in spite of its struggles for compromise, cannot hide the old *reductio ad absurdum*. Here is its list of occasions (pp. 186, 187) which demand fire-action : (1) Enemy entrenched ; (2) enemy occupying " broken or intersected ground " (*e.g.*, most of England and much of Europe) ; (3) enemy's convoy marching under escort ; (4) enemy occupying extended position (in other words, the enemy in his normal position in all modern war) ; (5) covering a retreat ; (6) enabling a scattered force to concentrate with a view to " decisive mounted action "; (7) in the case of numerical inferiority in Cavalry ; to which we must add (8) (from p. 215) " occupying localities for defence " ; (9) patrol work (where combat is necessary) ; and (10) (from p. 229) in pursuit, (where, following Bernhardi, the method is to be by fire, except in case of complete demoralization of the enemy). And yet, in the face of this exhaustive list, Cavalry are only to act by fire when the " situation imperatively demands it !" I think, perhaps, that of all the list No. (3) is the one which appeals most to the sense of humour— if it were a case for humour. It is the only unmistakable allusion to the Boer War in the whole handbook. Otherwise that war might never have been fought, for all the direct recognition it obtains. The idea is, I suppose, that reverses were specially associated with convoys, so that some special concession to fire is needed in that connection to lull the doubts of questioning minds. Unhappily the concession, if it is to be reconciled with the efficacy of the steel weapon at all, cannot possibly be expressed in intelligible language. Why in the world should "mounted attack" on a convoy involve abnormally "wide outflanking operations" (p. 188)? The escort, pinned more or less closely to a mass of transport, is, on the contrary, abnormally devoid of independent mobility, and abnormally open to direct attack at the will of the aggressor. And what is the meaning of this implied distinction between the "outflanking" character of a "mounted attack" and the direct character of a fire-attack? Cannot shock charges be direct, frontal? Observe the revenge which overtakes timid concession. Here is one more implicit betrayal of the steel, one more case of confusion between mobility and combat. Whether you attack the advance-guard, or rear-guard, or flank-guards of a convoy makes no difference to the weapon. If your shock charge is of any use, use it. And the bitter irony of it all is that it was in the attack upon convoys, or columns hampered by a large transport, that the Boers used the "mounted attack" with the most effect. But it was not the mounted attack meant by "Cavalry Training." It was the rifle charge, as at Yzer Spruit, Kleinfontein, Vlakfontein, etc. (Chapter XI. above).

Bernhardi, in many other respects, is a sounder guide to the value of fire-action than "Cavalry Training." He insists, for instance (p. 176), on the vital point that the firearm should be carried on the back, "as is the practice of all races of born horsemen," not attached to the saddle, as our Cavalry carry it, and shows thereby that he is more alive than they are to the real spirit of fire.

Although, regardless of consistency, he blurts out truths about fire which cut at the root of the steel theory, he generally succeeds in avoiding statements about steel which would nullify his conclusions about fire.

To illustrate this, let me return once more to the " shock duel," as between (1) independent Cavalries operating strategically, (2) on the general battle-field. The former case is dealt with in " Cavalry Training " on pages 193, 194, and in Bernhardi on pages 29-31 ; the later case on page 206 of our Manual, and on pages 82-84 of the German book. Bernhardi talks always in vague terms of the Cavalry duel, without mentioning shock, though I grant that he assumes it. But I am perfectly sure that he would not go so far as to say what " Cavalry Training " says on page 194 : " On such occasions dismounted action will at the best have but a *negative* result," and within the space of a few lines to contrast this " dismounted " action (so limited) with a " vigorous mounted offensive." Even with his non-recognition of mounted fire-action, this is just the kind of proposition which he seems, by a sane, if unconscious, instinct, to avoid. In point of fact, on page 267 he uses the epithet " negative " for exactly the opposite purpose, applying it to the " results obtained by our Cavalry in 1866 and 1870 . . . simply and solely because in *equipment and training* they lagged behind the requirements of the time," a passage which must be read with page 83, where he deplores the " mutual paralysis " of the duels of 1870. And all this, let it be remarked, while still believing, with " Cavalry Training," that fire-action is of an essentially dismounted, semi-stationary character, in spite of the lessons of South Africa. If his pen had begun to frame the word " negative " in the sense intended by " Cavalry Training," he would in that instant have been converted.

The solemn discussion of the indispensable *shock* duel in modern war reminds one of the polemics of medieval schoolmen. It is carried on *in vacuo*, without the remotest application to the facts of war, without even one backward glance at South Africa, without support even from the wars of 1866, 1870, and 1877, and without a gleam of encouragement from the Russo-Japanese War. Bernhardi on page 83 makes a pathetic effort to explain its failure at Mars la Tour, and the consequent absence of any decisive effect of the Prussian Cavalry upon the battle-field, in spite of their superiority, by saying vaguely that "neither their training nor the comprehension of their duties was on a level with the requirements of the time." For the real reason turn to his chapters on fire-action and to the passage I have just quoted from page 267, noting "equipment." The truth is that their training for shock was *too* good, and the comprehension of their shock duties so rooted as to be paralyzing. Why should the Cavalry, of all arms, have lacked dash when the rest of the Prussian army was afire with dash, when Infantry commanders had so often to be blamed for excessive rashness ? Why, indeed, save that Cavalry dash was founded on the wrong weapon ? As usual, when hard pressed, Bernhardi relapses into poetry, and urges his Cavalry to " stake their souls " and " risk the last man and the last horse " (p. 84). How strangely these antique dithyrambs ring ! Do not Infantry stake their souls, and risk their last man, and all the rest of it ? Not a whit braver than the Cavalry, did not they, simply because they had a good weapon, show more aggressive tackling power in South Africa than the Cavalry ? It is cruel to brave men to give them a bad weapon, tell them to found their dash on it, and then to blame them for lack of dash ; doubly cruel and doubly absurd to tell them that they are *par excellence* an arm of *offence*, as " Cavalry Training " tells them on page 187. They are not a more offensive arm than Infantry or Artillery. Defensive soldiers are a contradiction in terms.

How explain the mechanical repetition, decade after decade, in spite of all disillusionment, of this axiom—that it is peculiarly the province of Cavalry to sacrifice their last man in winning victories ? As a fact, all arms, in honourable rivalry, must and do make supreme sacrifices for supreme ends. The explanation is that the *arme blanche* is solely a weapon of offence, which has lost its utility and kept its fascination. The idea, I think, can be traced to the days when the duties of reconnaissance were relatively light, and when Cavalry were reserved on the battle-field for special steel functions, such as pursuit, or some desperate assault. All that is changed, by universal recognition. Reconnaissance is infinitely more difficult, exhausting, and important. On the battle-field special opportunities for the steel never, in fact, arise. But Cavalry must be busy, and busy with the rifle.

A last word on the " Cavalry duel." That it must be one of the grand objects of Cavalry to overcome the enemy's Cavalry is a truism. Whether, in the strategical action of independent Cavalry for the purpose of discovering hostile intentions and dispositions, it is best to pursue from the beginning a policy of wide dispersion, or to concentrate at the outset and drive the enemy's independent Cavalry off the field, has often been debated, and is settled now by Bernhardi and " Cavalry Training " in favour of concentration. It is all pure theory, unsupported by any facts either from Manchuria or from South Africa, where our reconnaissance was very bad. Let us, however, for the sake of argument, follow them. But that this collision, either of the concentrated independent Cavalries, or of concentrated Cavalries, in whatever capacity, on the battle-field, must take the form of shock, and can only be decided by shock, is, surely, a preposterous thing for serious men to waste time in proving. De Negrier, with the simplest illustrations from modern war, kills it with ridicule. In England, at any rate, you cannot get conditions of shock for large masses of Cavalry without deliberate selection from a small choice of areas. In practising as independent units, so as to represent rival strategical Cavalries, we choose suitable areas, and arrange for shock ground adaptable to it. In practising for the general battle-field we can obtain the conditions for shock between large masses of opposing Cavalry only by arranging friendly appointments between the two sides, as at Lambourne Downs on the third day of the general Army manœuvres of 1909. And in all cases, of course, we carefully impress upon both Cavalries that collisions without shock are "negative." Perhaps war in England is another "peculiar" war, like the Boer War. But in regard to terrain every war in Europe will be "peculiarly" bad for shock, as compared with South Africa.

Probe to the bottom this delusion about the "negative" effect of fire-action, and you will find for the hundredth time the confusion between mobility and combat. Suppose that one of the Cavalries consists at a given moment of Infantry, a paradoxical state of things which often happened with the Japanese in Manchuria. The action of this Infantry will not be *negative*, as against Cavalry using shock and only shock. Consult "Infantry Training" and the Manchurian War, and you will find that Infantry, averagely well led and trained, can go where they please, both in reconnaissance and combat, without fear of the *lance or sword*. Where they fail is in mobility, and that is why we use horsemen for all the duties of war which require high mobility. If the horsemen have Infantry rifles, and use them well, in conjunction with the horse, then, indeed, in combat as well as in speed, in tactical as well as in strategical mobility, they outmatch Infantry, and impose *negative* action on them. Not otherwise, and precisely the same thing applies *a fortiori* to mounted combats.

Another point : What are " masses " ? I take the word from Bernhardi, who seems not to contemplate shock without great masses, the greater the better. Between the mass and the patrol, where is shock to come in ? The patrol, where combat is necessary, according to " Cavalry Training," acts chiefly with fire, and Bernhardi says the same. For what size of unit does shock begin to be specially applicable ? " Cavalry Training " is dumb. Bernhardi, more frank, as usual, seems to imply that it is really applicable only to very large masses. But why this mystery ? Why should not even patrols use it ? Shock is silent, and therefore suitable. Does it make any difference whether the unit is 10, 50, or 100 strong, or 500, or 1,000, or 5,000 ? From the *arme blanche* point of view it is wiser to leave the question unanswered. The answer would throw a flood of light on the " peculiar " conditions of South Africa, where during a great part of the war the numbers engaged were comparatively small.

Once more I commend this topic to those Yeomanry officers who are asking for the sword, not with the ambitious dream of using it in " mass," but with the idea that for small casual combats it is a necessity. It was *never* so used in South Africa, and if they realized what inexperience with the rifle involved for the Yeomanry in that war—what miserable humiliations and losses—they would be silent. But why should they be silent, as things are ? High authorities tell them the war was peculiar, and recommend them to study German books. It is difficult to speak with restraint on this matter.

Let the reader study closely " Cavalry Training " and " Mounted Infantry Training " in the light both of Bernhardi and of the South African War. Without under-valuing their many excellences, let him apply the search-light to all parts which have any bearing on weapons, and ask himself whether that point has been thoroughly thought out, and brought logically into line with modern experience.   I have said little about "Mounted Infantry Training."   I wonder what Bernhardi would think of it. Tantalizing speculation!   Would he give them "the place of honour on the battle-fields of the plains" which he denies to Cavalry?   Would he give them or deny them reconnaissance and pursuit?   How would he class them? What would his feeling be when he found them exhorted in one breath to use saddle-fire in the manner of the Boers (with their congenital "habits and instincts"), and in the next to form square to repel Cavalry—a form of defence abandoned even by Infantry?

I now leave Bernhardi, whom, if he be intelligently read, with an eye to the Cavalry for which he wrote, I venture to regard as one of the most serious enemies the steel has ever had, and one of the best advocates of the rifle.

But when we compare him, in his two diverse moods, with the German Official Historians, with the Austrian Count Wrangel, with the British "Cavalry Training,' with the French system of training, with Colonel Repington, General French, and Mr. Goldman, and with the facts of modern war, what irreconcilable contradictions, what a tangle of self-refutation and mutual refutation!

And what is our grand motive in following this *enfant terrible?*   I repeat the words which were my text : "We must not be deficient in a weapon possessed by potential foes."   Probably the same motive dimly influences our potential foes.   Who knows how far this imitative instinct extends?   It must strike foreigners as a very remarkable fact that in spite of a three years' war without shock we have reverted to shock.   To whom do they probably look for the explanation?   No doubt to distinguished soldiers now in high authority, and so the process of mutual mystification goes on, the blind leading the blind.   But the proverb scarcely applies to the case of Bernhardi's influence upon our own Cavalry.   That, it seems to me, is the case of a guide with a sure instinct, but short sight, leading one who knows the way, but has wilfully bandaged his eyes.

Of European nations we alone know the full truth, because we alone have evolved the first-class mounted rifleman, and we alone know his supreme value. England bought that secret with two hundred millions of money and twenty thousand lives.   Why not make use of it ?

CHAPTER XIV

THE RUSSO-JAPANESE WAR

SOON after Bernhardi published his second edition of
" Cavalry in Future Wars," the Russo-Japanese War of
1904-5 broke out. Like the Boer War, it fulfilled to the
letter all his prognostications as to the value of fire for
Cavalry and belied all his theories as to the " collision of
Cavalry masses." Whether he regarded it as abnormal, I
do not know. But here, to our own *arme blanche* school,
as we might have expected, is another " peculiar "
war.

It was the second great land war between civilized races
since the invention of the smokeless, long-range magazine
rifle. It was attended by many circumstances which were
absent in South Africa. Both armies were constructed
on the European model ; both were regular, not volunteer ;
both were in very large force ; both possessed steel-armed
Cavalry. The war, in short, may be said to have been
the complement of the Boer War in illustrating all those
conditions which were not present in South Africa, but
which are likely to be present in a European war. Much
of the terrain was even better than South Africa for shock-
tactics. Though from the Yalu to Liao-yang the campaign
was fought in a mountainous area, from the Tai-tse-ho
northward vast open plains, unfenced, unobstructed, of
a character not to be met with in any likely European
war-area, were the rule.

What happened ? No shock. That is not quite

literally true of inter-Cavalry combats, for history records one almost laughably trivial case of pseudo-shock. There are said to have been others between patrols in the early days.* Not a single charge against riflemen on foot. The lance and sword were nowhere. In combat the rifle was supreme, banishing the very thought of the sword even from the minds of those who carried it, and inspiring the only effective action for Cavalry as for Infantry.

I ventured to describe the Boer War as presenting a mass of evidence, vast, various, cogent, against the steel, and in favour of the rifle. Here is another mass of complementary evidence, equally vast, various, and cogent, drawn from the very type of war which our soldiers now envisage—namely, one waged between European armies —in a temperate climate, at any rate in the matter of heat, and in which both Cavalries possess the *arme blanche*.

Before he begins even to think about explanations, I want the reader to grasp the broad *facts* in all their naked simplicity. Four years of war in all in South Africa and Manchuria, under every imaginable condition. No shock. In our war a few small cases of pseudo-shock, which belong strictly to the realm of the rifle. Numerous rifle charges, some very deadly. In both wars the rifle supreme, the steel negligible. What miraculous combination of circumstances could warrant our calling the Manchurian War in its turn " peculiar "?

In England, the *arme blanche* theory for a moment seemed to be in great danger. Some prompt and decisive counter-stroke was indispensable. There could be no compromise here, nothing but a bold lunge straight at the heart would suffice to fell the now formidable heresy.

---

* The recorded case (referred to later) was at Telissu. Colonel McClernand, the U.S. Official Cavalry observer, quotes the Colonel of the Japanese Cavalry of the Guard as having referred to a few steel combats between patrols in the early months of the war.

What form did the stroke take ?   I give it in the words of General Sir John French :

" That the Cavalry on both sides in the recent war did not distinguish themselves or their arm is an undoubted fact, but the reason is quite apparent.   On the Japanese side they were indifferently mounted, the riding was not good, and they were very inferior in numbers, and hence were only enabled to fulfil generally the rôle of Divisional Cavalry, which they appear to have done very well.   The cause of failure on the Russian side is to be found in the fact that for years they have been trained on *exactly the same principles* which these writers " (*i.e.*, advocates of mounted riflemen) " now advocate.   They were devoid of real Cavalry training, they thought of nothing but getting off their horses and shooting; hence they lamentably failed in enterprises which demanded, before all, a display of the highest form of the ' Cavalry spirit ' " (Introduction to Bernhardi, p. xxvii.).

It is true that these words were published in 1906, when information was still limited ; but they appear unmodified in the edition of 1909, and they are in strict accordance with the theory on which our Cavalry are at this moment trained.   To bring them into line with the facts as now known would be to declare the *arme blanche* theory a myth, and to shatter the system based on it.

But before approaching the facts, I propose, as in Chapter XII., to criticize the attitude of mind which permits a high Cavalry authority to brush aside with such confidence another great war in which the sword and lance fell into complete oblivion.   It seems to be perfectly useless for critics of those weapons to heap up masses of modern evidence against them and to prove that there is not a tittle of evidence for them, if we cannot also show to the public the kind of way in which the problem is viewed by those responsible for their retention.

General French held high command in a long, mainly mounted war.   Explain away the result as we may, this war did, in fact, produce by long evolution, under exacting stress, a certain type of soldier common to both belligerents—the mounted rifleman. It was a splendid type on both sides, and if we combine the best qualities of Britons and Boers we can, if we please, construct from it an ideal type. At any rate, what these troops did is on record. The greater their excellence in combining, for strenuous practical work, the rifle and the horse, the better the results. This was the criterion of success. Herein lay " dash "; herein, to borrow General French's words, lay the " highest form of the ' Cavalry spirit.' " It was by approximation to this standard, and by oblivion of all methods directly associated with the steel, that the regular Cavalry acquitted themselves best. It was our glory, not our shame, that we were able to produce this type, and to make it attain, even in the case of raw volunteers, to such a high standard. It was the glory of our brave enemies that, by virtue of progressive excellence in this type, they were able to make the task of the stronger nation so long, costly, and laborious.

How does General French represent this type when he is deploring the failure of the hybrid type in Manchuria ? The Russians, he says, " were devoid of real Cavalry training. They thought of nothing but getting off their horses and shooting," and had no " Cavalry spirit," and these, the General says, were " exactly the same principles " which admirers of mounted riflemen advocate. No wonder he resents such advocacy, if such are the " principles," and no wonder he objects to mounted riflemen who are taught to regard their horses as checks, not helps, to mobility and dash. So far from being his opponents' " principles," these are the very principles upon which, under the blighting influence of the *arme blanche* school, our fine force of existing Mounted Infantry is starved—theoretically, at any rate, into a sort of humble subservience to the steel.

Now, would it not be more natural and normal if, knowing what he knows by war-experience of what mounted riflemen can do, General French were to approach this Manchurian question from a somewhat different standpoint ? Should he not consider the possibility that the Russian Cavalry, which was armed "on exactly the same principles" which he advocates—and was not, as he seems to imply, trained only in the firearm—might have failed through lack of excellence in the whole-hearted union of the rifle and the horse, as the joint constituents of that aggressive mobility which constitutes the "spirit" of the mounted rifleman ? But no. He rushes at once to the conclusion least capable of proof, the conclusion for which there are no positive data since 1870, and very little then, since there were no smokeless, long-range rifles, nor any type of mounted rifleman to force the issue into prominence.

And to what strange conclusions his contemptuous definition of the mounted rifleman brings him ! In the admirable Colesberg operations, when the steel did nothing and inspired nothing, we know that his own Cavalry, under his own direction, were "continually getting off their horses and shooting." After their thirty-mile ride from Kimberley (and the steel did not help them to *ride*) to intercept Cronje, the same Cavalry did well only through forgetting their "real Cavalry training," and taking what he regards as the discreditable step of "getting off their horses to shoot." So did De Wet's men in their equally long rides to the fields of Paardeberg and Sannah's Post. It is true that on many occasions the Cavalry, when in superior force, were too ready, not through lack of spirit but through inherent faults of training, to dismount *prematurely* and take to the carbine. But at whose compulsion ? That of mounted riflemen. And why ? Precisely because they had not grasped " the highest form of the 'Cavalry spirit' "—reliance on horse and firearm in combination. The rifle charge, taught us by the Boers, is, to say the least, not described in an illuminating way by the words " getting off their horses to shoot." Saddle-fire apart, the words, nevertheless, are perfectly accurate. But the Boers shot to more terrible purpose than the Cavalry shot. Historical truth compels us to add that many of our own mounted riflemen excelled the Cavalry in this respect. The handful of Mounted Infantry, who after a chase of many days pounced on and pinned down De Wet at Bothaville, were working, I submit, on the right " principles." So were the Australians who hung on the same leader's heels in the desperate hunt of February, 1901.

If this is General French's mental attitude towards the Manchurian War, I am afraid we cannot expect to find him expressing himself lucidly and cogently on the subject. Turn back to the passage I quoted. The Japanese, he says, indifferently mounted, indifferent riders, and inferior in numbers—drawbacks, be it noted, which are as serious for genuine mounted riflemen as for Cavalry—did very well, but only as Divisional Cavalry. The meaning is not very plain (for they never did well with the steel), but I take it to be this : In our own army the Divisional Cavalry consist, not of Cavalry, but of Mounted Infantry. Their duties, as officially laid down, are " to assist the Infantry in the immediate protection of the division by supplying mounted men for divisional patrolling in connection with the advanced, flank, and rear guards and outposts ; to maintain connection with the protective Cavalry," and other small duties. Proceeding from this analogy, the General means, I gather, to convey that the Japanese Cavalry, acting in those minor capacities, did very well as mounted riflemen. That is all to the good, and presumably they would have done better still with better horses, better riding, and greater numbers.

Is there not also a presumption that with these added advantages they would have done better still in larger rôles as mounted riflemen ? But where is the argument leading us ? Here are the Russians. No praise for them, even in minor rôles, and even with their better horses, better riding, immense numbers, and, above all, their " years of training " as mounted riflemen. Surely the latter characteristic alone would have enabled them, *qua* mounted riflemen, to overcome the few and badly equipped Japanese Cavalry acting as mounted riflemen ? Overcome them, I mean, not merely in minor capacities, but in all the large and important functions of Cavalry ?

The General tacitly admits that neither side made use of the steel. And yet, why not ? One can understand that with these manifold sources of weakness which he details they did not attack Infantry with the steel, but why not attack one another ? Was the mutual " terror of cold steel " so great as to neutralize the steel ? The two Cavalries frequently met in different capacities and in different shades of numerical strength, strategically and tactically. Surely when both sides carry steel weapons this second total disappearance of the " shock duel," officially held to be an inevitable feature of modern war, both in the strategical and tactical phases, needs further explanation.

Pursuing our scrutiny with an eye trained to detect the *arme blanche* bias in its myriad fleeting forms, we detect a clue in the word " enterprises " near the end. This suggests neither the battle-field nor reconnaissance, but distinctly the big raid. We recall Mr. Goldman's complaint of the strategical mishandling of the Cavalry in South Africa, and his assumption that big raids must end in shock-tactics.

I do not know if this was in the General's mind when he wrote of " enterprises " which demanded before all a display of the highest form of the ' Cavalry spirit.' " If it was, I can only respectfully repeat my view, expressed frequently elsewhere, that there is here a radical confusion of thought between combat and strategy, between mobility in its broadest sense and tactics, and

Bernhardi would be the first to tell him so. Fortunately, this question of raids is as open to positive demonstration by Manchurian facts as any other point of Cavalry practice. But before even approaching the Manchurian facts, and taking my stand purely on South African lessons, I have shown, I hope, that *prima facie* the General's reason for the comparative failure of the two Cavalries is open to the strongest suspicion. The facts themselves dispose of the reason altogether.

It was never part of my scheme to deal in detail with the Manchurian story. I believe that for Englishmen, their own great war should be sufficient evidence. And yet, having reached this point, I feel inclined to regret that I did not begin with the Asiatic war, hardly complete as the material still is, and briefly summarize our own, so exaggerated seems to be the craving in many minds for foreign precedents and foreign models, so reckless the disregard for British experience, even when that experience is most stimulating and glorious. Happily, the Manchurian data are simple, uniform, and as absolutely free from complications or apparent contradictions as the South African data whose lessons they confirm.

What is the salient point? With all respect to General French, the salient point for Englishmen, who know by bitter experience that shock training has failed them, is not whether the Russians or Japanese were good shock horsemen, but whether they were good mounted riflemen. Our own Cavalry in South Africa were good shock horsemen, but that did not save the friends of shock from the necessity of finding elaborate reasons for the disappearance of shock during that war. Now for our salient point. Were the Russian Cavalry, who were far the most numerous and in some ways the better equipped of the two Cavalries, good mounted riflemen, by our proved standard of what is good? The answer, from all critics and observers, comes unanimously and emphatically, " No." In the first place, they were of the hybrid type, carrying swords and, in the great majority of cases, lances as well. Their legendary skill in fire-action proved to be a myth. The Boers would have laughed at them. Our own mounted riflemen would have regarded them as inefficient and ignorant. To the surprise of many people, they had none of the " habits and instincts " for modern war that the Boers had, nothing of the stalking power, the scouting power, the genius for ground and surprise, much less the charging power developed. The Historians of our General Staff (part i., p. 29) supply the explanation : " The system of tactical training was not unlike that of other European armies. Thus the Cavalry was trained both for mounted and dismounted combat, but *the musketry training necessary to make it efficient when on foot fell short of the requirements of modern war.* The Cossacks, who formed the greater part of the Russian mounted force, were trained on lines similar to the regular Cavalry, but did not attain to the standard laid down for the latter."

We must allow, of course, for general causes. The whole Russian army, by the testimony of its own leaders, was in a backward state, and the Cavalry was as backward as other arms. Its morale, by comparison with the Japanese morale, was low. In every arm the officers—that vitally important element—were ill-educated ; in every arm, together with much splendid devotion and zeal, some of the officers were neglectful of duty. The Cavalry suffered as much as any arm. Wrangel, the Austrian critic, describes the greater part of the Russian Cavalry engaged in the Manchurian Field Army, especially those Cossack organizations which consisted of troops of the second and third class of reserves, as being in the general sense " inefficient mounted troops."* Our own Official Reports, however, give a more favourable im-

* "Cavalry in the Russo-Japanese War," pp. 8-11.

pression.   The older reserve men were, no doubt, unfit for the field, but among the Don, Orenburg, and Trans-Baikal Cossacks there seems to have been some very good material.

Mr. McCullagh, in his book, " With the Cossacks," gives an interesting description of the great variety of religions, races, languages, colours, and military types which were embodied in the troops known broadly as Cossacks.   The Caucasians, though they carried carbines, appear to have been by tradition and choice steel horsemen pure and simple.   But whatever the training, there is no dispute about the incompetence of all the Cossacks as riflemen. Captain Spaits gives a distressing account of their failures.* McCullagh says : " They had no skill whatever in attacking entrenched Infantry.   *Once dismounted, they are lost.*" (p.182).   Both these writers accompanied them in the field.   On manœuvre and general employment there is an equally general agreement.   Unlike the Japanese, they were maintained for the most part in large independent bodies, in dim homage, we may presume, to that " collision of Cavalry masses " which is the basis of the shock theory.   So massed, they were generally idle, just as the Cavalries of 1866, 1870, and 1877 were too often idle, by the admission of Bernhardi, Kuropatkin, and Von Moltke.   There never appears a trace of talent for fire-tactics, or an attempt to play either the aggressive or the delaying rôle of the riflemen in South Africa.

What effect had that War had upon Russian Cavalry ? None.   No more effect than the brilliant performances of the Civil War leaders had upon the Austrian, Prussian, and French Cavalries in the wars of 1866 and 1870, or upon our own Cavalry in 1899.   How many Cossack privates had *heard* of our war ?   How many of their officers had studied it ?   Truly those words, " trained for years on the very principles these writers advocate," are a little hard on those Cavalry leaders in South Africa

* " Mit Kosaken durch die Mandschurei."

who led mounted riflemen with distinction. They are very hard, if he only knew it, on General French.

Kuropatkin (vol. ii., p. 151) is cruelly illuminating. It is true he never mentions armaments or the tactics derived from it. Nor did Von Moltke in his equally hard censure of the Prussian Cavalry of 1866 for the same grave delinquency—timidity on the battle-field. It was left for Bernhardi to disclose the true cause and the true remedy. Kuropatkin dwells on "training" and on commanders, most of whom he accuses of cowardice; for "the material of which our Cavalry was composed was excellent" (with certain exceptions afterwards named). What "training" and "command" meant becomes apparent. The Cavalry should have fought as "*obstinately as Infantry*," and by way of contrasting the two arms he gives pitiless statistics of relative casualties at the battles of Mukden and Telissu, where no observer or historian has ever suggested that there was any reason for or sense in shock. The single example he names of a good performance, that of the Cossacks at Yen-tai Mines, was one of defensive fire-action pure and simple, where the Cavalry "fought with greater bravery than some of Orloff's Infantry." Surely it was knowledge, not courage, that the rest lacked.

Look at the only large "enterprise" undertaken by the Russian Cavalry—Mishchenko's great raid, with 8,000 men and 34 guns, upon Ying-kou in January, 1905. No better example could be found for proving the fallacy of associating the success of independent strategical enterprises with the steel weapon. Of the conditions of success, one category has nothing to do with combat, but purely with mobility. The distance was 80 miles, as compared, for example, with the 100-mile raids imagined by Mr. Goldman for South Africa. There was a slow-moving millstone of a convoy, requiring protection and limiting speed, exactly our own difficulty when our

mounted troops, Cavalry included, cut themselves completely adrift from their communications, exactly the
difficulty which Bernhardi insists on when dealing with
the limitations to Cavalry raids. Scouting was bad.
Contrast the Boer scouting. Scouts, at any rate, do
not have shock duels. Passing to combat, we find no
shadow of a suggestion in any narrative that there was
the remotest opportunity for shock (except for a case
mentioned by McCullagh, where a Cossack brigade
charged a few Chinese brigands). The Japanese troops
met with were always Infantry, and were always in great
numerical inferiority. Until actually reaching Ying-kou,
they were met with in the shape of small detachments
guarding villages or railway-bridges. Result, small fire-
actions, in which the Cossacks showed incompetence.
Contrast De Wet's skill in raiding similar posts. One of
the three Russian columns, several regiments strong, was
kept back, says Captain Spaits, for three hours by half a
company of Infantry, which occupied a small trench—the
history of Dronfield and Poplar Grove repeating itself in
Manchuria. Another column was defied by a handful of
Infantry at Niu-chuang. Finally, at Ying-kou, after the
repulse of one Russian column by a precipitately de-
trained batch of Japanese Infantry, Mishchenko, with
1,500 men, made a night attack on the railway-station,
held by 300 Japanese Infantry. His dispositions were
painfully crude ; he was repulsed with heavy loss, the
retirement, says Colonel Shisnikoff, was " an utter rout,"
and that was the end of the raid. Contrast the Boer
night attacks, so rarely, even when unsuccessful, suffering
serious loss, so often highly successful. The results of
the raid, a few transports burnt and some trivial demoli-
tions on the railway, may be regarded as *nil*. The retreat
to the base was precipitate, headlong, and what was the
reason for the retreat ? The rumour that a force of
Japanese *Infantry* was preparing to block the line of
retreat. In view of what had happened, Mishchenko

was right not to risk that contingency. But is not all this a pitiful satire on the theory of hybrid training? Observe that the conditions were strictly normal. Raids on communications always have to meet stationary dismounted detachments of the enemy. What, then, is the use of a Cavalry which cannot attack and defeat Infantry by Infantry methods? The only abnormality was the absence of any hostile Japanese Cavalry throughout the whole course of the raid. And we are asked to believe that the grand *raison d'être* for elaborate and perfect training in the steel is to overthrow the enemy's Cavalry, who are also, by our official hypothesis, "thoroughly efficient" in the rifle, and who, on this occasion, were not present at all! And after overthrowing them by shock, then there is to be, in General French's words, "a brilliant field of enterprise for Cavalry as mounted riflemen." Brilliant! "The story of the raid," says Colonel Shisnikoff, "is a memory of shame to those who took part in it." And to crown all, it is General French's warning to our Cavalry that the Cossacks failed in the war owing to overtraining as mounted riflemen! *Quo non mortalia pectora cogis, ferri sacra fames?*

These are the Cavalry who, he suggests, were trained on *our* heretical principles. "Continually getting off their horses!" Is it a disgrace to dismount? Does he regret that Scobell's Lancers at Bouwer's Hoek did not use shock with the lance in storming Lotter's laager? Would Mr. Goldman have had these Russians charge loop-holed buildings on horseback? Once in the course of this raid, they are said to have charged a wall, and one account of the night attack on Ying-kou represents some of the Cossacks as having advanced on foot, "sword in hand." The true fighting moral of this enterprise was that the Cossacks should have been better riflemen. Contrast the great raids of the Civil War, when the firearm, although so imperfect, was the governing factor. Why were

there never any great raids in the Franco-German War ?
Study Bernhardi, that unconscious satirist of the steel,
and you will guess why. Lastly, contrast the Japanese
raid (described fully in our " British Officers' Reports,"
(vol. ii.) by 172 men, under Colonel Naganuma,
who, in the course of an expedition round the Russian
rear, beginning on January 9, 1905, lasting more than
two months, covering a vast distance, and including
several hotly contested fire-actions, achieved the substantial result of blowing up by night the great railway-
bridge at Hsin-kai-ho on February 12. The result was
to cause Kuropatkin to divert 8,000 men, including a
division of Cavalry, from the imminent battle of Mukden
for the defence of his communications. This raid and its
fellow under Hasegawa were in the style of Stuart and
De Wet. Compare, too, the ride of Smuts to Cape
Colony, and its subsequent results in diverting troops to
that quarter and in actual damage to our forces and
communications.*

Few as the achievements of the Russian Cavalry were,
whatever they did achieve was through fire-action.
Kuropatkin and all critics praise Samsonoff's defence of
the Yen-tai coal-mines during the battle of Liao-yang,
when he checked by fire the Japanese pursuit of Orloff's
beaten division. Rennenkampf, another leader of Cavalry
who showed signs of ability, in the course of the great
battle of the Sha Ho, led 1,500 Cossacks against the
Japanese communications on the upper Tai-tse-ho
(October 8 to 12, 1904). Wrangel commends his enterprise, but admits his complete failure. Our " British
Officers' Reports," vol. i., pp. 664-668, give a full account
of the whole episode, and describe the brilliant success of
the Second Japanese Cavalry Brigade under Prince Kanin,
first in anticipating Rennenkampf at Chaotao, which had
been defended by only seventy Infantry for two days,
then in driving the Cossacks back and forcing them to

* *Times* History, vol. v., pp. 302-319, 388, 394.

uncover one of their own Infantry brigades, which was attacking Pen-hse-hu, on the northern bank of the Tai-tse-ho. Prince Kanin, unmolested by the Cossacks, proceeded to surprise the reserve battalions of this brigade, and in the space of a few minutes killed many hundreds with his six Maxims. The result was the retirement of the Russian left and Stackelberg's eventual retreat. Needless to say, there was no question of shock between the two Cavalries, nor any suggestion from any quarter that there was any reason for it or possibility of it.

Wrangel credits the Russians with having "adequately solved some strategical tasks "—for instance, the guarding of the passes of the Fen-shui-ling Mountains against Kuroki and Nodzu, and the discovery, but nothing more than the bare discovery, of Kuroki's flank movement at Liao-yang, and of Nogi's terrible turning stroke at the battle of Mukden. In other respects they showed the most pitiful weakness at that last great crisis. No less than 25,000 strong, they were outmanœuvred and outfought by two brigades of Japanese Cavalry acting with Infantry. Of course no shock duel, and yet was the effect of the Japanese Cavalry " negative," in the words of " Cavalry Training " ? On the contrary, it was tremendously positive, and with larger numbers might have been as decisive as Sheridan's interception of Lee in April, 1865. Wrangel gravely remarks that *if* the Cossacks had first overthrown the Japanese Cavalry a great rôle would have been open to them in resisting Nogi's main force—not, he goes out of his way to say, with the *arme blanche*, but with fire-action. The old story ! If they could not overcome even the Japanese hybrid Cavalry with fire, how could they overcome Japanese Infantry ? As for shock, it is cynical levity to breathe the word in connection with that Titanic fire-struggle of March, 1905.

Wrangel himself throws some light on these perplexing conundrums. It is on page 24. He has just been deplor-

ing the fiasco of Mishchenko's raid, and has added that
throughout the war the Russian Cavalry showed none of
that " desire for action " which " we recognize as the first
and most important attribute of our arm." (As though,
forsooth, it was not the first attribute of Infantry and
Artillery!) We await resignedly the usual Cavalry
dictum—that they were ill-trained for shock, and were
" continually getting off their horses." Not a bit of it.
He goes on thus :

" On the other hand, a just critic, without any further ado,
must admit that the prevailing conditions made it extraordinarily difficult for the Cavalry masses of Kuropatkin to
play the part of Cavalry in battle. Indeed, we do not mind
openly declaring that, in our opinion, *no other European
Cavalry, supported by the principles of the Cavalry tactics of the
day*, would have been in a position to perform anything of
note on the Manchurian battle-fields " (" Cavalry in the
Russo-Japanese War," p. 23).

He goes on to say that Cavalry cannot attack " Infantry
masses " (but there were no masses during Mishchenko's
raid) unless utterly demoralized, and that " as long as
the two battle-fronts are struggling with one another, the
Cavalry arm is obliged to respect unrestrained the emptiness of the modern battle-field, . . . which is ruled by
the magazine rifle."

Really, what are we coming to ? It was something of
a shock to hear Bernhardi saying that Cavalry had been
driven from their place of honour on the battle-fields of
the plains, but that this arm, whose soul is offence, is to
respect unrestrained the emptiness of the modern battle-
field is surely a counsel of appalling levity. Mounted
riflemen, at any rate, do not carry respect for the dangers
of the battle-field to this length. If they had, there
would have been no war in South Africa at all. Our foes
would have respected the emptiness of the veld from
Pretoria to Cape Town.

Wrangel marches cheerfully on towards the inevitable *reductio ad absurdum :*

" As the lion-hearted Japanese Infantry never gave the Russian dragoons or Cossacks the pleasure of retreating in disorder to exemplify the last-mentioned principles, *it remained only for the latter to seek out the hostile Cavalry.* This also the Russian Cavalry divisions did not succeed in doing—whether through their own fault remains for the present undecided " (*ibid.*, p. 29).

This is not sarcastic ; it is the sincere thought of a serious Cavalry soldier, who believes in the *arme blanche*. Here is the admission, frank and unabashed, that Cavalry, because they are deficient in fire-power, are only formidable to Cavalry, who are equally deficient in fire-power ; that nobody cares a snap of the fingers for the lance or sword but those who, choosing to carry those weapons, agree to fear them. Clearly, even this exception is no exception, because one or both parties may by caprice or design break the compact and take to the firearm, which will then " rule the battle-field." In another passage on page 17, when commenting on the failure of the Russian Cavalry to use an " active screen " in the phase of strategical reconnaissance—*i.e.*, in non-battle-field encounters of the rival Cavalries—he gives as a cause the fact that the " Japanese Cavalry seldom committed themselves to shock tactics "—precisely the opposite cause alleged by General French—namely, that the Russians themselves were " continually getting off their horses." Wrangel perceives that the steel weapon is lost if this sort of thing goes on ; so in his final conclusion, quoted in my last chapter (p. 316), he urges his own Cavalry to remain deaf to the " so-called " intelligence of the advocates of fire training, which is impossible to combine with shock training, but to give the carbine an emphatically secondary place, and concentrate on shock. If all Cavalries agree on this self-denying ordinance, then, he implies, ground permitting, and far from the unseemly fire-scuffles of the battle-fields, we shall have, if both sides play fair, some grand spectacles of shock. There is less mental chaos in Wrangel than in most exponents of shock, because he ignores the historical achievements of mounted riflemen, and therefore feels no need for compromise ; but he cannot altogether escape self-contradiction. In order to proffer an illustration of the theory that shock should decide inter-Cavalry combats, he instances the first in the war—at Tschondschu (Tiessu) on March 28, 1904 (pp. 51-53)—a small affair where six squadrons of Cossacks were driven away from a walled town by the fire-action of three squadrons of Japanese Cavalry. We read that the Russians, being in larger force, should have " obtained a brilliant result " with the *arme blanche*, and also that the Japanese, after forcing the Russians to accept fire-action, should have charged and defeated the Russians. At the end we discover that the writer has no knowledge of the terrain beyond the fact that the town was situated in a " mountainous district," from which fact he infers that there must have been " ground over which the Japanese could have advanced unseen " for their charge. Truly a startling variation of the usual complaint of lack of " Cavalry " ground !

It is greatly to be regretted that Count Wrangel's ignorance of the attainments of British Cavalry permits him to class them among other European Cavalries as equally incompetent to have succeeded better than the Russians on the Manchurian battle-fields. Like de Negrier's biting criticism of the French Cavalry, the pronouncement throws a strange light on our own theory of imitating the armament of Continental armies. Our Cavalry have very good firearms, and are, so far as time allows, trained to use them a good deal better than the Austrians permit. And they *can* use them well, as they showed in South Africa, where they did engage in the " battle," and as they have shown in our recent manœuvres. But, that point made clear, I make no apology whatever for quoting at length the Austrian critic in a chapter starting originally from an appreciation of Manchurian problems by our foremost Cavalry authority, General French. The fundamental line of reasoning in both cases is precisely the same, but Wrangel is ruthlessly logical and careless of the logical consequences. General French's reasoning leads him inexorably to precisely the same conclusion as Wrangel— namely, that steel-armed Cavalry can be formidable only to steel-armed Cavalry. Both men believe in the indispensable shock duel, both underrate the rifle as a source of dash—for Cavalry. General French sneers at it in the words " continually getting off their horses "; Count Wrangel does not sneer at it. He respects it so much as to banish Cavalry from the sphere of fire altogether, for clean and decent encounters with a less formidable weapon. This is the inevitable tendency of the present reaction in England. "Cavalry Training " and Bernhardi's book admit, no doubt, of the most liberal interpretation in the right direction by officers who resolutely work out to their logical conclusion the directions given for fire-action, and ignore the conflicting directions for the steel. But whence is to come this liberal interpretation, when high Cavalry authorities denounce leanings towards fire as a betrayal of the " Cavalry spirit," and, so far from depreciating the sword, add the lance ?

Let us turn to the Japanese Cavalry. They were a very small force. Outside the thirteen, and eventually seventeen divisional regiments of 420 men apiece, which seem to have been in excess of divisional requirements (for Infantry did much of the work required), there were only two independent brigades of three regiments apiece —2,300 sabres together. The troopers carried good firearms, though of too short a range, but were trained principally for shock, and used the antiquated German drill-books denounced by Bernhardi. Lances wisely had been left at home, and only swords taken to the war. The men, constitutionally, were bad horsemen. Their horses were poor and were overloaded.* The astonishing thing is that they did so well under these conditions. As soon as they grasped the fact that fire governed action, the talent for fire which they shared with the Infantry, coupled with great keenness, was their salvation. Enormously outmatched in numbers, they overawed and outfought the enemy's Cavalry; they fulfilled sufficiently well, at any rate, in conjunction with the Infantry, the task of reconnaissance, both protective and offensive— and, in short, took a substantial part in enabling Japan to win the war. Needless to say, they were just as " lion-hearted "—to use Wrangel's expression—as other arms, but, having been trained and armed on false principles, naturally did not win laurels as great as those of the Infantry. Nevertheless, there is truth, I believe, in what Wrangel—always frank, at whatever cost—says in the following passage :

" The Japanese Cavalry, scarcely without exception, carried out their performances with the *carbine*, and in close touch with their own Infantry. To this circumstance, without doubt, we have to ascribe the principal reason why there has been hesitation among military critics in giving full recognition to their activity. A certain narrow-mindedness obstructs the means used to gain the end, which in no way is inclined to further the interests of the arm " (pp. 49, 50).

Extraordinary the words seem, in the face of Wrangel's ultimate conclusion about the *arme blanche ;* but the topic breeds paradox. Still stranger is what follows :

" ' *To be victorious is the chief thing.*' Under all circumstances this will remain our motto. If we do not succeed with the

* Both on horses and on horse-mastership opinions differ (see " British Officers' Reports," vol ii., and the U.S. Reports). The figures of wastage seem to show good management.

sword or lance, then let us try firearms. If we are too weak to gain success alone, then let us only be too thankful and accept without scruple the help of our Infantry. Accordingly, on these principles the Japanese Cavalry consistently acted. To reproach them because of this is extremely unjustifiable " (p. 50).

Then, forgetting that he has previously explained the absence of shock in the Russians by the Japanese adoption of fire-tactics, he adds :

" Besides, it must not be forgotten that they (the Japanese), as the weakest force, had the manner of fighting dictated to them by their opponents."

A whimsical side-light on all of which is thrown by General Sir C. J. Burnett (" British Officers' Reports," vol. ii., p. 543), who thinks the " much-maligned " Japanese Cavalry, " with their thorough knowledge of shock-tactics," must have found it " gall and wormwood to hang on to the skirts of their Infantry," instead of " riding straight at the opposing Cavalry whenever the opportunity offered."

Wrangel adds that men on " fast-galloping horses," and on " not too unfavourable ground," will be able to enjoy the " irresistible pleasure of charging home with the sword " against dismounted Cavalry. Elsewhere he speaks, in a passage I have quoted before, of the necessity of " eternally galloping." Our minds go back to the vast destruction of British horseflesh in South Africa, to the wild chimera of the " eternally galloping " horse in any war, to the hard incessant work imposed on scouts and patrols (who have somehow to combine scouting and patrolling with battle duties), and lastly to the charges at the canter made by the ill-fed, undersized Boer ponies. Again, I make no apology for quoting these passages. Wrangel is another of the *enfants terribles*, like Bernhardi. He betrays his own case, and the more fatally because he does not seem to have studied our war at all ; but his case *au fond* is the same as that of our own Cavalry school.

Among the achievements of the Independent Japanese Cavalry I have mentioned the case of Naganuma's raid, of Prince Kanin's important success at Pen-hse-hu, and of the energetic co-operation with the Second and Third Armies at Mukden. In this latter case Wrangel credits them with having pushed forward " in an extraordinarily quick and energetic manner," driving the Russian Cavalry before them. That the praise is well deserved is shown by the " British Officers' Reports " (vol. ii.). The Russian Cavalry are estimated at 25,000, the Japanese at 3,240. The latter, both in obtaining information and in action, did extraordinarily well, especially with Nogi's Third Army. The information is not wholly complete. Exactly how near the Cavalry came to interception does not appear.

Wrangel also gives high praise to the work of the First Cavalry Brigade at the battle of Telissu on June 14-15, 1904. Sir Ian Hamilton (vol. ii., p. 330, etc.) conveys the same impression in regard to the battle, though he, like Kuropatkin, dwells principally on the feebleness of the Russian Cavalry in not using plain opportunities for delaying fire-action against Oku's turning force. A preliminary combat of advanced guards on May 30 had led to the only recorded case of an *arme blanche* charge in the war, when two squadrons of Cossacks charged one Japanese squadron and, not having room to gather speed, used their lances as quarter-staves. Would not revolvers have done better ? The squadron was defeated, but the " general results of the engagement were indecisive."* In the culminating battle of the 15th the

---

* Our Official Historians (Part ii., p. 32), referring to the same incident, speak of a charge in " open order " over fifty yards of ground, and of lances being used with "great effect." The losses on both sides were evidently small.

Japanese Brigade checked a critical counter-attack by Glasko's Thirty-fifth Infantry Division, freed the flank of the Third Japanese Division, and took an energetic part in the pursuit of the Russians, driving back the rear-guard by fire.

All critics and historians mention the splendid behaviour of the Second Japanese Cavalry Brigade and of other divisional detachments at the battle of January 26 to 29, 1905, called by the Russians Shen-tan-pu, and by our historians Hei-kou-tai (see " British Officers' Reports," vol. ii., pp. 45-58). It was a vehement attack of four divisions against the left of the Japanese entrenched line, held by the Second Army, forty miles south of Mukden. The Japanese Cavalry brigade occupied a cluster of villages near the junction of the Hun and Taitsu Rivers, and in the course of a bitterly contested battle, lasting three days, had to take their share, sometimes with Infantry support, in meeting attacks by greatly superior forces. In this case the work they had to do was precisely the work of Infantry, and our minds go back once more to the directions of our " Cavalry Training "—that Cavalry may be called upon to " occupy localities for defence," but that their defences are on no account to be otherwise than of the " simplest description," so as not to weaken the offensive instinct of an essentially offensive arm—in other words, so as not to compromise the steel weapon. This is to organize defeat. If the Japanese had thought so lightly of fire and the concomitants of fire, they would never have had the offensive instinct which they showed at Pen-hse-hu, Telissu, and Mukden.

Everywhere the same moral. In screening, raiding, and battle, fire is master. No observer suggests on any definite occasion any definite opportunity for the use of steel by the Cavalry engaged. Sir Ian Hamilton, the senior of the large staff of British officers who watched the Manchurian War, himself a successful leader in South

Africa, has given his opinion officially (" Reports," vol. ii., p. 526) and in his published diary. He does not miss or evade the point ; he grapples with it directly, and is constantly contrasting South African mounted men and methods with Manchurian men and methods, and his conclusion is unreservedly in favour of the rifle. His opinion began to be confirmed at the first battle of the war, the Yalu, where neither Cavalry had any effect on events. His Japanese friends, he tells us, were very much surprised, and naturally, for they held German theories. But " the warmest advocate of shock must allow, when he follows the course of events on this occasion over the actual ground, that there was no place or opportunity where the horse could possibly have been of any value except to bring a rifleman rapidly up to the right spot " (vol. i., p. 137). Throughout the Manchurian campaign " the thought never " but once " occurred to him to long for Cavalry to launch at the enemy during some crisis of the struggle. Neither Infantry has the slightest idea of permitting itself to be hustled by mounted men, and it has been apparent . . . that the Cavalry could not influence the fighting one way or another, except by getting off their horses and using their rifles."

Nevertheless, two of the officers who were present do succeed in concluding that the war proves the supreme value of the steel weapon ; and if my readers wish to gauge the tyranny of a blind faith over the minds of accomplished practical men, whose Reports on any other point are lucid and convincing, let him read, in close connection with Count Wrangel's two contradictory explanations of the absence of shock, the remarks on the Japanese Cavalry by General Sir C. J. Burnett and Colonel W. H. Birkbeck (vol. ii., pp. 542-545). It would be a comedy, if such comedies did not have tragic consequences. Colonel Birkbeck seeks an interview with General Akiyama. That vigorous employer of aggressive fire-action states that his Cavalry learnt to draw their " greatest confidence " from the firearm. Wincing, however, under a reminder from Colonel Birkbeck of the religious " cult of the sword " in Japan, he pleads defensive necessities against the enormous numerical strength of the Russians, who, however, were " incapable of forcing an issue at close quarters " ! If they had been Cavalry " truly trained as such," besides being enormously superior, then—but the General is too clever to court the *reductio ad absurdum*—then " the case would have been different." General Burnett's comment I quoted on page 347, and to complete the comedy, Colonel Birkbeck, in a separate report (No. 10), has conjecturally attributed the inaction of the 25,000 Russian Cavalry at the battle of Mukden to their lack of training for shock ! In his interview with the more tactful Colonel McClernand, of the United States army, Akiyama speaks the plain, unvarnished truth.

Let the reader now take a bird's-eye view of the historical chain of authoritative comment on the performances of Cavalry.

Here is Von Moltke reporting to the King of Prussia, after the Austro-Prussian War of 1866 :

" Our Cavalry failed, perhaps not so much in actual capacity as in self-confidence. All its initiative had been destroyed at manœuvres . . . and it therefore shirked bold, independent action, and kept far in the rear, and as much as possible out of sight," etc. (" Taktisch-Strategische-Aufsätze ").

General French, in his Introduction to Bernhardi (p. xxvii), actually quotes this view as a warning to our Cavalry of the present day against " ultra-caution " with the *steel* in the presence of Infantry fire ; quotes it, I repeat, in the beginning of a volume whose central thesis is the futility of the steel in opposition to fire.

It may be added that an " Austrian officer of high rank," who is quoted in the French translation of the

Austrian Official History of that same war of 1866, attributed what he calls the " success " of the Prussian Cavalry to their reliance on the support of Infantry—that is, on *fire*. His compatriot Wrangel, forty years later, says the same of the Japanese Cavalry.

Bernhardi reminds his countrymen that in the war of 1870 their own Cavalry, and in the Russo-Turkish War of 1877-78 the Russian Cavalry, only obtained the poor success they did obtain because " not even approximately equal Cavalry " opposed them, criticizes their performances severely, and passionately advocates perfection in the use of the rifle.

We come to the South African War, where the firearm inspires the best achievements of Cavalry and the steel weapon is discarded, and where we find even the most convinced upholders of the *arme blanche* forced to construct an elaborate and often self-contradictory scheme of explanation for the failure of the British Cavalry—*qua* Cavalry—in that campaign.

The Japanese Cavalry only approaches other arms in so far as it uses fire well. And we end with Kuropatkin, who has condemned the Russian Cavalry in the war of 1877, and who, in the war of 1904-5, almost in the identical words used by Von Moltke, deplores the lack of confidence and dash in the Cavalry, and regards them as having *failed*.

Unanimity. Censure and excuses always. Of what other class of soldiers is this invariable complaint made ? And what is the common element in all these censured Cavalries ? Inefficiency in fire-action. Of the wars prior to the invention of the deadly modern rifle, which is the war where Cavalry are least censured and most praised ? The American Civil War, earlier than any of those I have named, where the Cavalries learnt reliance on the firearm, though their example passed unnoticed in Europe. After that invention, what type do we find winning its way to success in South Africa ? The mounted rifleman. Which weapon succeeds in Manchuria ? The firearm.

I have carried the reader of this volume through a very Wonderland of paradox. Let him collect the threads of one more paradox in our own domestic history.

In 1899, deaf to history and its most brilliant English exponent, Colonel Henderson, our Cavalry went to war equipped and trained like the present French Cavalry.

They and the nation suffered accordingly. After the war, Lord Roberts embodied in a preface to the " Cavalry Training " Manual of 1904 the ripe experience, not only of the South African War, but of a long life spent in military service. He inculcated reliance on the rifle as the principal weapon for all purposes of the Cavalry soldier. Two years later, although Manchuria had confirmed his words in every particular, the injunction was forgotten, and our Cavalry were sitting at the feet of a German writer who had nothing to tell them about the rifle which they had not already learnt by costly war experience, and who was addressing, not them, but a Cavalry ignorant of the ABC of modern fire-tactics. But, as a matter of theory, not of experience, he clung to shock, expounding it in terms irreconcilable with fire. Our Manual of 1904 was superseded by the Manual of 1907, with the directions of Lord Roberts expunged and Bernhardi's self-contradictory counsels embodied. In the August number of the *Revue des deux Mondes* of 1908 many people were astonished to find set forth in full by General de Negrier, as a model to the " dreaming " French Cavalry, Lord Roberts's preface to our Manual of 1904. That Manual is cancelled. So that to find in its living, authoritative form the verdict of our greatest living soldier, derived from facts, not from theory, on a technical and tactical question of vital importance, the student has to search the files of a French review.

CHAPTER XV

REFORM

I.—Study.

"Trust thyself. Every heart vibrates to that iron string."

I venture to address my first recommendation to professional soldiers, volunteer soldiers, and civilians alike. Study your own great war. Shut your ears to those who say it is abnormal. Study it with an open mind, forming your own opinion, and remembering that this is *your* experience.

With the facts and conditions of your own modern war thoroughly in your head, re-study other wars, including the last great war in Manchuria. Note the progress made during the last fifty years in the precision, range, and smokelessness of the firearm, compared with the unimprovable nature of the steel weapon. Ask yourself if the professional Cavalries in these various wars were alive to the lesson of this revolution, and whether their successors, judged by their own writings, are alive now to the lesson. And do not, I beseech, when you hear it said (with truth) that the " principles of war " never change, be misled into imagining that the steel weapon for horsemen is one of the " principles of war."

Picture past wars, such as the Franco-German War, by the light of the knowledge actually then in existence, but unused, as to the possibilities of the rifle in the hands of mounted men. Reckon the opportunities lost, and ask yourself if the successes gained by the steel might not have been gained equally well even in those days by first-class mounted riflemen.

Remember all the while in constructing out of precedents this " case law " that there is a " common law " behind, a physical principle, which is independent in the last resort of all psychological and historical associations. Follow it out, as I have often suggested in terms of vulnerability and mobility, constantly using the foot-riflemen as an analogy. But realize that the bayonet, which is used as the climax of a fire-fight on foot, is not the analogue of the sword or lance, which are used from horse-back only, on a system impossible to associate with fire. Superimpose the moral and psychological factors—in one word, the *spirit*—bearing in mind that the best weapon will promote the best spirit, and inspire the most fear in the enemy. Lastly, take training, and reflect whether it be possible for a hybrid type to attain perfection in two highly exacting and, under modern conditions, profoundly antagonistic methods of fighting. Weigh the terrible cost of not reaching perfection, the humiliation of being impotent even against inferior Infantry, and doubly impotent against superior mounted riflemen.

In studying the functions of mounted troops with the aid of the Official " Training Books," constantly distinguish weapons from mobility, the combat phase from the pre-combat phase. Do not be enticed into assuming that men armed with steel weapons can ride, drill, scout or manœuvre better, by virtue of those weapons. On the contrary, observe how steel weapons, not only by their mere weight in metal and leather, but by their manifold corollaries, react harmfully on mobility and intelligence, and in the case of the lance on visibility as well. Remember that in war every ounce and every inch tells, and that there is no other weapon on which to save weight. Nobody as yet suggests dropping the rifle. That is admittedly indispensable.

II.—NOMENCLATURE.

The grand distinction between the foot-soldier and the horse-soldier is the horse. The link which unites them is the rifle. We need some classification which emphasizes both the distinction and the link. All our terms, as at present used, are misleading. Those ancient and simple names, Cavalry and Infantry, are really all we want, but their significance is blurred by the modern intrusion of Mounted Infantry and its unofficial synonym, Mounted Riflemen, and Yeomanry.

"Mounted Infantry" is a very bad name, because, though accurate in a sense, it suppresses the common element, the rifle, and emphasizes the horse, which is the distinguishing element, by a sort of contradiction in terms, as though one were to say, horse-foot-soldiers. And in the very act of emphasizing the horse it belittles both that noble animal and its rider. It seems to say, " mount by all means, but above all dismount " ; " continually get off your horse "—" ignore the horse," to adapt expressions now familiar to the reader.

"Mounted Riflemen," though far better than " Mounted Infantry," is also unsatisfactory (1) because it suggests a non-existent distinction between foot riflemen and Infantry, (2) because it suggests a nonexistent class of mounted troops who are not riflemen.

Of course, the source of all this confusion is the retention of the steel weapon for our existing regular Cavalry, and the hybrid type which results.

I myself should strongly advocate the total abolition of all the modern jargon, and a return to the primitive simplicity of Cavalry and Infantry. Those names will live ; nothing can extirpate them, and if they stood alone their very isolation would force into prominence the really fundamental points of similarity and dissimilarity in the troops they represent. Of course, there will always be different qualities of Cavalry, as of Infantry, corresponding to length and continuity of training, and the most difficult and exacting functions will naturally be allotted to the best-trained troops. But do not let us make the sword or lance the criterion of excellence. Let us select any other criterion but that, paying at least so much of a compliment to modern war experience. Do not let us tell the relievers of Mafeking or De Wet that they cannot engage in a strategical raid; the Australians that they cannot pursue; De la Rey, the New Zealanders, and the riflemen of the Rand that they cannot charge. Do not let us impress upon our Mounted Infantry, with their South African traditions, that because they have no sword or lance, they cannot play the big, fast game they played in South Africa. By all means, if it is convenient, give them the limited functions of divisional Cavalry, but do not put it on the ground of defective armament. Give them a chance to realize their own worth, and do not commit the crowning folly—crime it might well be called— of singling them out from all the army for what is in effect a lecture on the " terror of cold steel."

III.—ARMAMENT OF CAVALRY.

I now come to the central object of my volume. My own belief is that reform here must be radical. If it were possible, as the United States Cavalry find it possible, to place the sword in a thoroughly subordinate position, and keep it there, accepting whole-heartedly all the logical consequences of its subordination, there would be little objection to its retention. Nobody can deny that it can be useful on very rare occasions, though I hope to have proved that the rifle, in expert hands, can do better, even on those rare occasions.

But experience proves that in this country it is utterly impossible to keep the sword or lance subordinate. Their fascination seems to be irresistible. They laugh at facts and feed men on seductive fictions. We know what the course of reaction has been. For a brief space after the South African War it was in fact made officially subordinate. Then the sword regained its old domination. Now the lance, from the cold shades of " ceremony," has become a combative weapon, also dominant, and in the case of Lancer regiments, sharing its supremacy with the sword, so that we have now what I venture to call the preposterous spectacle of horsemen armed with no less than three weapons, one of which, when at rest, adds several feet vertically to visibility. Of the respective value of the lance and sword in combat, where combat takes place, I say nothing, but on every other ground the lance is utterly indefensible. At the combined army manœuvres of 1909, for example, Lancers were operating in hedge-bound country, like that which covers so large a part of England, and where lances constantly make just the difference between concealment and exposure. They are incompatible with effective fire-action.

But that after all is a secondary matter. What makes compromise impossible is the fact that the steel weapon carries with it logically the whole theory of shock. Add the firearm and you are faced with dilemmas from which there is no escape. You cannot even take the elementary step of attaching it to the man, instead of to the saddle, without prejudice to the idea of shock. You cannot, as " Cavalry Training " tacitly admits, carry sufficient ammunition. Drop shock, and logic would tear aside the veil, and leave the steel weapon discredited. It could not live on " extended formations," eight-yard intervals and thin makeshifts of that sort. There plainly it would be trenching on the legitimate sphere of the rifle, and throwing its own inferiority into prominence. The steel involves shock, and shock involves a whole structure of drill, training and equipment, which are not only antithetical to fire-action, but prejudicial to general mobility. Splendid troops, with keen commanders and careful training, like our regular Cavalry, manage to attain a fairly high standard in both fire-action and shock-action ; no one can doubt that who witnessed the manœuvres of 1909. But reconnaissance was admittedly imperfect, and the conditions were peace conditions. Time spent in training for the steel is time robbed from other training. None know better than General French and other Cavalry officers with war experience how tremendously exacting is the standard of excellence required of the mounted rifleman, and how vital the importance of saving weight. War teaches us that only by exclusive and unremitting attention to the use of the horse and rifle in combination is it possible to make good mounted riflemen.

They can never know enough, never practise enough. And, when the last word is said, there remain those " out - of - door habits and sporting instincts " which are so difficult to imitate artificially, and for whose absence it is so difficult to compensate by drill and discipline.

But surely no better material exists in any European country than in this for the production of good mounted riflemen. We have the men, and we have the experience. We are leagues ahead of Germany, where steps are only now being taken to provide the Cavalry with a carbine equal in power to the Infantry rifle ; leagues ahead of Austria and France ; leagues ahead of Russia, unless since 1905 she has revolutionized her training. And yet we are blind to our good fortune ; not only blind but enviously imitative of the errors of foreigners, who in turn are ignorant of our elements of strength. Colonel Repington, our ablest military publicist, and one of the best friends the Cavalry or the army at large ever had, warns the Cavalry that their shock-action needs improvement, by comparison with Continental standards, while

Bernhardi and de Negrier passionately exhort their countrymen to wake up to the efficacy of the rifle. But Bernhardi cannot bring himself to give up the steel, so, as the most reputable exponent of compromise we can find, we copy into our drill-book those of his maxims on fire which can safely be quoted without fatally injuring the case for the steel. It is enough to make angels weep! Observe once more that we are courting failure in neglecting our own aptitudes. Our Cavalry school believes in the inevitable shock duel, and prophesies " negative " results for fire in the encounters of rival Cavalries. Continental schools believe the same, so that both Cavalries in a European war, oblivious, as of old, of their real battle duties, will seek the shock duel if level ground can be found for it. If our single division is beaten in a brute contest of weight we shall be reaping the fruits of compromise. But the more likely contingency is that the same old cruel and pointless censure will be meted out to both Cavalries, for " mutual paralysis " and " idleness " on the battlefield.

All this proves, I submit, that compromise is impossible. Sword and lance should be abolished, and the training book rewritten in the light of that abolition. With nothing but the rifle to depend on, a new, pure, equally magnificent, and far more fruitful spirit would at once permeate the whole force. There can be no such thing as a hybrid spirit, and the Cavalry know it ; hence the re-enthronement of the steel spirit. But inculcate unreservedly the true aggressive fire-spirit, or rather the horse-and-fire spirit, and you will get it in a form which would astonish the old European Cavalries.

From " Cavalry Training," even as it now stands, extract and marshal lucidly all the functions which Cavalry are now supposed to perform with the rifle, whether in offence or defence.* Realize the tremendous responsi-

* See p. 318.

bilities involved, and remember that in any even of these functions to pit half-trained riflemen against first-class riflemen, whether Infantry or mounted, is to court failure, and possibly humiliating and disastrous failure—for the sake of what ? Of obtaining not even perfection, but mediocrity in a class of tactics whose value rests on no proofs from any war since the invention of the smokeless modern rifle.

Dismiss these distracting and meaningless distinctions between the " Cavalry fight " and other fights, between " mounted action " and " dismounted action," which are now treated as though they had no connection with one another, and as though in the swift and various vicissitudes of war it were possible to sort troops into classes or to foresee from moment to moment which tactics to employ. Realize that under present arrangements there is, and can be, no provision whatever for that rapid transition from one to the other which battle conditions demand if Cavalry are to play the fast, confident game they should play. A man with a horse is a man with a horse. Make him feel it at all times. Do not tell him that a wound inflicted from the saddle counts in some mysterious way more than one inflicted on foot. Explain that mounted action and dismounted action may alternate with lightning rapidity, and merge in one another in a thousand ways. In teaching the charge with the rifle do not make the subaltern refer to two distinct chapters, one dealing with the ride into decisive range, another with his action when he dismounts—perhaps only a few yards from the objective—for the fire-climax. And for very shame avoid such puerilities as the direction that before embarking on dismounted action additional ammunition is to be served out.

Make the mere mention of " Cavalry ground " an offence punishable by fine. Tell Cavalry that all ground which a horse can approach at all is ground for them, and all equally honourable and fruitful ground. Tell them to welcome inequalities as the indispensable condition of surprise, not to hanker after open plains, where surprise is impossible. Get rid, too, of the equally demoralizing notion that in order to fulfil their supreme function in action their horses must perpetually be in a condition to gallop fast.

Saddle-fire for mounted troops is optional, according to capacity. But it should certainly be adopted by professional Cavalry, and practised regularly. I need not discuss the difficulty of learning saddle-fire. The mere fact that it is officially enjoined for picked Mounted Infantry in a three months' training proves its feasibility, to say nothing of its combat-value. Obviously it cannot be regarded as an absolutely essential concomitant of mounted action. A vast amount was accomplished without it in South Africa, and our own men, even in their best work, never used it. Nor was it used by either side in Manchuria, because neither side came near the South African standard of mounted rifle-tactics. But that it may be, if used at the right moment, skilfully, and for certain definite ends, of very great value, we know both from our own experience and from American history. It has genuine moral effect, and may have material effects of an importance out of all proportion to the actual loss of life inflicted, whether in horse or men. A few random bullets may stampede a crowd of led horses, or throw into disorder a regiment massed for shock. In the pursuit of mounted men by mounted men, in the running mêlée, so to speak, experience shows that skilled shots and riders can bring down men with aimed fire. A revolver might be better for this purpose, but the multiplication of weapons is on all accounts to be avoided. The rider must feel in every moment of his field-life that he and his rifle are one for all purposes.

It goes without saying, therefore, that the rifle should

be slung, as even the Russians and Japanese slung it, and, as Bernhardi recommends, on the back.

But for the *arme blanche* there would be plenty of time to learn not only saddle-fire, but much beside in the inexhaustible lore of the mounted rifleman. For example, a good *first-hand* knowledge of entrenchment is absolutely essential, as anyone can see who looks in " Cavalry Training " for the fire-functions allotted to Cavalry ; and at least one sharp lesson in South Africa drives home the same moral. To allocate a small detachment of Royal Engineers is to trifle with the subject. Entrenching tools, in the use of which the troopers themselves have been practised, should accompany every regiment or brigade. Remember the Cavalry at Hei-kou-tai and Pen-hse-hu. If you give men firearms at all, you must teach them thoroughly the defensive as well as the offensive use of firearms, for the two things are one. Men who cannot defend cannot attack.

A truce, then, to the rhetoric about Cavalry being essentially an arm of offence. *Ça va sans dire.* Every combatant arm is an arm of offence. Infantry would regard such an exhortation as a poor compliment. Of course we know and make full allowance for the reason of the exhortation—namely, that the *arme blanche* is by its very nature only a weapon of offence, and that in Cavalry theory the *arme blanche* is the supreme source of dash. Get rid of this theory, and you get rid of all excuse for the exhortation.

The *arme blanche* gone, the path of progress in every department opens out broad and clear. We want light, lithe, wiry men, and horses to match—horses at any rate in which nothing of any moment is sacrificed to size, and of which hardihood is the predominant characteristic. Small horses were far the hardiest in South Africa and Manchuria. High speed is altogether secondary ; looks are nothing.

The vexed question of the weight of general equipment (apart from the extra weight of steel weapons) I regard as outside the scope of this volume. The margin gained by abolishing steel weapons should be used for extra ammunition. In South Africa our men carried 130 rounds, the Japanese in Manchuria 150 rounds.

Should the troopers carry a bayonet? That is an interesting question, because it forces us to contrast the relative powers and duties of the foot-rifleman and the horse-rifleman. It is an open question, not vital, because the weight of a bayonet is small, and it does not impose a separate system of tactics. It may be said on the one hand that mobility and surprise are the grand advantages possessed by mounted riflemen over foot-riflemen, and should compensate for the bayonet, which, in point of fact, scarcely justified itself in South Africa. The Boers lost little by the lack of it, even in storming entrenchments at night, while their charges in the open were based directly on the idea, first of a swift stunning ride in, then on destructive magazine fire. That is the true idea, and we should not forget it. The bayonet suggests the slow, if less vulnerable, approach of men on foot. Even in the case of Infantry, critics of both the great modern wars associate over-close formations and unskilful skirmishing with an exaggerated idea of the importance of the cold steel. I except Port Arthur conditions, where horsemen were not wanted.

On the other hand, all British riflemen find confidence in the bayonet, and, as Lord Roberts truly says, it may be exceedingly useful in a dismounted night attack. War since 1865 proves that Cavalry must have the power to press home an assault against entrenched Infantry. As Mishchenko discovered, they cannot make the simplest raid without it. In strict logic, therefore, the trooper needs the bayonet if the Infantryman needs it. Only let us be sure that the utility of the bayonet is fully great enough to warrant the possible risk of making the trooper forget that normally his horse gives him a great tactical advantage over Infantry, and a range of opportunities unknown to them. Whatever we decide, let us not act in mimicry of "potential foes." If the new German carbine has a bayonet, as I believe it has, let us not make the bayonet a fourth weapon in imitation, but a second weapon to fortify the rifle.

On manœuvre not strictly connected with any special weapon I only wish to repeat the clear lesson of South Africa and the wise counsel of Bernhardi, that the less Cavalry, when in free and independent movement, are taught to rely on the support of Horse Artillery the better.

I need scarcely say that we should erase the last vestiges of the idea that Cavalry should count on the support of mounted riflemen. If we abolish the *arme blanche* that distorted and unwholesome idea dies a natural death.

The conditions of service constitute a most important point. For officers the force should be as cheap as any other part of the army, the career *ouverte à tous les talents*. Every stimulus should be given for the accession of the best men, both mentally and physically, and selection should be rigid. Cavalry is a very important arm, demands the most varied powers, and should command the highest talent. It is a relatively small force, it has highly specialized functions, and of all arms it is the least easy to replace in the thick of a war. It must be a comparatively expensive force to maintain, but the expense should fall on the State which it serves. That perhaps is a counsel of perfection for the State in its relation to officers of all arms, but if it softens anywhere, it should soften in the case of the Cavalry.

And the source of the present excessive standard of expense ? Analyze the whole matter carefully, and you will find at the back of it that enemy to progress, the *arme blanche*. Abolish that, and, with a little friendly help from the State, the evil will cure itself.

IV.—MOUNTED INFANTRY.

We touch here special questions of finance and administration which complicate the issue. But a clear mind on the question of armament and tactics will help immensely to simplify the problem. Let us begin by calling them for all purposes " Cavalry." That ought to be a simple and unobjectionable change, because in combined operations they are, in fact, called Cavalry, and are allotted the duties of divisional Cavalry. The name changed, what follows ? Logically, no doubt, that they should be merged in the Cavalry. Apart from the steel weapon, their characteristics are the same. Apart from the shock-charge, and assuming equal length of training, their functions and powers should be precisely the same. They are mounted riflemen, as the Cavalry should be. On the other hand, there is an advantage, no doubt, from the point of view of expense and simplicity, in the plan of abstraction from Infantry battalions for short periods of mounted service ; but I suggest that the advantage is small by comparison with the evils of the system. (1) In war, when fresh contingents have to be raised (as they surely will have to be raised), the abstraction, as we know to our cost, weakens the efficacy of the Infantry battalions. (2) Though the soldier's prior training (presumed to be thorough) as an Infantryman is of immense help to him in learning the work of a mounted rifleman, it is wholly impossible for him, in the short time available, to obtain all the trained aptitudes and instincts of a first-class mounted rifleman.

Is it not common sense that, if we go to the expense of providing professional soldiers with horses at all, we should go a little farther, and make them thorough professional horsemen, during their whole training ? Should we not rather add to the Cavalry than abstract from the Infantry ? I am sure it would pay us well.

But whether or no this step is taken, and whether or no the *arme blanche* is abolished, let us at all events revise their instruction in the light of war-experience, abandoning all this excessive stress on their character as Infantry, laying all the stress we will on their character as riflemen, and equal stress on their character as horsemen. Of course, as long as they remain, so to speak, improvised horsemen, their responsibilities must be appropriate to their efficiency, but they should not be taught to feel that they lose something by the lack of a steel weapon. By all means let them act as a " pivot of manœuvre " for regular Cavalry, where the two arms are acting together, if, as mounted riflemen, they are less efficient than Cavalry. But away with this absurd notion that their support on such occasions is intended to leave Cavalry leisure and opportunity for indulging in shock. Away, above all, with the demoralizing insinuation that if caught " in the open," whatever that vague and elusive phrase may mean, they are, owing to the possession of horses, actually more vulnerable to attack by the steel than Infantry ; that to meet this contingency, they must form square, an operation long obsolete in the case of the Infantry, except for savage warfare. This is just the way to make them lose all confidence not only in the very weapon which Infantry are taught to rely on so implicitly against the steel, but in the horse itself. I wonder if the existing Mounted Infantry believe in the suggestion after their previous training as Infantry. If any one of them, does, I can only say to him : " Read once more and learn by heart page 92 of ' Infantry Training ' (' Meeting an Attack by Cavalry '). Remember you now have a horse ; exercise your common sense, and you will conclude that unless you are ' surprised ' in a sense which would be a disgrace to soldiers of any class or type, mounted or dismounted, you have an immense advantage over Cavalry acting ' as such.' "

V.—YEOMANRY.

Here are volunteer mounted riflemen ; a keen, vigorous force, composed of some of the best elements in the nation, but without prior training as Infantry, obtaining a very small amount of field exercise, with horses specially provided for such occasions. They belong to the same type as Mounted Infantry ; but, through no fault of their own, are less efficient. Yet, for some inexplicable reason, they are called " Cavalry," and receive, in an appendix to " Cavalry Training," three special pages, which begin with the direction that " Yeomanry should be so trained as to be capable of performing all the duties allotted to Cavalry, except those connected with shock action." Let us follow out the effect which these words are calculated to have upon the mind of an average member of the Yeomanry. At the first blush the sentence wears an air of simplicity. Having no lance or sword, the Yeoman clearly cannot practice shock. But what are the " duties connected with shock action " which he must not perform ? If he were to begin by studying Bernhardi, he might very well come to the satisfactory conclusion that the only opportunity for shock was in the collision of huge Cavalry masses. But he need not read Bernhardi, because Bernhardi, he is informed, inspires " Cavalry Training." In " Cavalry Training " he searches in vain for an exhaustive list of these duties. He finds emphasis on the big shock duel, with its " positive " result, but no qualification in respect of smaller duels. He hears about the " Cavalry fight," which is clearly a shock fight, and also about Cavalry in " extended order," charging Infantry, and wonders if this, too, is shock, and presumes on the whole that it is. Eventually he comes to the conclusion, and the very reasonable conclusion, that he is lost without a steel weapon, irretrievably lost if he meets Cavalry, and at the best, perhaps, weak in aggression against Infantry. If he refers to "Mounted Infantry Training," it is only to find that even this arm, with its professional character and longer continuous training, is taught to fear the steel weapon. Reverting, therefore, to his original proposition, that the sword is absolutely essential, he appeals to be equipped with the sword.

But what, meanwhile, of that terrifically deadly weapon, the rifle ? With his eighteen days' field training, is he yet fit to meet on terms of fire professional mounted riflemen, to say nothing of swordsmen and Lancers ? Is he, with his limited practice and his double function of horseman and rifleman, fit to oppose even volunteer Infantry ? He has vague recollections of a war in which large numbers of volunteer troops under his own appellation met small numbers of skilled mounted riflemen, did remarkably well under the circumstances, but on the whole were completely outmatched. But the uncomfortable memory is soon stifled. That was an " abnormal " war. Cavalrymen say it was abnormal. He need not study that war, and in point of fact I am afraid it is true that the majority of our volunteer mounted officers do not study it. Why should they, when German theorists and German battles are presented to them on the highest authority as the best guides to education ?

I am fully aware that many Yeomanry officers resent the demand for a steel weapon, and take the line of common sense in the whole matter. But the opinions I have represented must be reckoned with, for they will grow, as the war fades farther into the past and the reaction to steel in the Cavalry gathers strength. In the summer of 1909, there was a correspondence in the *Times* initiated by an anonymous " Squadron Leader " of Yeomanry, who represented that to send swordless Yeomanry into war was sheer murder ; that in the face of Cavalry they were " unarmed sheep " ; that he cared nothing about the Boer War (of which, indeed, he was evidently quite ignorant); that it was " peculiar "; that our Cavalry and foreign Cavalries believed in the *arme blanche*, and that for his part he pinned his faith on authorities like General von Pelet Narbonne, the German author of " Cavalry in Action."

Of all the many pernicious effects of the survival of the *arme blanche*, this indirect encouragement to our volunteer horsemen to belittle the good weapon and hanker for the bad weapon is one of the worst. The responsibility rests absolutely on the *arme blanche* school of thought. There is no valid answer to the demand. They, least of all, can combat it. Nor would there be any valid answer if the Mounted Infantry raised the same demand. Every mounted man should have a sword, or none. In war you cannot sort out troops so that one class need only meet its own corresponding class. Germans, for example, have no steel-less Cavalry. By hypothesis, therefore, our Yeomanry cannot take the field at all against them. And how, on the same hypothesis, are our Mounted Infantry, acting as " divisional Cavalry," to meet German divisional Cavalry ?

Meanwhile, it is impossible to make any other recommendation to the Yeomanry than this. Regard yourselves as belonging to the highest type of mounted soldier—that is, to the mounted riflemen. Concentrate on the rifle and the horse. The more you do that and the more the hybrid professional horsemen waste their energies in compromise, or destroy their efficacy in concentrating on the steel, the fitter you will be to meet them in war.

VI.—IMPERIAL MOUNTED TROOPS.

It is for the Imperial General Staff to grapple with this question. We are dealing here with men who will never really believe that a steel weapon is the distinguishing mark of a superior Cavalry. How the steel weapon at present is to be submitted to them in an intelligible and natural way, I do not know. Without it the whole problem solves itself. It will be possible then to arrange for their inclusion in an Imperial army on some definite and reasoned basis, with functions defined according to their capacity as mounted riflemen.

VII.—Conclusion.

I hope I have written nothing in this volume which does not come within the bounds of fair criticism. I have written strongly, because I feel strongly on a point about which every Englishman, soldier or civilian, has a right to feel strongly. We have wasted too much energy, brains and splendid human material on the perverse pursuit of a phantom ideal. It is painful, at this moment, to see a great current of keenness and ability so misdirected and misapplied.

Let us trust our own experience, shake off this crippling superstition, and start afresh on lines which we have *proved* to be successful.

THE END

Printed in Great Britain
by Amazon

48712805R00225